SHORT-TERM AMERICA

SHORT-TERM AMERICA

The Causes and Cures of Our Business Myopia

MICHAEL T. JACOBS

Foreword by David W. Mullins, Jr.

HARVARD BUSINESS SCHOOL PRESS
Boston, Massachusetts

95 94 93 92 91   5 4 3 2 1

Jacobs, Michael T., 1958-
    Short-term America : the causes and cures of our business myopia / Michael
T. Jacobs.
        p.   cm.
    Includes bibliographical references and index.
    ISBN 0-87584-300-X (alk. paper)
    1. Industrial management—United States—Case studies. I. Title.
HD70.U5J33 1991
658'.00973—dc20   .   91-4207
                                                                 CIP

The paper used in this publication meets the requirements of the American National Standard for Permanence of Paper for Printed Library Materials Z39.49–1984.

To Stacy,
whose support and encouragement
made this book possible

Contents

Foreword

For the past few years the issue of American business competitiveness has become something of an industry in its own right, providing fodder for books, conferences, and magazine articles. Since the late 1970s, when the first signs of our slipping prowess relative to Japan, Germany, France, and other powerful industrial nations appeared, concern over U.S. competitiveness has taken many forms.

The first reaction, of course, was denial. Many simply refused to believe that a nation with America's depth of human and capital resources—the biggest guy on the block—could be bested at anything of importance by its rivals. A few still cling to this view.

By the early 1980s, the overwhelming presence of high-quality, foreign-made products in our homes, offices, and garages made believers out of most of us. Government trade reports and industry analyses merely confirmed what we had all observed with our own eyes. Asian-made consumer electronics were suddenly everywhere; American radios, televisions, and stereos were nowhere. There was little room left for denial. The sharp recession in the early 1980s aggravated the situation; many U.S. manufacturers in key industries like autos, machine tools, and semiconductors experienced dramatic market-share losses to competitors from abroad.

Fortunately, Americans are not chronic hand-wringers. Their awareness of the competitiveness problem has led to several years of debate, much of it very useful. One part of that debate has addressed the two areas in which government must be the major player: trade practices and industrial policy. These go to the heart of some fundamental and fiercely held beliefs about economics and the role of government. As a result, that debate has been highly politicized, often divisive, and has not approached a satisfactory consensus.

A second part has been the task of challenging and reforming management practices—particularly in the field of manufacturing. Reassessment of basic business issues such as quality, product development, empowerment of workers, and downsizing of bureaucratic organizations has resulted in dramatic improvements in business performance. Unlike trade and industrial policy, these are very tangible, firm-level problems that managers can identify, measure, and attack with tools they know how to use.

The debate on American business competitiveness has been highly visible. It provides ample proof that some of the best minds in the nation are concerned about the problem and are actively engaged in seeking solutions. This is all very encouraging.

But there remains one more trail to follow, and that one opens onto probably the most dimly lighted area of the entire competitiveness problem: short-term business thinking. Why is it, we may fairly ask, that American businesses and those who own them have developed a reputation for seeking short-term gain to the exclusion of long-term achievement? Why, for instance, did the U.S. innovators of the fax machine, the videocassette recorder, the digital wristwatch, and countless other breakthrough products either abandon their markets or sell the rights to foreigners to develop and harvest? How can we explain the paradox of rational corporate managers and equally rational investors making decisions that seem to impair their firms' future interests? And why is it that Japanese firms regularly jump with both feet into ventures deemed too risky or profitless by their American counterparts?

Probing the issue of short-term thinking, as this book so ably does, takes us into terrain that few readers have traveled. It examines the internal guidance systems of corporations and the institutions that provide them with capital. Michael Jacobs reveals those systems as flawed, explains why they are sending out the wrong directives, and offers some workable ideas on how they can be set aright.

This book concerns itself with a puzzle of several pieces: lending institutions, institutional investors, the take-over binge of the past decade, the American system of corporate governance, the cost of capital, and ways in which managers are paid. Each of these, of itself, has a constituency and a rich literature of research. Mr. Jacobs's contribution is in putting together the pieces to form a coherent picture. For him, each piece is part of a *systemic* problem that afflicts contemporary American business and investment practices. For example, few have explored the impact on America's high cost of capital of the regulations that affect bank lending and pension investment practices, or the government regulations that inhibit shareholders from acting like real owners. Similarly, the takeover game is analyzed as a phenomenon that arose because other elements of our system—and not just greed—made it inevitable. In putting together the puzzle, the paradox of why so many dedicated managers and investers so readily shoot themselves in the foot becomes evident.

I first got to know the author when I was Assistant Secretary at the U.S. Treasury. In response to the high level of activity in mergers and LBOs, the interest in corporate governance issues and the debate on U.S. competitiveness, we created a corporate finance group within Treasury to explore these issues. Michael Jacobs was appointed Director of Corporate Finance, with the mission to probe our financial system for any elements that presented barriers to greater U.S. economic competitiveness. He had a zeal for this mission that taxpayers outside the Beltway would find reassuring. He made it his business to be the synthesizer of the best research and the best experience in both business and government on this issue. In the process he has created a new perspective that is refreshingly original and free from doctrine. His is a satisfying new paradigm.

Scholars and business leaders are just beginning to probe the area of short-term behavior as a source of America's competitiveness problem. This book will get them off to an excellent start.

David W. Mullins, Jr.
Board of Governors of the Federal Reserve System
Washington, DC

Acknowledgments

Following the 1988 presidential election, I packed up my family and moved to Washington with the daunting mission of trying to develop policies to improve the competitiveness of American business. For the first time, the Treasury Department had established an office with an exclusive mandate to address this issue, and I had been asked to serve as its director.

Over time I learned what every policymaker eventually learns: Washington itself is very shortsighted. If ideas cannot be conveyed in a fifteen-second sound bite or are not a response to a crisis appearing in the daily headlines, they seldom attract significant attention. The senior officials at Treasury, from Secretary Nicholas Brady on down, cared immensely about the subject of competitiveness. But the need to develop a plan to address the savings and loan crisis, then the third-world debt crisis, then banking reform—intermingled with such crises as formulating budgets and financing operation "Desert Storm"—always took precedence.

Competitiveness was perpetually the next item on the policy agenda. Frustrated by the lack of attention to the subject my office was responsible for, I decided to write this book to share my views on the causes of and cures for the business myopia afflicting our nation.

After clearing all the hurdles with government ethics officers, I began what proved to be a much greater undertaking than I had imagined. Because I was unable to work on the book during the business day, my early-morning hours, late nights, and weekends became consumed by the project. For this, it is my wife Stacy and son Preston (and dog Tarheel) who deserve the most credit for their patience and understanding. Stacy deserves particular appreciation for having typed every word of the countless drafts of the manuscript.

The support and encouragement of colleagues and friends were also vital. I never would have had access to the leading thinkers on the subjects explored here were it not for the foresight shown by Secretary Brady, Under Secretary Robert Glauber, and Assistant Secretary David Mullins in creating an office to address these issues. At Treasury, French Hill was a partner and friend every step of the way, and Linda McDonough was instrumental to our team.

Various business groups, investor groups, government officials, and academics with an interest in competitiveness and short-termism helped me add to my knowledge about many elements of our economic system. Sorting through their views for "the truth" was not always easy, but it was a challenge that helped me form the ideas presented here.

Several people were of specific assistance in the preparation of my manuscript. Graef Crystal, Peg O'Hara, Jim Kaitz, Linda Quinn, Jeremy Stein, and Eric Zolt reviewed chapters or provided valuable data. Ken Lehn, David Mullins, and Jim Tyrone were kind enough to review the entire manuscript. And throughout, my editor at the Harvard Business School Press, Richard Luecke, was immensely helpful and supportive.

This book is my best effort to make sense of some very confusing and disturbing practices that contribute to shortsightedness in the United States. I have taken great care not to show any bias, as I have no axe to grind. If I have failed to offend anyone in the process, I apologize, because we all contribute to the problem and must recognize that fact. Only by questioning our own attitudes and behaviors, and the laws and policies we support, will we open ourselves to the changes necessary to cure our country's business myopia.

Michael T. Jacobs
May 1991
Washington, DC

SHORT-TERM AMERICA

1

Business Myopia and U.S. Competitiveness

America's number one export in recent years has been democratic capitalism, the system that made the United States the world's leading power. Throughout Eastern Europe and all across the globe, dictators are being thrown out of office and command economies are being abandoned by citizens supporting capitalistic ideals. As we look back over the decades of tension between East and West, we can see clearly that the decisive contests between capitalism and communism were fought and won not on the battlefield, but in the world's factories and marketplaces. In the end, it was economic prowess, and not military power, that mattered most.

But as the final chapters of the cold war are being written, critics at home and abroad are questioning America's ability to maintain its economic status in the "new world order."

America is experiencing a mid-life crisis. In its year-end 1990 review on competitiveness, *Business Week* observed that "you can feel America's eroding status in your bones." A Gallup poll shows most Americans now regard Japan, rather than the United States, as the world's leading economic power. Even before the Berlin Wall had been dismantled, U.S. citizens regarded Japan's economic prowess as a greater threat to the future of the nation than Soviet warheads by a factor of three to one.[1] And pollster Louis Harris observes that Americans fear we will soon drop to number three, behind Japan *and* Germany. Today, less than one-fourth of the American public has "a great deal of confidence" in the people running major U.S. corporations.[2]

These fears are fueled by the daily headlines. In 1980, the United States was the world's largest creditor nation; by 1990, it was the largest debtor. It was only four decades ago that the United States pumped billions of dollars into Japan and Germany to resurrect their war-ravaged economies. Yet fiscal problems at home forced the United States to appeal to these same countries—an effort referred to inside the government as "Project Tin Cup"—to finance operation "Desert Storm."

Right or wrong, the growth of foreign investment in the United States unnerves many who are worried about America's ability to compete. The United States has quietly funded massive budget deficits in recent years largely with foreign capital. Yet when their claims on U.S. wealth became more visible through their purchase of Rockefeller Center, Columbia Pictures, and MCA, the Japanese were accused of economic hegemony. Intuitively, we know that many of our economic problems are of our own making, yet the anxiety of seeing national treasures sold to foreigners and our stature in critical markets slip often engenders an emotional response.

Declining U.S. Competitiveness

Competitiveness can be measured in a number of ways, but none of them is fully adequate. Economists look to measures such as productivity, investment, per capita income, trade balances, and global market share. Regardless of which yardstick we choose, the story is the same: relative to many Asian and European countries, the United States is losing ground.

Productivity growth in the United States has been anemic in recent years. America is still the world's most productive nation, but not by much. Output per hour grew less than half as fast in the United States as in Japan from 1973 to 1989. This is primarily because Japan invested far more money than the United States in capital equipment and employee training relative to the size of its economy, as illustrated in Exhibit 1.1. From 1976 through 1987, Japanese investment in machinery and equipment ranged from 14.9 percent to 20.6 percent of GNP; in America it ranged from 7.5 percent to 9 percent. In 1989, Japanese companies actually spent $4.6 billion more on plant and equipment in absolute dollars. Japanese companies now employ almost three-quarters of the world's robots, more than five times the number operating in the United States. Today, Toyota produces half the number of vehicles manufactured by General Motors with only 5 percent of the number of workers.

In industry after industry U.S. market share slipped precipitously during the 1980s (see Table 1.1). The loss of global dominance occurred not only in mature industries, but also in the technology sectors that will define the information age.

Exhibit 1.1
Investment Nondefense R&D Expenditure

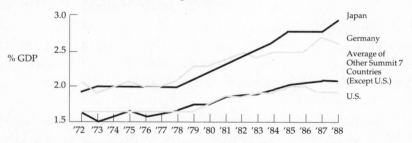

Source: Council on Competitiveness and the National Science Foundation.

Table 1.1

Declining Market Share of U.S. High-Tech Industries

	1980	1988
Fiber optics	73%	42%
Semiconductors	60	36
Supercomputers	100	76
DRAMS	56	20

Source: Council on Competitiveness.

The quality of life, which encompasses both economic and noneconomic factors, has declined for many Americans. Real wages have been sliding for most U.S. workers, a factor that ripples through people's lives in a number of ways. According to a Heritage Foundation policy paper, over the past generation the number of hours parents spend with their children each week has declined from 30 to 17, primarily because of the economic difficulties confronting families with children. Competence in math and science among our youth lags behind that of most developed countries and even some lesser-developed countries. Health care costs in the United States have approached 12 percent of our GNP, more than in Canada, France, Italy, Japan, Sweden, the United Kingdom, and Germany. Yet the United States has a higher infant mortality rate than any of these countries. The murder rate in America is 10 times higher than the average in other advanced nations. Many experts blame this on the economic plight of the American underclass.

Some people define competitiveness in terms of "product quality." The decline in quality of American products is so widely acknowledged that Buick was proud to advertise that it ranked *fifth* among best-made cars in the world in 1990, ahead of all U.S. competitors. A recent half-page ad in the *Washington Post* read: "Who says 'Made in the U.S.A.' doesn't cut it anymore?" Ironically, the ad was promoting Honda lawn mowers produced in Swepsonville, North Carolina. Although the 1991 federal budget agreement included an excise tax on all cars sold for over $30,000,

Detroit was noticeably silent. The only cars Americans are now willing to pay that much for are made overseas. Not long ago the stamp "Made in Japan" connoted cheapness. Today Japanese quality is the benchmark for many American companies.

The Technology Administration branch of the Commerce Department released a report entitled "U.S. Report Card: Trends," comparing the relative strength of Japanese and American producers in 12 emerging technologies.[3] The report concluded that the United States was "losing badly" in advanced materials, biotechnology, digital-imaging technology, and supercomputers. In six other technologies U.S. companies were "losing," while holding their own in only two areas and gaining ground in none.

Some observers dismiss the debate over declining U.S. competitiveness by arguing that it is no longer possible to categorize a company as either American or Japanese. Is a Toshiba plant in Tennessee Japanese or American? With 45 percent of its employees located overseas, is IBM truly an "American" company? In a January 1990 article published by the *Harvard Business Review*, Robert Reich asks, "Who Is Us?"[4] Reich argues that it does not matter where a company is headquartered: what determines a nation's competitiveness are the skills of its work force. Why not give U.S. government money to Japanese companies that want to engage in basic research as long as they spend it in the United States, he asks. But Michael Porter, author of *The Competitive Advantage of Nations*, argues that successful corporations usually do have a distinct national identity. And Robert Noyce, the founder of Intel, likened the sort of argument put forth by Reich to "selling the farm and becoming sharecroppers."[5] Although the United States may continue to maintain jobs, all the profits from their labor would flow overseas, eroding the wealth of our nation.

Furthermore, jobs do not always remain with the most advanced nation. An American invented the radio (1920), the television (1923), the digital computer (1940), the integrated circuit (1958), the videocassette recorder (1963), and the personal computer (1975). Yet today the majority of production workers manufacturing these products are located overseas. And the faster technologies change, the quicker production flees our borders. In 1984, 85 percent of laptop computers were made in the United States; today fewer than half are made in America.

Others view the loss of control of technologies as a threat to America's national security. Not a single U.S. company converts sand into silicon, the basic ingredient for the electronics in our missiles and warplanes. Only one U.S. machine tool company is left that has the technology needed to meet Defense Department standards in manufacturing certain equipment critical to the production of nuclear weapons, and the Japanese have attempted to buy 40 percent of its stock. When the U.S. government contacted producers of military equipment in early 1991 to ensure that they could supply the parts and equipment necessary to carry on an extended war with Iraq, they discovered that a surprisingly large number of the companies that supply our defense industry have overseas area codes.

Although it is important to acknowledge that U.S. competitiveness is waning, it is equally important not to adopt a defeatist attitude. It is useful to remember that it was the U.S.-sponsored Marshall Plan that served as the framework for rebuilding the German economy. In Japan, General Douglas MacArthur crafted much of the economic system that has led to that nation's success. And it was an American, Edwards Demming, who taught the Japanese the lessons of quality. Just because the United States is down, it is not necessarily out. America still boasts the best universities in the world and remains the leader in innovation. And very few Americans would trade the standard of living they now enjoy for that of the Japanese, who often commute two hours each way to work a 14-hour day in Tokyo, only to come home to a house the size of a two-car garage.

If defeatism is counterproductive, complacency is equally dangerous. Many deny that America has a competitiveness problem because they see U.S. workers and corporations as still the most competitive in many areas. These people will never admit we have a problem until historical statistics show that other nations have already eclipsed the United States in all absolute measures. By then, of course, it will be too late. Vision requires acknowledging where we are heading and taking corrective action before ending up where we do not want to be.

The spirit that produced America's successes in the past continues to inspire leaders throughout the nation to search for ways of making our country more competitive. Unfortunately, no national consensus has emerged as to which direction to take. A number of prominent scholars and corporate leaders want the government to become more involved with business, to select and support key "strategic" industries. Others regard government as the problem and believe a national industrial policy will merely put our economic future in the hands of bureaucrats and politicos ill-equipped to steer private industry. Everyone agrees that we need to improve our educational system, eliminate drug abuse, and lower the cost of health care in the United States; however, achieving consensus on how to accomplish these goals has proven elusive. Because virtually every aspect of public policy influences the ability of American workers and corporations to compete, attempting to develop a national "competitiveness policy" is overwhelming.

Radically different biases do not make the process any easier. Democrats and Republicans, liberals and conservatives, executives from high-tech companies and union leaders in smokestack industries all preach the gospel of competitiveness. But mixed in with their well-intentioned rhetoric are proposals that would lead us in totally different directions. The only belief common to all these sermons is that American businesses and investors need to adopt a longer-term perspective. We cannot develop the technologies, penetrate the markets, or produce the products necessary to compete on a global basis by focusing on results one quarter at a time. A preoccupation with short-term results and instant economic gratification is undermining the long-run viability of American companies and, in some cases, entire industries. America is suffering from a chronic case of myopia.

The technology community clearly thinks short-termism is a serious problem. In a 1990 survey on what has caused the erosion of U.S. technological leadership, members of the Industrial Research Institute were asked to rank five categories in order of importance. Within each category were several factors that were also to be ranked. The overwhelming majority regarded "general management practices" and "external financial pressures" as the most important categories, ahead of government policy and others. The factor cited as the greatest overall threat to competitiveness in technology was management's "short-term horizons." Close behind were factors such as the "growing dominance of institutional investors in equity markets and their demand for short-term returns" and the "high cost of capital."

The financial community concurs. In 1990, the Financial Executives Institute (FEI) queried 2,000 of its members on issues related to competitiveness. FEI is comprised of America's top financial executives, including corporate financial officers who are accountable for company performance and private pension fund managers who comprise the largest group of investors in the nation. Not surprisingly, 98 percent of those polled said that America faces a competitiveness problem. But a more interesting response came when participants were asked to rank the factors that inhibit the ability of American companies to compete in world markets. The list included unfair trade practices, the budget deficit, exchange rates, and untrained workers. Yet two entirely different factors tied for the dubious distinction of being blamed most often for America's competitiveness problems: shortsighted investors and shortsighted corporate managers. The fact that the leading executives and investors in the nation were willing to blame themselves and each other supports the notion that short-termism—what I call "business myopia"—is at the heart of our competitiveness problem.

The Causes of Short-Termism

Many people believe short-termism is endemic to American culture. But the fact that shortsightedness has not always been so pervasive in the United States belies this view. The ability to think and act with great long-term vision inspired the building of canals, and later, the great railways and interstate highways. An American would not have set foot on the moon in 1969 had it not been for long-term thinking and planning. A great deal of patience and persistence was required to transform IBM from a typewriter company into the world's most powerful provider of office technology. And the U.S. military would not have experienced such a decisive victory in operation "Desert Storm" if it had not relied on strategies and weapons developed over several decades. Americans are not innately myopic. But today terms such as "visionary" and "prescient" are rarely used to describe either corporate executives or investors in the United States.

Some people—mostly academics—argue that the notion of short-termism is more perceived than real. They contend that there is no such thing as a short- or a long-term decision, only economic and uneconomic decisions. In theory this is true. In a world of markets unencumbered by obtrusive regulations, and in which everyone is fully informed, investors and business managers would not differentiate between the short run and the long run; they would always make economic decisions that maximized their welfare. But business executives and capital providers do not live in a theoretical world. Each day they encounter government regulations, communications problems, and self-interested parties that influence them to behave in uneconomic ways.

When I joined the Treasury Department, my mission as director of the newly formed Office of Corporate Finance was to examine the U.S. financial system, looking for elements that were undermining America's ability to compete. Following extensive study and countless discussions with business leaders, academics, and government officials, I became convinced that America clearly suffers from shortsightedness. I believe the primary cause of business myopia is the distant relationship between the providers of capital (shareholders and lenders) and the users of capital (corporate managers). This book will explain how distrustful and often antagonistic relationships between these two groups motivate them to make decisions that gratify only their own parochial, short-term interests, instead of cooperating to achieve goals that are in their mutual, long-term interest. These disharmonies also raise the risks of investing, which drives up the cost of capital for U.S. businesses, making investment in long-term projects less economically attractive.

Lack of communication prevents investors from understanding management's long-term goals and objectives. Shareholders trade stocks so often and hold such broadly diversified portfolios that they cannot possibly keep up with the business activities of the companies they own. Because most U.S. investors are detached from the businesses they fund, they rely on outward manifestations of what is really going on within the company; namely, quarterly earnings and other accounting measures of performance. These numbers only measure the past; they do not explain the future. When they are dissatisfied with corporate performance shareholders sell stock, rather than trying to discern the causes of poor performance and using their collective voice to communicate their concerns to management.

Companies exacerbate the problem by stacking their boards with directors handpicked by top management and insulating themselves from the oversight traditionally provided by shareholders and lenders. In recent years companies have consistently disenfranchised their owners; they want access to capital with no strings attached. But a lack of trust makes investors hesitant to fund projects with no visible results for extended periods of time.

This is in stark contrast to the practices followed in Japan and Germany where banks and shareholders are long-term investors. Capital providers become intimately involved with the companies in which they invest, either directly or through agents, thereby establishing a much greater degree of comfort and mutual trust.

Informed and involved investors are much more willing to allow companies the flexibility to pursue strategies with no immediate payoff. Patience comes with participation.

Short-Termism and the Cost of Capital

The lack of knowledge and involvement on the part of capital providers in the United States creates uncertainty as to whether the investors' money is being allocated efficiently. And their lack of influence increases the risk that capital providers will have little recourse if the corporations controlling the use of their money are not well managed. Both of these factors are translated into a higher cost of capital in the United States.[*] And high capital costs explain a lot about short-term business behavior. In its 1991 report, "Gaining New Ground: Technology Priorities for America's Future," the Council on Competitiveness concludes that many of the areas where the United States is "weak" or "losing badly" have high capital needs and require extensive investment in technology for an extended period of time.

---

[*] For the academic reader: the cost of capital is commonly defined as $R(f) + \Lambda P$, which represents a risk-free return plus a risk premium. $R(f)$ is the risk-free return required by investors; Λ is the price of risk and P is the amount of risk. Most attempts to identify international discrepancies in either $R(f)$ (the risk-free return) or Λ (how markets price risk) have failed to show compelling evidence of national differences in capital costs, indicating that Adam Smith is an internationalist. Yet most studies of observed required returns indicate disparities in international capital costs. When discussing the cost of capital, I will focus on differences in P, or the amount of risk, unique to each country's financial system—specifically the systematic risk pertaining to how capital is allocated and monitored. This risk has not been widely discussed in most cost-of-capital studies for two reasons: 1) it is not the area of expertise of most macroeconomists who study capital costs, and 2) it is difficult, if not impossible, to quantify. However, because factors such as agency costs, the costs of financial distress and information asymmetries influence the returns an investor requires, they do affect the cost of capital.

One of the most perplexing issues for Americans frustrated by declining competitiveness is why U.S. companies forego investments that their Japanese and German counterparts undertake. The common explanation is that American investors and corporate managers are not as patient as their foreign competitors. But the reality is that economics drives many of these decisions.

In late 1990, Cincinnati Milacron became the last in a long line of American manufacturers to abandon the industrial robotics industry when the company sold its robotics division to Asea Brown Boveri AG of Switzerland. Westinghouse, General Electric, and United Technologies had already thrown in the towel. Robotics is a product area believed by many to symbolize the future of manufacturing. The company's reason for exiting the market sounded familiar: it could not make an adequate return to justify the major investment in technology required to compete with overseas producers.

To understand the economic forces that drive this type of investment decision, it is imperative to understand how profoundly capital costs influence time horizons. Throughout much of the 1980s, U.S. companies paid substantially more for capital than did their German and Japanese competitors.

If we assume that Cincinnati Milacron faced a 10-percent, after-tax cost of capital and that certain of its foreign competitors were required to provide only a 5-percent return to their suppliers of capital, i.e., their shareholders and lenders, then straightforward financial analysis illustrates how their time horizons would differ based solely on disparities in their capital costs. Assume that both companies were considering an investment of $100 million in the exact same robotics technology that would produce an annual return of $15 million a year after the technology was commercialized. The American company would have to bring its product to market in about four years in order to show a positive return; otherwise, its stock price would decline. In stark contrast, the foreign competitor could take *20 years* to commercialize the same technology, and the investment would still be economically viable, solely because of its lower cost of capital. Even small differences in capital costs have an exponential impact on investment horizons.

There have been a number of arguments put forth to dispel the notion that short-term or high-cost capital is a systemic problem. Some point to America's dominance in innovation and note that the United States still generates the largest number of new products and technologies. But the fact that so many new technologies and startup businesses are dying on the vine or being sold to Asian companies at the point where large amounts of capital are needed for long-term efforts to commercialize these products or technologies actually supports the notion that the U.S. capital markets are short-term oriented. Ampex spent the time and money to develop the VCR, but when it learned of the amount of capital required to commercialize the product, Ampex licensed the technology to a Japanese company.

Others point out that some industries subject to the capital markets prosper in global competition, citing exceptions to disprove the rule. But if one looks closely at the businesses cited, one finds that each of these industries is able to differentiate itself in a way that could overcome capital cost disadvantages. For example, the U.S. pharmaceutical industry is able to invent superior products, secure lengthy patents to lock out competition, and then market products at very high margins to fund new product development efforts internally.

The entertainment industry is another often cited American success story. No amount of capital can clone Walt Disney, Madonna, or Michael Jackson. And Coca-Cola was built on marketing, not on capital-intensive production.

Aerospace is a capital-intensive industry that the United States has dominated for years. However, planes are designed on supercomputers that for many years were only available in the United States. As the Japanese gain the technology required to build airplanes, which they have already begun doing, we may not continue our domination of the market. When one looks beneath the surface, short-term capital does indeed appear to be a systemic problem.

The causes for international discrepancies in capital costs is a subject of great debate. The concept of the cost of capital is itself not well understood. Frequently, the cost of capital is erroneously regarded as synonymous with interest rates. Interest costs are but one of many factors that influence a corporation's cost of capital. The cost of equity—the capital supplied by owners—is equally important, as is the relative percentage of both debt and equity in a corporation's capital structure.

Traditional macroeconomic explanations for why capital costs differ among nations fall woefully short. The most common assumption is that interest rates have been higher in the United States because of a dearth of domestic savings. The massive federal budget deficit and paltry personal savings rate produce more than a $100-billion annual shortfall in national savings. If we were operating in a totally domestic economy, this would pose a serious problem. However, because of the rapidly integrating global capital markets, sufficient foreign savings have been pumped into the United States to minimize the real effects of interest rate differentials between nations. When this factor is combined with the depreciation of the dollar and the ability to finance investments in foreign currencies, the impact of interest rate differentials on capital costs faced by competitors in the same market becomes negligible, as discussed in Chapter 6.

Similarly, taxes are frequently blamed for international disparities in capital costs. However, there is no compelling evidence that the total tax burden is any higher on capital investments in the United States than it is overseas. In fact, tax rates are much higher in Germany and Japan.[*] In 1989, corporate taxes consti-

---

[*] Corporate tax rates range up to 50 percent in Germany and 37.5 percent in Japan. Individual rates in these countries top out at 53 percent and 50 percent, respectively. In the United States, the top federal corporate rate was 34 percent, and the maximum individual rate was 33 percent as of 1991.

tuted 7.6 percent of GDP in Japan, more than in any other OECD country, and only 2.5 percent in the United States. So, although lowering capital gains taxes and eliminating the double taxation of corporate profits are highly desirable and would clearly lower the U.S. cost of capital, experts have found that the tax code does not explain present global differentials in capital costs. Tax-driven remedies are often merely Band-Aid solutions that fail to address the underlying economic problem.

Even when macroeconomic factors give certain countries a cost-of-capital advantage, such factors are often fleeting. From 1984 to 1987, the Bank of Japan pumped up the money supply at an annual rate of more than 10 percent and lowered the official rate it charged other banks to 2.5 percent. The Japanese stock market soared while interest rates were negligible, causing capital investment to skyrocket. Meanwhile, the yen appreciated against the dollar, making imports more expensive; yet inflation was kept under control. Few observers expected the Japanese to continue to experience such a favorable environment forever. In fact, in 1990, the Japanese stock market plunged 40 percent and interest rates began to climb, reducing the Japanese advantage in capital costs. In early 1991, Tsunehiko Ishibashi, general manager for finance of a major Japanese petrochemical company, noted: "As a result of the higher cost of capital, the profitability standards for new investments must be raised."[6]

When simply considering macroeconomic factors, one might conclude that there is no lasting cost-of-capital problem in America. Yet even the most recent cost-of-capital studies show substantial international discrepancies. There are two consistent explanations among these studies, and both are compatible with the view that differences in the structure of various nations' financial systems—and the impact these disparities have on relationships between capital providers and capital users—explain at least part of the problem. First, the studies show that financial returns demanded by equity investors (even when adjusted for differences in national accounting standards) are much higher in the

United States. Second, they conclude that since debt is always cheaper than equity for a given company, and since German and Japanese companies have historically been capitalized with *more* debt than American companies, capital structures explain some of the differential. Unfortunately, most studies stop here. They fail to explain why companies in Germany and Japan use more leverage or why shareholders in these countries are willing to accept lower returns than shareholders in American companies.

This book will explore why the financial system in the United States makes both equity and debt investments riskier than comparable investments in overseas companies. These risks explain why shareholders demand greater returns and why companies in America find leverage more burdensome than do German and Japanese competitors. Not surprisingly, the exact same factors explain why both investors and corporate managers are inclined to put their parochial short-term interests ahead of their collective long-run well-being.

Myopia—A Growing Problem

The problem of business myopia appears to have gotten worse in recent years, which would imply that relationships between capital providers and capital users are growing increasingly distant. There are two primary reasons that American businesses and investors are more myopic today than in the past: 1) market evolutions and new technologies permit stocks and business loans to be treated as financial commodities rather than investments in a corporation based on relationships involving dialogue, oversight, and control; and 2) new laws, changes to existing laws, and broader interpretation of regulations in recent years have made it harder for capital providers and capital users to communicate effectively. The growth of global competition from companies that do not suffer from these problems has magnified the dangers of business myopia and raised the consciousness of those who operate under these conditions.

Any businessperson or investor knows that Wall Street has changed dramatically over the past decade. One of the biggest changes has been the emerging dominance of powerful institutional investors. The growing influence of pension funds and insurance companies has been compounded by the retreat of the individual investor. Legions of individual investors now invest in equities through mutual funds (themselves institutional investors) or in debt by way of uninsured money market accounts, which primarily invest in securities rather than direct loans. From 1983 to 1989, the net value of equity holdings by private investors in the United States declined by $550 billion, or about 40 percent. According to *The Economist*, "Would these trends continue, the last American to own shares directly would sell his last one in the year 2003."[7]

Program trading, risk arbitrage, and the futures markets increasingly influence equity trading activity. Huge "baskets" of stock representing an entire index of 5,000 companies can now be purchased with a single order. The number of shares changing hands on a typical day in 1990 would have represented three months' worth of trading in 1960. Simply buying and selling individual stocks to hold as long-term investments is a fading tradition.

Many investors are perplexed by what is going on in the financial markets. Some people have even come to believe that modern securities markets are irrational, driven by forces beyond the control of corporate managers or investors. On the other hand, many academics still cling to the notion that markets are perfectly efficient, instantly incorporating all relevant data into the pricing of securities. They argue that with existing technologies the market is able to respond more quickly to new information, which is the true cause of gyrations in stock prices. As Chapter 2 will discuss, although there is anecdotal and theoretical evidence to support both these views, in reality the markets are neither "irrational" nor "perfect"; they are rational but often uninformed. And the less investors know about what is taking place inside a company, the more dramatically they will respond to quarterly earnings.

The popularization of programming computers to generate buy and sell orders based solely on quantitative factors, and the trend to invest through funds that purchase stocks regardless of the merits, simply because they are listed in an index, mitigate the need for shareholders to familiarize themselves with companies whose shares they own. The ownership component of a stock is becoming de-linked from the financial interest. The quality of managers, workers, strategies, technologies, and everything else associated with the enterprise takes on less importance. Investors who hold shares for a day, a week, or even a month, or only because the stock is in an index, are less likely to take the time to study a company's industry and competitive position.

Voting one's shares also loses its meaning if an investor intends to sell a stock within the next few months or hold it forever regardless of who serves on the board. An Employee Benefit Research Institute study reported that 31 percent of private pension plans did not even know if their proxies had been voted; and of those respondents who had voted at least some of the proxies, only 28 percent did so in accordance with a written policy. This decline in familiarity with and commitment to a company also makes selling one's shares to a bidder offering a premium for the company's stock a more mechanical decision.

Ironically, short-term trading practices thought to be precipitated by greedy investors out to make a quick buck regardless of the effect on corporations actually produce abysmal returns for most stock traders. Every year approximately three-fourths of the professional money managers who invest the funds of major institutions produce returns that are below the market *average*. Similarly, individuals continue to pump billions into mutual funds even though for the past eight years they would have made more money if they had selected stocks by throwing darts at the financial pages of a newspaper. Such poor performance is not surprising when you consider that at the peak of stock trading in

1987, $25 billion was spent in trading stocks, an amount equal to one-sixth of corporate profits and 40 percent of all dividends paid out that year.[8]

It is easy to say that there are too many short-term investors in the United States, but it is much more relevant to ask why investors continue to trade rather than hold stocks when most trading strategies have proven ineffective. Chapters 2 and 3 will examine government regulations that prevent institutional investors from behaving as owners, investment industry practices that provide economic incentives for securities firms and money managers to engage in unnecessary trading, and subtle pressures placed on institutional investors to sell their shares when they disagree with management rather than try to effect change.

Because America's shareholders have effectively abdicated their role as owners, independent buyers of corporations—"take-over artists" and "corporate raiders"—have attempted to fill the void. These self-styled policemen of capitalism dominated the financial headlines during the 1980s. Most people who lament the myopic behavior of American corporations blame at least part of the problem on leveraged buyouts (LBOs) and the people who propagated these transactions. The most common criticism of leveraged buyouts is that they are financially driven and ignore the products, technologies, and people that make companies competitive. Chapter 4 will examine the merits of these accusations.

Managers of public companies are among the most outspoken critics of LBOs. In these days of rapidly changing world events, it is easy to have a short memory. Financially engineered transactions are not a 1980s' phenomenon. During much of the 1960s and early 1970s, executives of some of the very same companies that condemn leveraged buyouts engaged in a frenzy of mergers and acquisitions driven almost exclusively by financial considerations. There is not a tremendous amount of business synergy between a baking company, a hotel chain, an insurance company, and a finishing school, yet companies such as ITT merged together businesses as diverse as these. General Electric became the citadel of financial planning, building a staff of 350 number-crunchers who viewed every business through a quantitative lens. Today, most of these people are gone. Because diversification was thought to be the best way for a company to grow and to preserve its existence, corporations took on markets and technologies they did not understand. As a result, U.S. companies lost their focus, and the owners of American companies lost their patience. The Dow Jones industrial average dropped considerably in real terms during the conglomerate era and was even lower in *nominal* terms in 1982 than it had been 15 years earlier.

The effects of the mergers of the 1960s and 1970s are evident in a paper published by Frank Lichtenberg in which he shared the results of his study of 17,000 manufacturing plants.[9] Lichtenberg found convincing evidence that productivity, thus profitability, suffered incrementally as a company expanded the number of industries in which it operated. In other words, the inability of general managers to operate a business they did not know more than offset whatever financial synergies that were thought to exist.

With conglomerates as sitting ducks, a nation of dissatisfied owners, and armed with a new financial instrument known as a "junk bond," buyout groups began to spring up across the nation. At first, these groups went after mature, stable businesses that operated with little debt. By taking over these companies and replacing equity with debt, buyers were able to achieve much higher returns on equity without having to acquire rapidly growing businesses about which management knew nothing. William Simon, former Secretary of the Treasury, was one of the pioneers of leveraged buyouts. In 1982, he purchased Gibson Greeting Cards for $80 million. The next year he took the company public at a valuation of $330 million, earning his firm Wesray $250 million on an investment of only a million dollars.

Following their successes in reaping enormous financial returns by leveraging cash-generating businesses, financial buyers began to target the conglomerates.[10] Takeover artists argued that many of the operating businesses owned and run by unwieldy bureaucracies at diversified companies would be worth more if they were set free to be run independently by a focused management group. The "bust-up" LBO became the rage, and many of the conglomerates assembled in the previous two decades were dismembered. In fact, 55 percent of the leveraged buyouts completed in 1988 were divestitures. With all this buyout activity occurring, countless companies scrambled to restructure voluntarily to avoid being taken over.

While all this leveraging and restructuring was taking place, the stock market tripled in value, reflecting the market's belief that "focus" was a better strategy than "diversification." However, as is often the case, matters went too far. Investors and lenders, giddy from the returns they received throughout the early and mid-1980s, continued to pump money into LBOs. At one point in the late 1980s, there was enough money invested in LBO equity funds to purchase 10 percent of the public companies in America. However, given levels of LBO activity and the growth in takeover defenses during the past decade, the number of available targets diminished. Prices escalated and buyers began to bid for companies in more cyclical industries, loading them with debt that could only be paid back on schedule under the most optimistic scenarios.

Both commercial and investment bankers had become addicted to the fees generated by takeovers. To get their fix, deal makers would put companies into play, regardless of the long-run benefits to the company or the economy. By the end of the 1980s, the stock of the typical company taken private in a highly leveraged transaction had a beta of greater than 1.0, meaning it was a riskier-than-average business to begin with. Adding substantial debt was only asking for trouble.

While Wall Street deserves much of the blame for the excesses of the late 1980s, it was not alone. Often overlooked is the fact that some of the excessive leverage taken on by American corporations was not imposed on companies by takeover artists, but was the product of either management's desire to enrich itself or its refusal to give up control of companies, regardless of the price they had to pay. Numerous LBOs that have encountered serious difficulties involved defensive recapitalizations, where insiders paid more than a corporate raider was willing to pay in order to preserve their jobs and avoid a change in control. Fruehauf, Interco, Harcourt Brace Jovanovich, and USG are classic examples.

Similarly, companies such as Charter Medical gorged themselves on debt in transactions where management was able to cash in on large shareholdings yet still preserve control of the business—in this case transferring much of the risk to employees by using an employee stock ownership plan (ESOP) to buy the stock. The event that signaled an end to the excesses of the 1980s was the failure of a management group at United Airlines to finance an exorbitant $300-a-share offer to take the company private in order to escape the grasp of unsolicited suitors. When the deal fell apart in October 1989, the Dow Jones average plunged almost 200 points in a matter of hours; investors realized the party was over.

The events of the 1980s severely strained relationships between corporate managers and shareholders. Relations that had been increasingly characterized by benign neglect since the days of J.P. Morgan deteriorated into antagonism, and, in some cases, hostility. Corporate boards and executives—largely the same group of people—sought refuge from policy makers. They pleaded for new laws that would prevent, or at least deter, leveraged buyouts.

During the conglomerate era, some powerful business leaders were the predators, while others were the victims. Politically, this produced a stalemate. Policy makers enacted federal legislation in the form of the Williams Act of 1968, which was designed to level the playing field between buyers and sellers.

The situation in the 1980s was much different. The predators were takeover artists and Wall Street firms, with institutional investors serving as accomplices. Institutional investors typically sold their shares to corporate raiders who offered them a premium. Many pension fund managers believed that it was their fiduciary responsibility to sell under these circumstances. There was so much confusion on this issue that the Departments of

Treasury and Labor issued a joint statement in January 1989 stipulating that private pension funds were not required to sell stock at a premium if they believed holding it long term would produce a superior value.

The fact that corporate executives and workers were regarded as the victims of greedy Wall Street deal makers and institutional owners tilted the political power heavily in favor of target companies. Adroit business and labor groups avoided asking for federal intervention where the balance of power would be looked at from a national perspective. Instead, they targeted their lobbying efforts at the state government level, where they could threaten to move corporate charters and jobs to other states if they were not protected from hostile bidders. Laws were enacted or tightened in 40 states to prevent takeovers. In more than a dozen cases, state corporate law was changed to accommodate the needs of a single company under siege. Washington protected Boeing; Massachusetts accommodated the Norton Company; and Pennsylvania provided cover for Armstrong World Industries.

In their haste to protect local companies, many state legislatures and corporate boards implemented provisions making collective action by shareholders more expensive, more difficult, and, in some cases, virtually impossible. Majorities of 85 percent are now required at some companies for certain decisions such as a change in control. Shareholders of countless companies are now deprived of the opportunity to call special meetings. Owners who acquire a significant percentage of shares in certain companies automatically lose their voting rights. In one state, any bidder for a company that fails to gain complete control will have its profits repatriated if it attempts to sell its shares within 18 months.

Most of the takeover defenses written into corporate charters and state law in the 1980s threw the baby (shareholders) out with the bathwater (corporate raiders). These laws have heightened the futility felt by the few remaining shareholders who are willing to hold their shares long term in exchange for some measures for holding those who control their money accountable for how it is used. American owners are already much more fragmented than owners in Japan and Germany. Large shareholders in those countries do not have to rely on takeovers and proxy battles to effect change; they do so behind closed doors in private meetings or in the boardroom. Chapter 3 will describe how the existence of more effective accountability systems in Japan and Germany lower the risks of owners having their capital misappropriated.

Borrowing Has Become Riskier

While the relations between corporations and their owners were growing more acrimonious, relationships between corporations and their lenders were also disintegrating. As discussed in Chapter 5, the 1970s and 1980s witnessed the end of relationship banking and the emergence of transaction-driven borrowing. America's depression era laws have produced the most fragmented and regulated financial services industry on earth, rendering U.S. banks unable to offer their customers a broad range of products and services. These laws, coupled with a legal system that exposes banks to extensive liability if they purchase stock in their customers, also deter banks from being owners as well as lenders, a practice applied universally throughout Japan and Germany.

With U.S. banks unable to offer their corporate customers meaningful relationships and a broad range of services, American corporations began to *disintermediate* their banks, accessing capital directly from the markets or from a foreign bank rather than through a U.S. financial intermediary.* The increasing sophistication and rapid integration of global debt markets in recent years have provided a discount shopping mall for any creditworthy

---

* Rates available through public bonds, private placements, and commercial paper are typically lower than the cost of a bank loan. Interest rates charged by many foreign banks in recent years have also been more competitive than the rates of domestic lenders.

company in need of capital, expediting the demise of relationship banking in the United States. Loans have become little more than transactions, and U.S. banks have increasingly focused on how to get their money back, rather than on how to help their customers prosper in the long term.

Since the well-known and well-run companies were better positioned to circumvent the banking system, this left the weaker companies, along with commercial real estate developers, third-world countries, and other less dependable borrowers as the banks' primary customer base. Needless to say, the erosion of the banks' traditional franchise has led to serious financial difficulties for the U.S. banking industry. As banks have lowered their prices to compete with alternative sources of debt, and taken on riskier loans to continue their growth, their credit ratings have declined, raising their costs. Facing a squeeze on profits and stricter globally mandated capital standards, U.S. banks have shuttered offices overseas and pulled in the credit reins at home. Unable to serve their multinational customers' foreign needs, and less reliable as a source of financing for domestic borrowers, U.S. banks have become increasingly viewed by corporate America as irrelevant.

This perilous spiral does not only hurt banks. In Japan and Germany, when borrowers encounter difficulties, their lenders work with them to restructure existing loans or advance additional funds to minimize the disruption to their business. In the United States, on the other hand, transactional lenders are not as accommodating. Consequently, U.S. companies view debt as a noose that limits their flexibility to pursue aggressive corporate strategies.

U.S. companies that have circumvented the banking system altogether find their debt more restricting than the borrowing of their foreign competitors. The rules that govern a standard bond restructuring in the United States discourage compliance among bondholders. Owners of 90 percent or more (depending on whether the company is in bankruptcy) of each layer of debt have to consent to new terms. And if bondholders fail to go along with a plan that is approved, they preserve the original terms, which are usually more favorable, providing them with an incentive to hang tough and not work with companies in times of trouble.

Where the Japanese and Germans tend to rely on informal negotiations to solve disputes between borrowers and lenders, in the United States we resort to formal documents and litigation.[11] Furthermore, secured creditors of U.S. companies are often intransigent because their customers are worth just as much dead as alive—they simply confiscate their collateral. This mind-set is anathema to German and Japanese lenders, who own stock in their customers and stand to lose a great deal in a liquidation.

A reliance on rigid debt covenants rather than relationships has limited the operating flexibility of U.S. corporations. In other words, because of weak relationships between borrowers and lenders, debt in the United States is a riskier source of capital than it is in Japan and Germany. And since debt is a cheaper source of capital than equity, the fact that U.S. companies have been unable to take advantage of borrowed funds to the extent that their foreign competitors do has raised their relative cost of capital.

No Quick Fixes

When you combine disengaged owners who are actively trading shares with a dysfunctional corporate governance system, severe restrictions on takeovers, and the declining use of financial intermediaries, there are not many options left to harmonize the interests of corporate managers and those who provide them with capital. Many people believe that one of the few remaining vehicles to bridge the widening gap in the relationship between corporations and investors is management compensation plans. If you marry their economic fates, they reason, managers and owners will share the same interests. Although this sounds logical, there is little evidence that existing executive compensation plans have any real effect on management performance, and there are severe impediments to using executive pay to influence behavior, as detailed in Chapter 7.

The way in which executives in the United States are rewarded frequently has little to do with their performance. Consider the largest corporation in America—General Motors. Until Robert Stempel was named chief executive in April 1990, the company had been run by finance people for 37 years. During their reign, quarterly earnings received a great deal of attention, but the company forgot how to build competitive cars. General Motors witnessed its domestic market share drop precipitously. During the 1980s alone, GM's U.S. market share plunged by 10 percent— equivalent to almost the entire domestic sales of Chrysler. Yet when then-CEO Roger Smith retired in 1990, the GM board of directors voted to double the pensions of over 3,000 top managers and boost Smith's annual retirement benefits to approximately $1.25 million a year. Compare this to Japanese compensation practices: when Mazda Motor Corporation of Japan was warned by the Transport Ministry a few months later to pay stricter attention to the safety of its cars in connection with a recall of 3,500 vehicles, Chairman Kenichi Yamamoto and 17 other top executives immediately took a 10-percent pay cut.

Base salaries for U.S. executives have continued to escalate, regardless of performance. In 1989, the average salary for *Business Week*'s top 1,000 chief executives rose 7 percent over the previous year. Yet during 1989, the average profits of the companies they ran were down 5 percent, and their shareholders lost 11 percent of the market value of their holdings.

Although some top executives such as Reebok's Paul Fireman and Chris-Craft's Herb Siegel pulled in over $10 million (excluding stock-related gains), Warren Buffett was paid a salary of only $100,000 to run Berkshire Hathaway. Buffett, the CEO most renowned for having a long-term perspective, and the third-wealthiest man in America, has tied his economic fate to that of his company's owners. However, Buffett, who owns about half the stock in the company he runs, is the exception. The median percentage ownership of CEOs in their own companies is only one-quarter of 1 percent, or less than two years' pay, according to

Forbes's Executive Compensation Survey. But shareholders are ignored when they complain about the amount or structure of management compensation. Perhaps this is because two-thirds of the directors of America's public companies, who establish management pay, are themselves top executives of other public companies.

No matter how pay is structured, compensation has to influence one's lifestyle before it will have a meaningful impact on behavior. The average U.S. chief executive's salary is approximately four times his German counterpart's and eight to ten times that of top Japanese executives according to Graef Crystal, a leading expert on compensation issues. Even the most creative compensation packages will have less of an effect on the behavior of someone whose income already greatly exceeds their living expenses. Compounding this problem is the fact that most reward programs can provide perverse incentives to top managers and directors, which may motivate them to take actions that do not maximize the total return to shareholders. Highly touted stock options, for example, can encourage executives to retain earnings that the company may not be able to reinvest profitably, rather than pay them out as dividends to shareholders, since option holders do not receive dividends.

Short-termism is too pervasive to be resolved by tinkering with financial incentives for top executives. Because of the magnitude of the problem, the solution will have to be more dramatic. To cure the chronic myopia that is undermining U.S. competitiveness, we need to improve the relationships between the providers of capital and the users of capital so that investors and corporate managers will communicate better and trust each other enough to put their mutual long-run interests ahead of their parochial short-term objectives. Closer relationships and reduced risks of investing will lower U.S. capital costs, affording companies the opportunity to invest long term. Also, investors will better understand corporate strategies with distant payoffs. Jonathan Charkham, who advises the Bank of England on corporate governance and other related issues, characterizes the problem colorfully: "If relationships are prostitutional, you do not get the benefits of marriage." A series of one-night stands between capital providers and capital users is not the same as having a supportive, long-term partner.

Throughout this book the practices followed in the United States are compared to those of other countries only because they provide valuable lessons on how cooperation works better than confrontation in building competitive enterprises. International comparisons are not intended to serve as a template for reform. The cultures, histories, and traditions of Germany and Japan are different from those of the United States. The cure for America's business myopia is not to simplemindedly mimic the practices followed in these countries, or to replicate their financial systems. *What America needs is a uniquely American solution.* America's investors, corporations, and political leaders must work together to find and implement creative ways to reform the practices of the investment industry, improve the corporate governance system, and restructure the laws and regulations governing our financial services industry to better facilitate dialogue and teamwork.

Institutional investors, bankers, business leaders, and government regulators have all contributed to the problem. We must all be a part of the solution. During the two years I served as director of the office responsible for competitiveness policy at the U.S. Treasury Department, I never once received a visit from anyone who volunteered that they were, in any way, responsible for short-termism. It was always someone else's fault. The following chapters will show that there is more than enough blame to go around. But pointing fingers is counterproductive. Rather, the goal of this book is to show how everyone contributes to business myopia and to stimulate ideas on how to restore the American financial system to one that promotes the long-term economic health and well-being of the nation's economy.

2

The Commoditization of Corporate Ownership

A share of stock is not what it used to be. Originally, a share of stock was more than an economic investment, it was an ownership interest in a company embodying both rights and responsibilities. Today, a share of stock is a financial commodity, little different from an ounce of silver or a pork-belly futures contract. The increasing legal and regulatory barriers that prevent stockholders from behaving as owners, coupled with new technologies that make it less expensive and easier to trade stocks, are transforming the stock market into less of a place to raise capital and exercise corporate oversight than a gambling casino.

Stock trading surged in the 1980s, while the amount of equity pulled out of the public markets far exceeded new stock issues. As equity investors look to trading as a source of wealth rather than working to improve on the success of the businesses they own, shareholders are growing more disengaged as owners.

The trend serves neither investors nor corporations well. Year in and year out, America's powerful institutional investors turn in abysmal results. A study conducted by William Mercer Asset Planning, Inc. showed that returns realized in 1989 by 122 bank and insurance company investment managers were almost 20 percent below the Standard & Poor's 500 stock index, making it seven consecutive years that they had underperformed the market average. Stock mutual funds dropped 6.3 percent in 1990, while the market declined only 3.1 percent, according to Lipper Analytical Services. Since mutual funds are required to hold a portion of their assets in cash to meet potential redemptions, they *should* outperform the average when stocks decline.

The evidence indicates that those who hold stocks for longer periods of time outperform speculative traders. In 1990, Morningstar Inc., a Chicago mutual fund research firm, examined the performance of 278 domestic stock funds. They found that a "buy-and-hold" strategy outperformed all other strategies, including those of "rapid-fire traders" and those funds with moderate turnover. Pitcairn Financial Management Group examined the performance of stocks with a significant group of (at least 10 percent) long-term owners. Pitcairn Group concluded that the share prices of these companies appreciated more than twice as fast as the S&P 500 index from 1979 to 1989; they did better in both bull and bear markets. Despite the overwhelming evidence that trading strategies fail to produce acceptable, let alone superior performance, the United States commits substantial economic and human resources to shuffling stock certificates.

Stock turnover is a concern of the corporate community as well. Business leaders complain that pressures from shareholders to meet short-term performance bogeys are undermining their ability to build competitive enterprises. They claim that shareholder preoccupation with quarterly results makes investment in innovative products and technologies with distant payoffs more difficult.

Many academics contend, however, that investor horizons have little, if any, impact on investment decisions. Much of the confusion on this issue stems from misperceptions about how the stock market functions. One day spent on the trading floor of a Wall Street firm would dispel any notion that markets are perfect, that all meaningful information is instantly disseminated and incorporated into the price of securities. The best-selling book *Liar's Poker* provides a glimpse of how securities are bought and sold for those who have never had a chance to witness the action behind the scenes at a brokerage firm. However, the view that speculative trading generated by mindless computers and greedy investors produces stock prices that are wildly different from their true economic value is overstated.

Bad information undermines the effectiveness of even the most efficient markets. Without this framework by which to assess market behavior, it is easy to misconstrue the signals the market sends. A belief that markets are irrational makes it easy to dismiss important market feedback. Believing that markets are perfect ignores the fact that much of the information incorporated into stock prices is incomplete or inaccurate.

Short-Run versus Long-Run Value

A commonly held perception is that corporate managers try to maximize the long-run value of a company and that most investors, large institutions, and corporate raiders in particular focus only on short-term value. Whenever a takeover is discussed, the issue of long- versus short-term value is raised. But is there really a difference?

The business schools attended by most corporate executives and money managers alike teach that the price of a company's stock reflects the value of *all* future cash flows that a shareholder can expect to receive, whether in the short run or in the distant future. Obviously, the further away an expected cash flow is, the more heavily it will be discounted, to compensate for the time value of money and the uncertainty that it will materialize. But within this theoretical framework, it is possible to incorporate both immediate and long-term payoffs into present valuations. The belief that there is a difference between short- and long-term value implies that the market fails to do this analysis properly.

One explanation is that shareholders no longer take the time to do the analysis, but instead rely on quarterly earnings reports to signal the future prospects of the company. With the growth in the equity portfolios of large institutional investors, it is increasingly difficult for them to stay abreast of events at hundreds, if not thousands, of companies, leaving them little choice but to look for proxies for future value.

The reasoning behind looking to historical earnings as an indicator of future performance appears logical. Assume, for example, that you contract with a builder to construct a new home for your family. After agreeing to the blueprints and a detailed list of features, the builder quotes a price. Equate this to an annual earnings estimate. The final price you will pay, however, is subject to what it actually costs to build the house. If the first phase were completed at a cost 50 percent above the estimate, would you not fear the worst—that the entire house could cost an additional 50 percent? Absent any other information, you might assume that the original estimate was overly optimistic, based on the interim result.

It is doubtful that the builder would suddenly drop this news on you without explaining the overrun on the first phase and how some or all of the unexpected costs would be made up in future stages in order to meet the original budget. Corporations also attempt to justify unexpected results. However, companies often do a poor job of explaining interim results, and frequently shareholders fail to take the time to listen. As a result, the relevance of short-term results to the long-term prospects of the company can be exaggerated.

This becomes more of a problem if communication between managers and shareholders is infrequent or superficial. Often investors rely on third-party research reports for insights into management's plans and the prospects for the company. The quality and integrity of third-party research has increasingly been a subject of debate.[1] Equity analysts on Wall Street typically are compensated based on the commission revenue generated by their firm's institutional brokers. Occasionally they are also paid according to the transaction volume produced by the firm's corporate finance department. Neither factor depends on the insightfulness of their research. Compounding the problem is the structure of research departments in investment firms—analysts tend to cover multiple competitors in the same industry. While this practice makes sense from the brokerage firms' perspective, it alarms executives at many of the companies they follow who do not want their confidential strategies exposed to competitors.

In a speech to a group of chief financial officers of *Fortune* 500 companies, I asked if they were forthright with stock research analysts, telling the analysts all they would want their owners to know. Uproarious laughter broke out. One participant summarized the views of the group: "We tell them as little as possible; they talk to all of our competitors." Everyone nodded in agreement. Yet stock analysts are the primary conduit for information between the managers and owners of U.S. corporations.

Without ongoing, in-depth, and straightforward dialogue, management and investors will operate with different information, which might lead them to different conclusions. This problem is addressed in a paper co-authored by Jeremy Stein, a finance professor at the Massachusetts Institute of Technology who worked with me on this subject when he was a member of the President's Council of Economic Advisors.[2] Presented below is a brief synopsis of the problem academics refer to as "information asymmetries," as paraphrased from Stein's paper.

Suppose a company's board approves a $100-million expenditure that it believes will produce $300 million in added revenues, leaving $200 million as profit. (For simplicity, ignore the time value of money in this example.) If management is able to communicate the strategic and economic merits of the project to the market—and the shareholders listen—then when the project is announced the value of the company's stock should rise by $200 million. This is the paradigm of market behavior that academics and investors generally espouse. However, if management fails to communicate the benefits of the capital investment to the marketplace—because it does not want to publicly disclose its competitive strategy, because shareholders ignore the press release, or because investors have lost faith in management's projections—

then the market will not incorporate the full value of the project into the stock price.

In the early stages of the project, the shareholders note a decrease of $100 million in the company's cash flow. Not knowing otherwise, they construe this as a decline in the company's business prospects and adjust their valuation of the stock downward. Not until the profits from the capital investment show up in reported earnings would the market fully incorporate the merits of the capital expenditure into the value of the stock. The market is behaving rationally, given available information, but from the perspective of corporate managers, investors are behaving myopically.

This is a particular problem for intangible investments that fail to show up on the balance sheet. Research and development, employee training, and other expenditures that are not capitalized as assets according to today's accounting norms are important investments in the long-term health and competitiveness of a company, yet they are immediately charged to earnings. Absent a way to communicate the merits of these expenses to shareholders, corporations would tend to minimize the amount of funds allocated to intangibles. This becomes a greater concern as shareholders place increasing emphasis on reported earnings, and disproportionately penalizes companies that invest heavily in training and research.

The problem lies in the quality of information the market uses to value companies, not in the greediness or impatience of investors. Institutional investors are sophisticated enough to understand valuation techniques, and they certainly have the manpower and computers to perform the math properly. But if the assumptions on which their formulas are based are inaccurate, the resulting valuation will misrepresent the true value of a company.

In many cases, current earnings are a poor proxy for the long-run prospects of the company, which is why relying too heavily on them can produce valuations that misrepresent a firm's true economic worth. Obviously, weak earnings can signal problems ahead. But to the extent that the market inappropriately reads weak interim results caused by long-term investments as discouraging news about the future, it will penalize the stocks of companies that are truly investing for the future. And to the extent that corporate officers care about the value of the company, seeing the stock price decline will make them more hesitant to commit resources to strategic initiatives with distant payoffs. Ironically, although many managers blame stock market pressures for short-termism, the most rapidly growing component of executive compensation is stock options, whereby they make themselves more vulnerable to these pressures.

As they say in Washington, perception is reality. And the perception among many corporate executives is that if they fail to produce consistently higher quarterly earnings, their share price will suffer. Anecdotal evidence leads corporate managers to believe that investing long term and maximizing stock price are mutually exclusive goals. Consider the following excerpt from a story in *The Wall Street Journal*:

> A lower-than-expected profit rise at Motorola, Inc. spooked investors. . . . That news . . . sent Motorola shares tumbling in heavy trading $7, to $52.75. The decline . . . clipped some $950 million from the company's total market value. . . . In addition to igniting a debate over Motorola's prospects, the stock market action highlighted a conflict between investors and such large-growth companies as Motorola. Even as the company's executives profess to manage for the long term, investors can't help but react to the short-term reality.[3]

Why do investors rely so heavily on interim results and spend little time understanding the long-term plans of corporations? One answer is that the less time investors plan to own a security, the less time they are able to devote to understanding the dynamics of a given firm's strategies and establishing relationships with company executives and directors that would provide them access to firsthand information. As a practical matter, investors holding shares for a day, a week, or even a few months cannot afford the time required to learn about the specific plans of a given company in their portfolio. Another factor involves the number of stocks in one's portfolio. As investors increasingly invest through index funds, which own hundreds or thousands of stocks, they find it more difficult to track companies in their portfolios. Also, as a legal matter, shareholders privy to internal data are prohibited from trading based on "inside information," so active stock traders are precluded from knowing anything about a company's long-term strategy or plans that is not made public.

Without insight into corporate plans and strategies, it is harder to determine which companies will generate shareholder wealth over the long term. Thus, more attention is focused on earnings reports, which can change significantly from one quarter to another. A popular way to make money on stocks, therefore, is to predict whether reported results will be higher or lower than the analysts' short-term earnings forecasts. Not surprisingly, the analysts who serve stock traders want to cater to their informational needs, so they focus greater attention on predicting quarterly earnings accurately and less on becoming knowledgeable about a company's competitive prospects. The result is that corporations strive to produce predictable, consistent quarterly earnings because with disengaged owners, it is simply too difficult to explain unexpected results.

Although the lack of quality information about a firm's long-term prospects produces valuation inaccuracies, it is important not to exaggerate the degree of misvaluation that occurs. In 1988, *Fortune* magazine asked Alfred Rappaport, a professor of accounting and finance at Northwestern University and author of the well-known book *Creating Shareholder Value,* to determine what percentage of a stock's price is based on the company's long-term prospects and what percentage reflects the returns investors could expect to receive in the next five years.[4] Evaluating the 20 largest U.S. companies based on market value, Rappaport found that anywhere from 66 percent to 89 percent of a company's stock price could not be explained by existing prospects for dividend payouts over the upcoming five-year period. Not surprisingly, the company whose stock was least influenced by short-term expectations was Boeing, a well-managed company positioned as a market leader in virtually the only industry in which the United States had gained market share in the previous 20 years. Equally unsurprising was the company whose stock value was tied most closely to the short term, Occidental Petroleum. This company was run more as a fiefdom by its octogenarian CEO than in a manner designed to optimize value to the shareholders in the long run (see Chapter 3). It is important to note that in none of these companies was the portion of value attributed to the short term equal to the average takeover premium paid during the 1980s.

Why Owners Become Traders

The debate over the ills of short-term trading has been waged over the wrong issue. To date, more attention has been paid to market volatility than to informational problems, which is the real concern. Typically, critics of short-term trading claim that rapid stock turnover increases the volatility of the equity markets, which theoretically raises the cost of capital. However, the evidence indicates that by most measures, the volatility of the stock market is no greater today than it was in the past. The reason people perceive the market to be riskier nowadays is that there have been two periods—in October of 1987 and 1989—when stock prices fell precipitously. These sudden, dramatic drops create a perception of volatility, but the monthly trading ranges in recent years are not out of line with those since the depression. Also, because the Dow Jones industrial average has been much higher in absolute terms since 1982, a 40- or 50-point move no longer represents a 4 or 5 percent drop.

Those who defend active trading strategies always point out the little-known fact that stock turnover is *higher* in Germany and

Japan, countries typically credited with having a long-term perspective. This defense, however, has a major flaw. In Germany and Japan, the individuals and institutions that speculate on stocks are a sideshow; in the United States, they are the main event. In Germany, banks with long-term customer relationships typically control, through direct ownership and proxies of individual shareholders, a majority of the stock in most public companies. And as Table 2.1 shows, short-term investors in Japan comprise a much smaller percentage of ownership than they do in the United States, and they seldom control a significant portion of a given company. Long-term investors control 70 percent of all publicly traded Japanese companies; in any event, more than 99 percent of Japanese companies are privately held. In Germany and Japan, speculative traders can churn stocks all they want, but they will have little impact on the behavior of corporate managers.

In the United States, on the other hand, ownership is much more fragmented than in Germany, Britain, or Japan. Although stocks are becoming increasingly concentrated in the hands of U.S. institutional investors, these investors are not investing in the same way their counterparts overseas do. The reasons for this are important to understanding what is behind the growth in speculative trading and the poor communication between owners and managers in the United States.

Early in the twentieth century, much of the stock in U.S. companies was held by relatively few people. The Morgans, Carnegies, Vanderbilts, Fords, and other families controlled an enormous percentage of corporate assets in the United States. By mid-century, publicly traded shares had been dispersed among a broad cross section of individuals. Today, for the first time since the Great Depression, control over America's corporations is once again becoming concentrated, this time in the hands of large institutions that invest on behalf of millions of individuals.

Overall, institutions own about half of the publicly traded equities in the United States and control a majority of its large companies. In 1987, institutions owned 53 percent of the shares in

Table 2.1

**Comparisons of Ownership Patterns of Equity Securities,
U.S. and Japan, January 1988**

	U.S.	Japan
Purely Investment Return-Oriented Investors		
Institutional investors (e.g., pension funds, mutual funds)	44%	15%
General public investors	19	3
Other	4	4
	67%	22%
Relationship-Oriented Investors		
Financial institutions with business relationships (e.g., banks, life insurance companies)	12%	47%
Nonfinancial corporate holders	9	11
Parent and other group companies	3	17
Owner–Founder	10	4
	34%	79%

Note: Figures may not add due to rounding.

Source: Industrial Policy Bureau, Ministry of International Trade and Industry, Tokyo, Japan, from a survey of 300 of the largest manufacturing companies in both the United States and Japan. Cited in Burton G. Malkiel, "The Influence of Conditions in Financial Markets on the Time Horizons of Business Managers: An International Comparison." Paper prepared for the Time Horizons of American Management project, sponsored by the Council on Competitiveness and the Harvard Business School (1990 draft).

the 100 largest U.S. companies as measured by market value. In one out of 10 of the largest 1,000 companies, institutions controlled over 70 percent of the stock. During the 1980s, the total assets of institutional investors grew from less than $2 trillion to more than $5 trillion. And since 1950, the equity ownership of the pension funds alone has soared from $1 billion to $1 trillion. Today the 20 largest pension fund managers in the United States control over $600 billion in assets. These pension funds, combined with the 10 largest professional money managers, now control more than 15 percent of America's 10 largest companies.[5] This consolidation of economic power has occurred virtually overnight, and neither the institutional investors nor the rules and regulations governing them are equipped to deal with it.

Institutional investors are not a monolithic group, but the major sectors do have similar investment objectives and risk profiles. Pension funds, which invest the retirement savings for America's workers, comprise the largest segment. The second-largest category is insurance companies, which invest the vast sums received from premiums so they will have the money to pay future claims and benefits. Insurance companies also manage portfolios on behalf of some of the pension funds.

Investment companies, most of which are known as mutual funds, are an increasingly popular mechanism for individuals to purchase stocks. By pooling resources, individuals are theoretically able to attain much of the power available to larger investors (although in most years individuals outperform institutional investors). With more than $1 trillion invested in this manner, one in four American families now owns a mutual fund, according to the Investment Company Institute. Bank trust departments, a shrinking category of institutional investors, manage investments for both individuals and institutional customers, but they do not invest the bank's own capital. Finally, foundations and endowments affiliated with universities and other tax-exempt entities comprise the smallest segment of institutional investors. Most of the discussion in this chapter will focus on the pension funds since they are the largest and most influential segment of the institutional marketplace.

One would expect these institutional investors to be the ideal long-term shareholders. Pension funds and insurance companies collect money that does not need to be paid out for many years into the future. However, on average, these institutions hold stocks for much shorter periods than individuals do. Labor Department statistics show that the annual turnover of pension fund portfolios is more than 50 percent.

The fact that institutions, which should have long-term horizons, invest on such a short-term basis perplexes many in the business community. However, a close look at the constraints and pressures that influence institutional investors reveals that they have little choice. The federal and state governments regulate institutional investor practices with such a complex web of laws and regulations that it is virtually impossible for pension fund managers and other institutional investors to emulate the long-term, patient investors we find overseas.

Because we have failed to understand the hurdles institutions face in being long-term owners, policy makers have proposed a variety of ways to punish the seemingly counterproductive behavior of stock speculators. The most popular idea is to impose an excise tax each time an equity security is traded. But this is a simpleminded way of using the tax code as a Band-Aid solution to a deeper problem. If long-term investors do not find active stock trading profitable, yet persistently allocate funds to money managers who constantly buy and sell stocks, there must be a reason. When I was at the Treasury Department, I used this argument in my efforts to persuade Secretary Brady to oppose a "short-term trading tax" on pension funds which had been proposed as a cure-all for short-term trading. An effective solution requires defining the problem properly.

Chapter 3 will explain why holding stocks indefinitely with the hope of providing meaningful accountability to corporate managers is futile. The corporate governance system in America is stacked against the owner. It is easier to sell a stock and move on to a company where you believe management is focused on the interests of the owners than it is to change management's behavior. This practice of "voting with your feet" is popularly known as the "Wall Street Rule"; it is the path of least resistance taken by most investors. But the biased corporate governance system is not the only reason institutions trade so much.

Declining commission costs is the most commonly cited reason for the recent increase in turnover. The volume of shares traded in the U.S. equity markets exploded fourfold during the 1980s even though the total number of shares in the stock market shrunk because of stock buybacks and leveraged buyouts. Others attribute the growth in turnover rates to computer technology, which now allows money managers to oversee and execute a far greater number of transactions. In recent years we have also seen the advent of stock index futures, financial instruments that allow an investor to purchase an entire basket of different stocks in a single trade. Because the price of these instruments is often slightly different from the aggregate value of all the stocks comprising the index (because of trading anomalies in either market), the opportunities for arbitrage profits exist. Computer programs can trigger orders to purchase the index futures and sell the basket of individual stocks or vice versa. The constant buying and selling of the stocks that comprise the index raise turnover rates.

Another factor that contributed to the turnover of the 1980s was the large number of takeovers. The surge in buyouts not only precipitated the sale of securities to new owners, but frequently involved numerous intermediate trades. An entire business known as "risk arbitrage" evolved out of the takeover era. In this practice, investors amass significant stakes in potential takeover targets in order to sell them to a corporate raider or other buyer. Although the profits on each trade might not be substantial, the holding period is short enough for arbitrageurs to make hefty returns.

Some have suggested draconian measures to reduce trading such as banning computer-generated trades or outlawing arbitrage. If measures are taken to put a halt to the use of computers, we will drive the investment industry offshore. In the same vein, if arbitrage activities are banned or more heavily regulated, we will de-link the futures market from the cash market, which should theoretically function as one market. Such action would only exacerbate the potential for sudden jolts to either market. Solving the problems associated with short-term trading requires an understanding of the reasons why institutional investors with long-term horizons prefer to shift their portfolios rather than behave as true owners, including the following:

- The securities industry's livelihood depends on generating commissions;
- Regulatory impediments make it difficult for institutions to exercise their rights as long-term owners;
- Pressures are placed on institutional investors, particularly pension funds, to produce attractive quarterly results; and
- Pressures are placed on institutional investors not to challenge management.

The Drive for Commissions

The livelihood of Wall Street is dependent upon commissions derived from trading securities. No one but the owner makes money when an investor holds stocks. As Robert Monks and Nell Minow note in *Power and Accountability,* trustees do not receive bonuses for voting proxies judiciously. Not surprisingly, America's stockbrokers, research analysts, and advisers have engendered the perception that the way to make money on stocks is to buy and sell, rather than to buy and monitor, which is what ownership is all about.

The bias of securities firms to promote stock trading is easy to understand, but none of us knows the extent to which this occurs. For example, since fixed commissions were abolished, a new industry of soft-dollar brokers has emerged. An enormous but enigmatic market, the soft-dollar business involves the use of brokerage commissions by money managers to pay for products and services instead of purchasing them directly. By charging commissions that substantially exceed the cost of executing a trade, brokers can provide kickbacks in the form of products and services to money managers who trade stock through them. The "free" research that old-line Wall Street firms have been providing their customers for years is an example of this concept. More than 700 products and services are now involved.

Soft-dollar transactions occur when a money manager, investing on behalf of an institutional investor, directs a trade to a soft-dollar broker. The broker credits the money manager's account for a percentage (generally 50 percent) of the commissions generated by the trade. The credits in these accounts can then be used by the money manager to purchase research, consulting services, seminars, software, and even computer hardware from the soft-dollar broker without paying cash. The more overhead a money manager can cover with soft dollars, the more management fees they can pocket as profit.

The reason soft dollars are so enticing is that the party who receives the benefits of the credits, the money manager, does not have to pay the commissions that generated them. The bill is sent to the institutional investor whose account is being traded. Accumulating soft-dollar is like spending your employer's money on air travel and getting to keep all of the frequent-flier perks, except that you don't have to leave town. Clearly, if institutional investors do not monitor their money managers' use of soft dollars, abuses will go undetected. A recent survey conducted by Callan Associates, Inc. indicated that 50 percent of the pension funds have no soft-dollar policy, and 80 percent of the pension plan sponsors do not know how their investment managers utilize soft-dollar commissions.

The money management industry is somewhat closed mouthed on the subject, so it is difficult to determine how extensive this practice is. Since soft dollars are an unmonitored supplement to money managers' fees, they have an incentive not to publicize it, especially since the practice has received substantial criticism. Even the consultants who monitor the performance of money managers are disinclined to expose abuses in the soft-dollar industry; they are often paid with soft dollars.

Investment Dealers' Digest estimated that soft dollars are a billion-dollar-a-year business.[6] *Business Week* estimated that one-third of all institutional brokerage business involves soft dollars.[7] It seems that anything worth paying for in soft dollars would have the same value in real dollars. Why not simply price each product and service separately and let the money managers pay for what they need? As long as there is a perception that play money exists, and that more of it can be generated by churning stocks, there will be a temptation to trade stocks unnecessarily.

Compounding the problem is the fact that soft-dollar brokers occasionally extend credit to money managers, enabling them to receive products and services *before* the trades occur. When accounts are settled at the end of the month, money managers who have not covered all of their soft-dollar credits are clearly tempted to generate a few extra trades to avoid having to pay cash to make up the shortfall.

In a 1990 report presented to the Labor Department and the Securities and Exchange Commission (SEC), Morgan Stanley and Goldman Sachs argued that the soft-dollar business is damaging to the markets for a variety of reasons, including the fact that liquidity is hurt by money managers directing "easy" trades to soft-dollar brokers and only the more difficult trades to traditional brokers. To execute large orders, brokers often need to deploy their own capital, which increases their risk. Yet the commissions they receive are no higher. But Wall Street is divided over whether to curb such practices, because several large investment firms make an enormous amount of money from the soft-dollar business.

Regulatory Impediments to Ownership Behavior

In the survey conducted by the Financial Executives Institute mentioned previously, top financial officers were asked what type of investor they find most desirable. The respondents overwhelmingly selected long-term *active* shareholders. Since America's corporations say they welcome investors who behave like owners (and the evidence indicates that investors obtain better results with this approach), one would expect government officials to encourage rather than inhibit ownership behavior. Yet, in addition to the myriad corporate governance provisions promulgated by the SEC and state governments, which will be discussed in Chapter 3, ownership behavior is also impeded by regulations emanating from the Justice, Treasury, and Labor departments.

The Federal Trade Commission (FTC) is responsible for enforcing the Hart-Scott-Rodino Act, legislation enacted to prohibit monopolistic behavior by America's corporations. One of the issues the FTC deals with is whether an acquisition of stock is made truly for investment or as a foot in the door to secure competitive information or to aid in a potential takeover. The Pre-merger Notification Office of the FTC has interpreted Hart-Scott-Rodino broadly—far more broadly than its authors intended. By applying the regulation to pension and mutual funds, which have no interest in taking control of companies, the FTC has put up another roadblock to ownership behavior. Specifically, the FTC stipulates that the following activities, normally associated with ownership, "could be viewed as inconsistent with an investment-only intent":

- Nominating a candidate for the board of directors;
- Proposing corporate action requiring shareholder approval;
- Soliciting proxies; and
- Having a controlling shareholder, director, officer, or employee of the investor serve as a director of the company in which they have invested.

But that is not all. In January 1990, John M. Sipple, Jr., chief of the Pre-merger Notification Office, elaborated:

> I want to stress that this [above] list was not intended to be an exhaustive list of the types of conduct that could be construed as inconsistent with investment-only intent. For example, if a significant shareholder makes suggestions to the issuer's management that it undertake certain actions, whether or not they require shareholder approval, such conduct may be construed as evidencing an intent inconsistent with an investment-only intent. A passive investor can meet with management to gather information about its investment and it can vote the stock its holds, but it cannot

attempt to influence the basic business decisions of the issuer. Thus, we will not limit ourselves only to the types of conduct listed in the Statement of Basis and Purpose in addressing the issue of intent. . . . It seems to me that if mutual funds assume more active roles with respect to the companies in which they make investments they may no longer qualify for the investment exemptions. . . . Similarly, it has been reported that some of the nation's pension funds have assumed a more active role as major corporate shareholders. Again, it seems to me that their activities should be closely scrutinized to determine whether they qualify for the investment exemption for future acquisitions of stock in companies in which they may assume a more active role.[8]

With all the braying and posturing in Washington, it is no wonder institutional investors are paranoid about behaving like active owners. And the FTC is not alone; the Internal Revenue Service also throws up a few roadblocks that discourage institutions from behaving like the sophisticated institutional stock owners overseas. The unrelated business income tax (UBIT) is a provision of the tax code which stipulates that if an institutional investor actively engages in providing direction to a company in which it owns stock, it may in fact be entering that business. Engaging in a business would expose a pension fund or endowment to paying tax on that investment. Pension funds guard their tax-exempt status carefully and avoid any action that could be deemed taxable. Although the intention of the UBIT was not to prevent institutional investors from acting as owners, that has been the outcome of an overly broad interpretation by present regulators.

Private pension funds are also careful not to violate the Employee Retirement Income Security Act (ERISA), the law that charges the Labor Department with making sure that pension managers invest their funds for the exclusive benefit of the plan's beneficiaries. Although the intent of this law is noble, it produces a herd mentality. Because they are fiducaries, private pension managers are hesitant to experiment. In other words, pension fund managers realize there is safety in numbers. Consequently, plan sponsors continue using investment practices that consistently underperform the market rather than breaking with the pack.

Public pension funds have been more active than private plan sponsors in using innovative approaches, in part because they are not subject to ERISA. Public funds, however, are frequently governed by state laws that establish comparable standards, so not many of them have followed the lead of the California and New York State retirement plans in speaking out for change. As with any fiduciary, more attention is spent on reducing the risks of legal exposure than on finding new ways to improve economic performance.

The Quarterly Performance Bogey

Each quarter, if not each month, the trustees of pension plans receive a report on how the performance of their plan compared to overall market indices. For pension fund managers whose compensation and jobs often depend on their performance relative to such indices, this report is an important milestone. Naturally, there is a temptation for institutions to pressure their money managers to produce attractive quarterly results. So money managers are inclined to purchase stocks that they hope will produce short-term gains, rather than those that might have superior long-term prospects.

The Financial Executives Institute found that the average tenure of money managers hired by private pension funds is about seven years. So, contrary to popular belief, money managers are not fired on a regular basis. Rather than proving that institutional investors do not demand immediate results, this fact may simply indicate that money managers follow investment practices that prevent them from deviating from market indices by a meaningful percentage. Money managers typically are paid on the basis of the amount of assets under management, not on performance. Since managers are measured quarterly, avoiding bad quarters is more important than outperforming the market.* Rather than investing long term in fewer companies that could be followed closely, money managers engage in active trading of broad portfolios, which is more likely to produce consistent quarterly results.

Compounding the problem is the fact that some pension fund managers view their jobs as merely a way station on the road to becoming treasurers or chief financial officers. Obviously, if they are only going to hold their jobs for a few years, they will not be around to receive credit for successful long-term investment strategies that only produce results after they leave.

One of the many paradoxes of the debate over short-termism is the fact that the trustees of the pension funds who pressure their managers to produce short-term results, and who rotate people through the job of pension manager, are frequently top corporate executives. This is the same group that complains the loudest about pension funds being so shortsighted. During the 1980s, annual pension contributions ranged between 5 and 18 percent of pretax corporate profits, making the pension fund the largest asset of most corporations. Yet top management often pays little attention to how that asset is being managed.

Coopting the Owners

Stock market forces, investment industry practices, and regulatory barriers that discourage long-term ownership are documentable. But there is a factor that even fewer people are willing to talk about than soft dollars, one which also discourages pension fund managers from becoming long-term active owners—their bosses do not want them to. Many corporate pension fund managers will privately admit that, although the top executives of their company

---

* The "twelve/twenty-four rule" is common among institutional investors. Money managers who are 12 percent below the Standard & Poor's 500 index for 24 months are replaced.

have not paid much attention to how they invest, they have discouraged them from becoming involved in the controversial issues of other companies. Managers of public funds, bank trust departments, insurance companies, and investment firms also face subtle pressures to be silent owners.

Chief executives do not want to hear from a friend on the Business Roundtable that their pension fund manager is stirring up trouble. Every pension fund manager I have talked to was sensitive to the concern that challenging management at other companies might get them in trouble with their bosses. In other words, private pension fund managers are torn between doing what they were hired to do, which is to maximize investment returns, and succumbing to pressure from above not to operate as true owners, which seems to produce the highest returns. This also applies to the money managers they use. In Chapter 3, I describe a situation in which a money manager almost lost several important clients because he planned to oppose management in a hotly contested proxy battle.

Managers of union and public plans face similar pressures from above to consider agendas other than producing attractive returns. Union plan trustees are obviously union members; frequently they are more concerned with preserving jobs than maximizing the returns to the pension plan. Consequently, many union retirement fund managers support measures that insulate companies from a change in control, even if it hurts the value of their investment in those companies.

When the executive director of the Council of Institutional Investors, whose members are primarily public and union pension funds, expressed opposition to a state anti-takeover statute that blatantly disenfranchised owners, and shortly thereafter opposed a securities transfer excise tax being considered by Congress because it would have cost council members dearly, many of the union fund members tried to have her fired because they regarded these measures as preserving jobs.

The trustees of public funds are typically appointed by political leaders and frequently have political agendas that find their way into investment behavior. This is one reason why public pension funds are among the most active proponents of corporate resolutions that involve social issues such as disinvestment in South Africa. When the manager of the Pennsylvania employees' retirement fund testified that a highly restrictive anti-takeover law under consideration by the Pennsylvania legislature would discourage him from investing in companies based in his own state, his political superiors made it clear that such comments would not enhance his career; most members of the legislature as well as the governor supported the bill.

New York's Cuomo Commission is an example of how politicians sometimes regard other people's retirement savings as an economic resource to further their own political goals. The commission produced a report tacitly endorsing the idea of using government employees' retirement savings, rather than taxes, to rebuild the state's infrastructure.[9] Given the state of New York's finances, such a plan might be politically expedient, but many of the critics of the commission argue that forcing pension plans to make investments in other than an arm's-length transaction could open the door to potential abuses by politicians.

Although this discussion has focused on pension funds, similar factors influence the behavior of other institutional investors. Mutual funds and insurance companies are severely restricted in the amount of stock they can own in a given company. Both bank trust departments and endowments face substantial pressure from various constituents not to become involved in any controversy such as opposing management. It is very easy to sit back and accuse today's institutional investors of being shortsighted. They trade stocks frequently; they focus an enormous amount of attention on quarterly results; and they seldom spend the time and resources needed to learn a company's business and to participate as true owners. Basically, they view stocks as financial commodities. But these investors have a number of reasons for behaving as they do.

As we have seen, there are tremendous pressures imposed on large shareholders by the investment industry, federal and state government regulators, and pension fund trustees that discourage long-term ownership.

Indexing Is Not the Answer

Unfortunately, institutional investors have responded to criticism of being short-term owners neither creatively nor boldly. Since most of them realize that the Wall Street Rule fails to produce acceptable returns on a consistent basis, many institutional investors have adopted a practice called "indexing." Essentially, indexing is based on an "if you can't beat 'em, join 'em" mentality. Index funds effectively buy one of everything, guaranteeing that they will do no worse and no better than average. And as we have seen, being "average" in the investment industry means outperforming all but the top quartile of money managers each year.

Index funds are simply portfolios of stocks designed to mirror the performance of certain stock indices. Most attempt to replicate the Standard & Poor's 500 stock index, while broader indices such as the Wilshire 5000 are also becoming popular. On the surface, indexing appears to be a logical investment strategy for a pension fund manager. Indexers can eliminate expensive research departments, portfolio managers, and most transaction costs and still outperform most professionally managed funds. According to an unpublished survey by the Financial Executives Institute, in 1984 only 14 of 36 private pension fund members surveyed reported using index strategies for some portion of their portfolio. By 1989, 27 of the 36 were indexing.

Unfortunately, indexing may have negative effects on the market that could lower everyone's returns. What may be in the interests of a single investor may be detrimental if too many people operate the same way.

Indexers may assume that they can coast along on the efforts of shareholders who monitor management, sell shares when companies announce uneconomic investments, and buy shares when companies improve their situation or need new capital. But as more investors index, who will monitor management? Who will decide which companies in the index need additional cash? How will companies not part of an index raise equity?

Because indexed investors are "guaranteed" that they will do no better or no worse than average, there is no economic incentive to participate in corporate governance, learn a company's strategy, or vote their proxies. With indexing, investment dollars are spread so thinly across a large number of companies that improving the performance of a few would hardly influence their overall return.

Not surprisingly, index fund managers commit virtually no resources to voting proxies, meeting with corporate managers, or monitoring the business practices of companies in which they invest. Their objective is purely numerical—they make sure their stock portfolio mirrors the index, and they do not worry about what happens to the index. To meet this objective, managers must minimize their overhead, which means eliminating expenses associated with the responsibilities that normally go along with being an owner.

Pension funds and other institutional investors have neither the staffs nor the skills required to monitor the hundreds, if not thousands, of companies they own through an index fund. Some institutions that index have tried to participate in corporate governance in spite of the overwhelming difficulties. The California Public Employees Retirement System (CalPERS) is now so large that it is willing to commit substantial capital to policing the performance of some companies in its index. With about $60 billion in assets, $17 billion of which is invested in equities, CalPERS Executive Director Dale Hanson believes CalPERS can influence corporate behavior even though 75 percent of the fund's equity investment is through an index. But even Hanson admits that his fund gets involved only in the case of consistent underperformers. That means that all the average and slightly below average performers receive virtually no attention. And CalPERS is the exception. Few other institutional investors commit *any* time or resources to monitoring indexed portfolio companies; they simply coast along on the efforts of the few remaining shareholders who fulfill their intended roles as owners.

Knowing that so many investors are indexed gives corporate management one more excuse to ignore its owners. Indexed investors are "locked in," regardless of management practices or performance. To sell a company's stock would only distort the index fund, making it harder to replicate the performance of the index.

If the practice of indexing continues to spread, it will lead to the virtual elimination of corporate accountability. Even the limited accountability provided to corporations by the Wall Street Rule—dumping stock of underperforming companies—is lost with indexing. Before indexing, U.S. investors voted with their feet. With indexing, there is nowhere to walk.

Indexing strategies also make it more difficult for growing companies to raise equity, since each company in an index receives its pro rata allocation of capital regardless of need or merit. The purpose of the capital markets is to provide money to the companies that need it for investment and growth. Indexed investors do not purchase large blocks of newly issued stock when growing companies attempt to raise equity because doing so would distort the index.

Despite these criticisms, many applaud indexing as being long-term oriented since its practitioners do not trade stocks. In fact, the 1990 Nobel Prize in economics was awarded to the pioneers of the financial theories that made indexing fashionable—they showed how broader diversification lowers risk for a single investor. These theories assume that stocks are commodities and that company-specific risk can be diversified away. However, shares of stock also represent ownership stakes in the corporate assets that drive our nation's economy. The risk of unaccountable management and uninformed capital allocation cannot be diversified away. In fact, indexing only compounds these risks. Perhaps one day the Nobel Prize will be awarded to someone who examines how stock indexing has affected the capital markets, the relationship between owners and corporations, and the increasing tendency for both parties to focus on the short term.

The absence of engaged owners places American companies at a severe competitive disadvantage relative to foreign businesses, whose owners not only keep them on their toes but are also committed to their success. Whether one views this void as contributing to a higher cost of equity in the United States or providing cover for sleepy managers who fail to build competitive enterprises, the effect is the same—the performance of companies suffers. The result is less investment, less innovation, and a less competitive economy.

America's pension funds, insurance companies, and endowments collect funds today for benefits that will be paid out many years from now. They are the ideal source of the patient capital our country needs in order to be competitive. But patience requires participation. And present barriers to participation make it unlikely that institutional investors will take an active ownership role. In the absence of a significant regulatory overhaul, the short-term cure for this problem will involve finding a surrogate that can fulfill this role on behalf of institutions. Chapter 8 describes one such approach. But even then, these investors would still encounter significant barriers to participating as owners through our nation's system of corporate governance.

3

How Corporations Are Really Governed

The corporate governance system establishes the ground rules that dictate the relationships among the owners, the board of directors, and corporate management. This system of corporate accountability, which is supposed to keep the goals of the professional managers in sync with those of the owners, was radically altered in the 1980s.

Over the past decade the tension between owners and managers reached its zenith. From the perspective of many in corporate America, Wall Street had gone mad. Countless companies were targeted by corporate raiders to be involuntarily restructured or dismembered. A baffling technological revolution swept Wall Street: a company's stock would change hands at a tumultuous pace, not triggered by a fundamental reason but because of the whims of computer programs, which impersonally regarded shares as part of a basket of securities. The fate of corporations that had existed for decades was often in the hands of arbitrageurs who had purchased their stock only days before a shareholder vote.

Some boards and directors viewed shareholders as adversaries, not owners. Because they willingly sold their shares to corporate raiders in order to make a quick buck, shareholders were perceived to be accomplices of the takeover artists. Others in the business community regarded shareholders as irrelevant. Because they either held on to their shares for shorter periods of time than in the past or only owned stock through an index fund, they were easier to ignore. Twenty-five years ago, shares of companies traded on the New York Stock Exchange were held an average of eight years; by 1987, the average holding period had declined to a little more than a year. Those who complained one year were often gone by the next.

Wall Street was its own worst enemy. Investment bankers were portrayed as villains whose only ambition was riches, regardless of the cost to others. A line in the movie *Wall Street*, "Greed is good," (taken from an Ivan Boesky speech) epitomized how most people characterized investment bankers. The newspapers were full of articles supporting this view. Martin Siegel, the head of mergers and acquisitions at Drexel Burnham Lambert was jailed for accepting a suitcase full of money in exchange for inside information on pending transactions. The famous arbitrageur Ivan Boesky was indicted for illegally manipulating stock prices. Michael Milken, who claimed to be the financier of entrepreneurism, was sentenced to 10 years in prison for the illegal practices he used in building a junk bond empire that earned him over a half a *billion* dollars in a single year. Even the old-line Wall Street firms were tainted by corruption when investment bankers at Goldman Sachs and Kidder Peabody were arrested and handcuffed in their offices.

Investment bankers who since the days of J.P. Morgan had been corporate America's closest advisers were viewed increasingly as predators. Bankers—including Morgan Bank—represented hostile bidders in attacking old clients. The patrician firm of Morgan Stanley, which served as adviser to America's top corporations, was the subject of a scathing article in *The Wall Street Journal* for its role in taking Burlington Industries private.[1] Morgan Stanley had acquired control of Burlington Industries in 1987 with only $46 million of its own money invested in a $2.2 billion deal. Through advisory fees, junk bond underwritings, special dividends, and other services the firm pulled more than $175 million out of the company in the following three years. In the process Morgan Stanley had sold many of Burlington's prized assets, leading Burlington's chairman Frank Greenberg to ask the question on the minds of many corporate executives, "How did all this madness happen?"[2]

To protect themselves from the perversities of Wall Street, corporate boards and managers insulated themselves from their owners. It did not matter whether a shareholder was hostile or friendly, new or old, large or small, they were stripped of many of the traditional rights of ownership. Management circumvented their owners by adopting measures such as "poison pills," which could be unilaterally imposed by the board without shareholder approval. Business leaders convinced state legislatures to alter corporate laws to insulate companies from their owners. Corporate political action committees persuaded state legislators to go along with these measures, knowing full well that the company's owners would have balked at them.

Because these changes took place incrementally—on a company-by-company or state-by-state basis—they have gone largely unnoticed. Yet collectively they have had a profound impact on the balance of power in America's corporations. Such extreme measures have been taken that in many cases corporations are virtually unaccountable to their owners. From the perspective of shareholders, a dysfunctional corporate governance system that weakens their ability to take corrective action if management fails to perform adequately raises the potential risks of owning stock. This boosts a corporation's cost of capital.

The Power Triangle

There are a number of interesting parallels between what is going on today between owners and managers and what has taken place over the past several decades involving management and labor. Three key groups are involved in any business enterprise— the investors, the managers, and the workers. In an ideal business world, the interests of all three groups would be aligned as closely as possible with a common goal of producing a highly competitive company. By working together to maximize the success of the business, each party would ultimately claim the rewards it seeks— the investors would receive handsome returns; executives would gain operating freedom and be well compensated; and workers would have quality jobs with attractive wages. But in our imperfect world people tend to exploit power; and relative power determines whose short-run interests are taken care of, at the expense of everyone's collective long-term benefit.

Throughout the early part of the twentieth century, management and the shareholders sided against labor. They had the money and the power. Having been exploited for decades, workers formed unions to facilitate collective action. By 1940, more than 35 percent of the U.S. labor force had been unionized, giving labor a strong political base. Flexing their newfound muscle, workers stood up to corporate executives, which set the stage for decades of antagonism between the two groups. In many cases, unions demanded rigid job descriptions, redundant workers, and enormous wage increases. Management fought them every step of the way. Strikes crippled production. Morale sagged; productivity plunged; and labor costs skyrocketed. Not surprisingly, competitiveness waned.

Both labor and management began to realize how counterproductive their behavior was when the streets of Detroit became filled with Japanese automobiles and America's skyscrapers rose upon pillars of foreign steel. After shipping countless jobs overseas in order to lower labor costs, corporate managers realized that this solution had some practical limitations and that eventually the problems with labor relations at home would have to be confronted. Meanwhile, the unions woke up to the fact that in the final analysis, structurally uncompetitive companies offer little job security. Unions backed off some of their demands. Managers became more responsive. Companies formed quality circles, encouraged employee involvement, and initiated open-door policies. As a result, there has been a resurgence in quality and a corresponding boost to the competitiveness of many American companies.

Some would argue that today's remaining labor–management problems stem from union militancy; others that they are the product of management neglect. Who is to blame for past and present labor–management problems matters far less than the lesson we should have learned from our mistakes—having workers and managers at cross purposes undermines the competitiveness of a company. One would hope to benefit from this experience in confronting the increasingly caustic relations between corporate owners and managers. Unfortunately, looking at present trends in corporate governance, we appear poised to repeat the same mistakes.

The feud between the owners of American corporations and the managers who run them has grown bitter. In many ways the takeovers of the past decade are similar to strikes; both reflect a lack of shared objectives. If owners and managers worked together to build the most competitive enterprise possible, there would be no need for most takeovers. By banning takeovers, we have attacked the symptom but exacerbated the problem. When workers do not trust management, they demand rigid work rules, which raise labor costs. When owners do not trust management, they demand higher returns, which raise capital costs.

The Need for Constructive Tension

It is important to strike a balance of power in the relationship between owners and managers. Totally passive shareholders fail to provide the accountability necessary to ensure that companies maximize their performance. Managers who are unaccountable are more likely to deviate from value-maximizing strategies, which can result in uncompetitive companies and depressed share prices. Yet if uninformed shareholders meddle in corporate affairs, they can force decisions on management that are inconsistent with the company's long-term strategy. What is needed is an ongoing *constructive* tension where the owners provide meaningful direction and oversight through informed board representatives but leave daily business decisions to management.

The role of the board is critical because it is impossible to eliminate the conflicts of interest that are inherent between shareholders and corporate managers. Senior executives control corporate accounts. There will always be a temptation to take actions that lead to personal enrichment or ego gratification at the expense of the owners. The average CEO of a *Fortune* 500 company owns about one-fourth of 1 percent of his company's stock. If the chief executive decides to spend $100,000 of the corporation's money on a corporate yacht, which adds absolutely no value to the company, the market value of the corporation would theoretically fall by $100,000. However, the out-of-pocket cost to the CEO is his pro rata share of the drop in market value, or about $250. Since the CEO has complete use of the yacht, this is not a bad deal.

Anyone who has read *Barbarians at the Gate* is familiar with the RJR Nabisco "air force" and the 24 country club memberships the company paid for to supplement Ross Johnson's lifestyle. While the former chairman of RJR Nabisco was certainly more egregious than most in spending the money of faceless shareholders, he is not the only executive to do so. In 1989, the board of Occidental Petroleum voted to spend $86 million of the company's money to build a museum to house the personal art collection of its chief executive, Armand Hammer. Some of the art was also paid for with corporate money. A substantial amount of the shareholders' money had already been spent on some of Hammer's hobbies, such as Arabian horse breeding, cattle farming, and film production. In 1987, when Dr. Hammer slipped in his bathtub and cracked three ribs, news of the accident boosted the market value of the company by $306 million.[3] When he died in December 1990, Occidental Petroleum's shares rose about 10 percent on volume of more than 8 million shares, or about 12 times the stock's average daily activity. The market obviously did not feel Dr. Hammer ran his company with the interests of the owners in mind.

Lone Star Industries filed for bankruptcy in 1990. The company, once among the nation's leading cement manufacturers, had sold most of its valuable assets to cover losses. Share prices had plummeted 90 percent over the previous two years, yet CEO James Stewart continued to spend the shareholders' money lavishly. Stewart spent about $3 million in 1989 on hotels and private planes to accommodate a lifestyle that involved working in Connecticut and living in Florida. His board, like RJR's and Occidental Petroleum's, was filled with corporate dignitaries such as Robert Strauss, former chairman of the Democratic National Committee, and Dwayne Andreas, CEO of Archer Daniels Midland. Instead of reversing the downward course of the company, Lone Star's board chose to insulate the company from a takeover by allowing a series of asset spinoffs.

Not all misuse of corporate resources is so blatant. Many people argue that much of the unrelated diversification in the 1960s and 1970s was precipitated by the desire of top executives to increase their pay and prestige by amassing larger companies, regardless of the strategic merits. During this period of conglomeration, the shareholders paid a steep price. In 1982, the Dow Jones industrial average was lower than it was in 1966, yet executive pay had risen handsomely. These inherent conflicts can only be resolved by a functioning accountability system.

This chapter will detail numerous hurdles, in addition to those already mentioned, that prevent shareholders from providing effective accountability measures to corporations. It will then be easier to appreciate why shareholders have become so disengaged, and why they have abdicated the true responsibilities of ownership. Chapter 4 will show how accountability brought about by *revolutionary* changes such as takeovers is disruptive and less desirable than a viable corporate governance system that provides for *evolutionary* changes to align the interests of managers and owners.

Before reviewing the U.S. system of corporate accountability, it is useful to look at how companies in Japan and Germany are monitored and directed. There is a common misperception that because takeovers are seldom read about in these countries corporate managers are largely left to their own devices, free to pursue the strategies of their choice. Many claim this is why German and Japanese companies are long-term oriented. Nothing could be further from the truth. Executives in both countries face more rigorous accountability systems than their U.S. counterparts.

Corporate Accountability in Japan

It is commonly acknowledged that Japanese corporations are not accountable to their *public* shareholders.[4] Japanese companies are thought to exist first for the benefit of corporate managers and employees, then for the lead bank, customers, and suppliers, and finally for the public shareholders.

The status of public shareholders in Japan is vividly illustrated by the treatment they receive at annual shareholder meetings. More than 80 percent of the publicly listed Japanese companies hold their annual meetings on the same day, making it impossible for shareholders to participate in more than a couple of these events each year. And Japanese companies often do not mail proxy materials until two weeks before the annual meeting. Furthermore, they frequently hire "sokaiya," which are mafia-type organizations that suppress dissent at annual meetings by threatening to rough up outspoken shareholders in exchange for payoffs from the company. Although Americans have a hard time believing that such Byzantine practices exist, Japan recently amended its Commercial Code to curb the overt practices of sokaiya, proof that their existence is more than a myth.

Besides being free of the influence of speculative shareholders, Japanese companies are virtually immune from hostile takeovers. In fact, to date no foreign company has ever succeeded in an unsolicited buyout of a Japanese firm. By law, a Japanese company can only be acquired with the consent of every director, many of whom are company insiders.

Coupled with this legal restriction are some practical impediments to unsolicited buyouts. About two-thirds of the shares of public companies in Japan are held by related businesses, leaving only a minority of shares in public hands. Under Japan's Securities and Exchange Law, tender offers are legally possible, but the fact that only two have succeeded since 1970 proves that it is virtually impossible to acquire control of a company on the open market.

The impotence of public shareholders and the absence of takeovers in Japan are commonly cited as justifications for disenfranchising the owners of America's corporations. Freed from accountability for economic performance, the argument goes, American managers could concentrate on the long-term objectives that make a business competitive. Perhaps Andy Sigler, the chairman of Champion International and former head of the Business Roundtable's corporate governance committee, is correct when he asserts that the United States would be more competitive if shareholders were caged.

The problem with this argument is that it ignores an important part of the story. Public shareholders may not be the mechanism for accountability in Japan, but Japanese business managers are definitely held accountable for their performance. According to the Japan Fair Trade Commission, about 1,000 mergers occur each year in Japan, a number not at all out of line with takeover activity in the United States, given the number of companies in each country.

These transactions are not precipitated by corporate raiders or takeover artists; they are typically engineered by the government or the lead bank. Frequently, companies whose performance is not up to par are politely contacted by the Ministry of International Trade and Industry or the Ministry of Finance and encouraged to find a "merger partner." In some cases they are even told who that partner ought to be. Although this approach lacks the fanfare and publicity of a hostile takeover, it has the same effect. Weak managers are replaced and uncompetitive companies are reorganized. If the Japanese system is so appealing, perhaps those who are enamored of it would be willing to let the Treasury Department and the Department of Commerce decide which companies should be merged and which managers should be replaced.

Furthermore, the shareholders of Japanese companies really do exert a great deal of control over the company. We often dismiss their impact on corporate decision making because we associate ownership with publicly traded stock. But in Japan, the shareholders are predominantly related companies, and they have enormous influence over board decisions, often exercised through the group's lead bank.

The Japanese system of cross shareholding provides rigorous accountability because the largest shareholders are informed and involved. Japan's Fair Trade Commission reported that companies that belong to a keiretsu, or web of affiliated businesses, have an average of 23 percent of their stock held by other firms in their group. In fact, two-thirds of these companies actually employed executives from affiliated businesses in a full-time capacity. With access to senior management and confidential data, these related-company shareholders are better prepared to monitor and influence corporate decisions than a fragmented group of public stock owners.

Furthermore, the Japanese are moving toward showing greater respect to public shareholders. In July 1989, the Tokyo district court overturned an attempt by two companies to immunize themselves from takeover threats by selling large blocks of their respective stocks to each other at below-market prices. The reason the court cited for its decision was that the proposed transaction was unfair to the existing shareholders. And in 1990, the Ministry of Finance began to exert pressure on Japanese businesses to boost their paltry dividends to benefit public stockholders.

It is unlikely that American corporations would be willing to grant their bankers, customers, suppliers—and most of all their government—the degree of power that these parties wield in Japan's corporate accountability system. Nevertheless, business leaders defend takeover defenses and shareholder disenfranchisement by claiming that they are instrumental to long-term behavior in Japan.

It would be unwise to try to replicate the Japanese system in the United States. In fact, the benefits of the Japanese system are diminishing. A number of scholars have suggested that because the Japanese practice *managerial* capitalism (where executives of related businesses are the key providers of accountability, rather than the shareholders), they have a distinct advantage in global competition. Japanese corporations can theoretically invest for growth, market share, and other nonfinancial objectives. Japan's closed system may have provided Japanese businesses an advantage in the past, but it is unlikely that it will continue to do so to the same extent in the future. As the world's capital markets become more highly integrated, capital will flow more quickly to the markets that provide the highest returns. Market integration is inevitable, and it favors the American system of *shareholder* capitalism. One of the reasons Japanese stock prices escalated so rapidly during the 1980s was that regulated Japanese investors bought very few foreign stocks, locking the growing equity pool within Japan's borders. Japanese investors who can receive superior returns overseas will not continue to invest domestically forever as markets are deregulated. For America to reverse course, just when the tide is turning in our direction, would be a mistake.

Corporate Accountability in Germany

The German system of corporate governance is quite different from that in Japan, but the same principle applies: management is rigorously held accountable for its performance by informed parties. In Germany, most companies are privately held. Only about 700 of an estimated 380,000 companies are listed on a public stock exchange. Clearly, in privately owned companies, owners and managers do not suffer from the same conflicts of interest that exist between owners and managers of publicly held corporations, because they are often one and the same.

German companies that do have publicly traded shares operate with a dual system of boards. A management board, which is analogous to the senior management team of an American company, is appointed by a supervisory board, which is comprised *exclusively* of outsiders. Since the shareholders elect a majority of the members to this powerful group of independent directors who oversee management, they have little need to become directly involved in corporate affairs.

Interestingly, German companies are required to include representatives of the employees on the supervisory board. For companies with more than 500 employees, one-third of the directors are designated by the workers. It is mandatory that companies with more than 2,000 employees allow employees to elect half of the board members, with tie votes broken by a chairperson chosen by shareholders.

As a practical matter, the large banks in Germany control who is elected to the supervisory board. Because of the universal banking system in Germany in which banks also engage in securities activities, most institutional and individual shareholders leave their stocks on deposit at the bank. In essence, the shareholders grant the bank power of attorney to vote these shares. With the ability to control a majority of shares in most public companies, the banks can unilaterally remove directors, thus management, if they wish. In addition, a representative of the lead bank typically serves on the supervisory board.

Deutsche Bank executives, for example, sit on over 400 corporate boards. Among the companies that Deutsche Bank owns at least 20 percent of directly are Daimler-Benz (Germany's largest industrial company), Karstadt (Germany's largest department store), and Phillip Holzman (Germany's largest construction company). When bank-owned shares are combined with the proxies of public shareholders, German banks sometimes vote up to 90 percent of a company's stock.

So although the shareholders seldom become personally engaged in corporate governance, they do have substantial power over management through their agent, the bank. Furthermore, if they are dissatisfied with the performance of the bank in monitoring management, individual investors can engage in collective action with far fewer legal and regulatory impediments than in the United States. Minority shareholders can call special meetings, nominate directors, and request the removal of auditors. In practice, however, the owners seldom exercise their rights because they are confident that the supervisory board is looking after their interests. German law specifies that the banks are to vote their proxies for the benefit of the shareholders.

German banks provide enormous accountability to corporations, in a manner that has not existed in the United States since the Great Depression. The likelihood that corporate managers will be able to stack their boards with their cronies does not exist in Germany. In fact, managers are typically employed under contracts (usually five years) with the supervisory board, and the contracts are not renewed when managers fail to perform. Consequently, there is little chance that senior executives could pursue uneconomic strategies for extended periods before outside discipline would be exerted.

Just as with drawing analogies to Japan, interpreting the lack of takeovers and shareholder activism in Germany as a lack of accountability is misguided. The United States has decided that neither the banks nor the government should control commerce in this country, but that the role of holding corporations accountable rests with the owners themselves. Yet in recent years we have systematically undermined the ability of owners to perform this function without finding a replacement, leaving corporations virtually unaccountable. Capitalist systems in which those who control the capital are not responsive to those who provide the capital can degenerate into imperialistic systems. As management guru Peter Drucker notes: "Power without accountability always becomes flabby or tyrannical and usually both."[5]

Diminishing Accountability in America

It is useful to step back and contrast how America's corporate governance system is supposed to function with the way it works in practice. The system is designed so that shareholders can influence how a company is run by establishing the ground rules (the charter and bylaws) and by electing directors to the board who will represent their interests. The board's function is to make certain decisions on behalf of the shareholders and to oversee the performance of the company's management. Consequently, the shareholders do not have to get involved personally except in unusual situations, which suits both them and management.

In practice the system does not work this way. For three principal reasons, shareholders are no longer able to provide the constructive accountability that was central to the original design of America's corporate governance system.

1. Boards of directors are influenced more heavily by management, and increasingly by other constituents, than by shareholders.
2. The proxy system by which shareholders vote is ladened with regulations that frustrate dialogue among the owners and undermine their ability to take collective action.
3. When the proxy system fails, the owners' options have been severely limited by new restrictions on shareholder power designed to deter changes in control.

The Board of Directors

As with any centerpiece, if boards are not functional they can become purely decorative. Unfortunately, corporate managers and shareholders do not always agree on how boards should function. One of the most heated corporate governance debates today is about the ultimate objective of the board of directors. Traditionalists argue that the only constituency that should matter to the board is the shareholders, since they are the true owners of the company. However, there is an increasingly popular view that the board of directors has the responsibility to determine what is in the best interest of a broader group of constituents that also includes the employees, customers, creditors, and communities in which the company conducts its business. In a recent Opinion Research Corp. survey, directors ranked the concerns of the shareholders behind those of employees and customers. With this perspective, a board will be forced to make trade-offs that are not in the interests of the shareholders.

The debate over whether boards should put the interests of other constituents on an equal footing, or perhaps ahead of those of the owners has arisen because many people question whether maximization of corporate value is still an appropriate societal goal. As boards attempt to maximize the value of the corporation, sacrifices will occasionally be required from individual employees, customers, suppliers, or communities—all large constituencies with enormous political power. As a result, in recent years there has been a proliferation of state laws that force boards to consider other constituents on an equal, if not superior, footing with the shareholders. For example, a 1990 Pennsylvania law explicitly stated that directors have the prerogative to subordinate the owners' interests to other groups. Indiana already had a similar law on its books.

Resolving this debate requires going back to the fundamental goal of our nation's economic system, which is to produce the highest standard of living for American citizens. The question then becomes whether maximization of corporate value produces the highest standard of living for *all* parties. In the short run, perhaps not, but what about over the long haul? Virtually everyone agrees that the standard of living in the United States *ultimately* depends upon the competitiveness of our national economy. Quality jobs, attractive wages, and a tax base capable of supporting the arts and public amenities are among the fruits of a competitive economy.

A country seeking to maximize its economic competitiveness must: 1) *increase* the economic potential of its human and other scarce resources through means such as education, training, and the cultivation of natural resources; and 2) *fulfill* that potential by deploying existing resources to their highest and best uses. The latter is accomplished by efficient capital markets and effective governance of the corporations that control the country's resources.

In spite of the many shortcomings of our present equity markets described in Chapter 2, the collective wisdom of our markets is still the best judge of economic value. Poor information, rather than poor judgment, is the root of inappropriate valuations. If we allow companies to ignore their stock price, there will be no mechanism to force them to deploy resources more efficiently. Consequently, pursuit of other goals at the expense of maximizing the value of the corporation would not only violate the directors' fiduciary responsibility to the shareholders, it would also undermine the capitalistic system which we have always relied on to satisfy the *long-run* interests of employees, communities, and customers.

Too often people inappropriately characterize competitiveness by focusing on individual corporations, rather than considering the collective competitiveness of all U.S. companies. An individual corporation may improve its "staying power," for example, by becoming larger or more diversified. This was the logic used to justify many of the conglomerates formed during the 1960s and 1970s. For example, a company that combined insurance, oil, and tobacco could withstand enormous economic fluctuations without going out of business. If preserving a company's existence is the goal of the board, which Jay Lorsch notes in his book *Pawns or Potentates*, is an increasingly popular view among directors, then this is an appropriate strategy. However, if the size or diversity of the business results in suboptimal management of the resources under the company's control, such a strategy would hurt our nation's overall competitiveness. In other words, if each individual business could be managed better if operated on a stand-alone basis by a focused management team, collectively they would create more value, more productive jobs, and more wealth. The overall system would benefit, even if it meant that more companies without large parent organizations would fail. Our economic system was designed to maximize the staying power of the overall economy, not the staying power of individual companies.

Another common mistake is to assume that all research or capital improvements that enhance the products or technology of U.S. companies relative to foreign competitors are good. If we measure competitiveness solely on who has the best products, which is tempting to do, one would assume that virtually any investment would boost America's competitiveness. However, if the investment fails to achieve a return at least equal to its cost of capital, it is an inefficient use of our nation's scarce economic resources. Perhaps we would be better off allocating that capital to another industry. A company that produces world-class products that sell for less than they cost to make may increase its market share and corporate pride, but it robs the nation of capital that could be deployed more profitably elsewhere. Although most companies have political action committees promoting their parochial interests, there are few lobbyists who represent the overall welfare of the nation. As a result, competitiveness policy has itself become myopic by focusing on the needs of individual corporations rather than the nation as a whole.

Laws that inhibit market forces from maximizing corporate values in order to serve the interests of management, labor, local communities, or any other constituency, therefore, are symptomatic of the lack of long-term vision, which is at the heart of America's competitiveness problem. Directors sound noble when they profess to serve the greater good, but when boards place the short-term needs of these constituencies at the head of the line, they do so at the expense of the long-run success of our economy.

This in no way implies that constituencies other than the shareholders do not matter. Companies should always strive to satisfy the needs of their employees, customers, and communities. Doing so makes the company more successful in the long run. Value-maximization is a goal, not a corporate strategy. And maximizing value does not mean maximizing this quarter's earnings.

Smart capitalists know how to motivate employees, customers, suppliers, and communities to work together in a fashion that ultimately produces the greatest value for the owners. Delta Airlines is a good example. Several airlines that tried to solve cash flow problems by cutting back wages or laying off workers have been crippled in the past by labor unrest. Delta, on the other hand, has a policy of lifetime employment, pays higher wages than many of its competitors, and cherishes its worker morale. When a sluggish economy and soaring fuel prices forced domestic air carriers to cut back on flight schedules in the 1970s, Delta pilots helped out by sorting baggage. In 1983, after fare wars had decimated industry profits, Delta flight attendants initiated a fund-raising campaign and purchased a $40-million jet for their employer. Delta is consistently among the most profitable airlines in the country. Delta makes its shareholders happy by making its employees and customers happy, instead of making the owners happy.

"Multiple constituency fiduciary" is an oxymoron. No one can serve two masters. For example, corporations should not be encouraged to keep open an unproductive plant that is unable to earn a return equal to its cost of capital. It may be in the short-run interests of the employees and the surrounding community, but the larger community suffers when the nation's skilled workers—expected to be in short supply in the coming years—are committed to losing operations. If those workers could be pushed by the market into more profitable endeavors, the country as a whole would be better able to compete with foreign rivals. Even in the Soviet Union and Eastern Europe people now realize the magic of markets. Yet in America state laws are being passed to instruct directors to overrule the judgment of the markets.

One reason our corporate governance system has deviated so far from its original economic underpinnings is that because the subject has for so long been dominated by lawyers and judges, it has been dismissed as a legal issue by economists. Few economists I dealt with in Washington knew how the U.S. corporate governance system functions. A proper legal perspective is essential, but not sufficient. We should avoid the temptation to restructure our economy to serve new laws, rather than structuring our laws to serve the historic economic principles on which the country was built.

Responsibilities

Directors clearly have legal responsibilities, including the duty of loyalty and the duty of care. The duty of loyalty means that the interests of the corporation come before the personal interest of the director. The duty of care, simply put, charges board members to behave responsibly, prudently, and in good faith. Directors, however, as part of their fiduciary duty to maximize the value of the corporation also have an economic responsibility to:

1. review and approve strategic plans;
2. select senior management, evaluate its performance, and establish its compensation;
3. monitor the financial results of the company; and
4. ensure the integrity of financial data and the existence of adequate record keeping and control systems through verification by an independent auditor.

Simply by refraining from fraudulent or manipulative behavior, the board does not accomplish any of these four objectives. The legal system cannot be used to ensure the economic performance of a company. The "business judgment rule" is a judicial doctrine that makes legal sanctions for inept business decisions virtually impossible. This doctrine essentially protects directors from liability even if they use poor business judgment, as long as there is no evidence of fraud, illegality, or bad faith.

There are cases where a board has been held liable for exercising poor business judgment. In 1985, the Delaware Supreme Court ruled that the directors of Trans Union Corporation acted too hastily in accepting a takeover offer. The court held the directors liable for the unrealized value of the company, even though the shareholders received a significant premium to the prevailing market price, because they accepted an offer without hiring professional advisers or seeking to receive a superior bid.

Following the Trans Union case, the Delaware legislature amended state corporation law to permit a company to eliminate a director's personal liability for monetary damages to the shareholders if the director breaches his or her fiduciary duty of care. Similar "director protection statutes" have subsequently been passed in 42 other states. Most of these statutes do not apply to the duty of loyalty, intentional misconduct, or unlawful payment of dividends and purchases of stock.

According to Korn Ferry International, 85 percent of the companies in their survey of corporate boards have amended their bylaws or articles of incorporation to take advantage of the state laws that permit companies to indemnify nonofficer directors; 96 percent of the respondents to the same survey already had directors' liability insurance. In other words, directors have virtually no legal obligation to make good business decisions, and if they are sued, they are protected from economic loss by an insurance policy paid for by the shareholders.

How then can we rely on legal remedies to enforce business decisions? The answer is we should not have to. If directors make poor business decisions, they should be replaced, not sued. Owners, not a judge, should evaluate the performance of a board. A reliance on legal remedies not only undermines the board's economic responsibilities, it also diverts the attention of directors. Having to live in fear of being sued for the business decisions they make biases board members to select risk-averse strategies when the optimal route might be to pursue a more aggressive approach. And relying heavily on the legal system to achieve accountability also makes it more difficult for boards to attract competent candidates.

We have historically relied on the courts by default. The primary reason so many battles over director decisions involve lawsuits is that it is virtually impossible to replace a director. The belief that the owners truly decide who sits on corporate boards and are able to replace an ineffective director is one of the greatest business myths in America. As Lorsch notes, the way in which boards are selected in American corporations more closely resembles a "pre-glasnost Russian election" than the democratic process we are accustomed to in the United States.[6]

Selection

When I was at the Treasury Department, some lobbyists from one of the most powerful business groups in the country told me that shareholders have all the power they need because they control who sits on the board. I challenged them to tell me how many times shareholders had been able to replace a board of directors against management's wishes except in the case of a takeover where a third party financed the proxy contest. They could not name a single instance. Several months later they returned with a high-priced Washington securities lawyer bearing a list of a dozen examples that had occurred over a five-year period. In almost every case, either the company was virtually bankrupt or a top executive was under indictment before the shareholders were successful in replacing a majority of the board.

It seems a bit extreme to have to wait for such circumstances to shake up those charged with monitoring our nation's economic resources. Even though most board members are highly competent and committed, there should be a mechanism to either wake up directors who fall asleep at the wheel or to remove them from the driver's seat. If the board is not accountable, the chances that it will hold management accountable diminish. In order to make directors accountable, modifications must be made to the procedures for nominating, electing, and compensating directors.

The chief executive, or in some cases a nominating committee of the board, which usually includes the CEO, selects potential director candidates. Not surprisingly, a 1990 Board of Directors survey conducted by Korn Ferry International on how potential board candidates are surfaced listed "recommendation of chairman" as the most common method. It did not even list "recommendation of shareholders" as one of the seven most common sources. Robert Monks claims there is no example of a company electing a board member who was proposed by the shareholders, absent a contest for control of the corporation, which is why he nominated himself to serve on the board of Sears and solicited votes personally.

The only way for shareholders to provide an alternative candidate is through the proxy process, which is prohibitively expensive for a shareholder who does not own a significant percentage of the company's shares or who is not interested in taking over the corporation. To win a proxy contest not only involves hiring lawyers to prepare mailings to be sent to other shareholders, but also commonly entails purchasing ads in *The Wall Street Journal* and hiring a solicitation firm. These expenses can add up to more than a million dollars. And given the lack of interest of many shareholders in voting their shares, the chance of securing a majority of votes is stacked against anyone who challenges management's nominee. Furthermore, the company has massive resources available to defeat shareholder-proposed candidates. Sears budgeted $5.6 million and assigned 30 people to work toward keeping Robert Monks—who already had served as a director at several major corporations—off its board. In fact, even if you do succeed, the battle is not over. According to the Investor Responsibility Research Center, 57 percent of the 1,500 publicly traded companies they surveyed elect only one-third of the board each year, which means that at least two proxy contests are required to change a majority of the board.

With the sponsorship of business groups, state legislatures have been actively devising ways to make boards even less accountable to the owners. For example, a law enacted in Massachusetts in 1990 *mandates* staggered board terms so that only a minority of directors will stand for election in a given year, and *prohibits* shareholders from voting to opt out of the law.

A well-known takeover defense lawyer, Martin Lipton, has been promoting a concept to policy makers that would involve director elections being held only once every five years. Rather than promoting greater dialogue between the owners and corporate managers, the proposal reflects a belief that dealing with the owners is a necessary evil—like going to the dentist. Although Lipton does propose some modifications to make those five-year elections more meaningful, in many ways his proposal is no different from children promising to brush their teeth daily if their mother promises they will only have to go to the dentist every five years. If problems arise and are allowed to fester for five years, a great deal of damage can be done.

Function

Regardless of how they get there, or how long their terms are, it is important to remember the principal function of directors. Somehow we have come to believe that a board member is supposed to be an adviser to the chief executive. CEOs can seek advice from management consulting firms and their peers in business organizations. A good adviser may lack not only the time but the independence to be a good director, i.e., to fulfill responsibilities to shareholders of holding management accountable for its performance.

When directors are close personal friends of the CEO, it is harder for them to truly focus on the shareholders' interests. But perhaps a greater concern about the ability of boards to fulfill their responsibilities lies in the amount of time directors commit to board duties. The typical board member is employed full time as a top executive in another company. (Estimates of the percentage of directors who are themselves chief executives range from two-thirds to 80 percent.) He or she sits on several other boards and is involved in civic and business organizations. As an example, Robert Ted Enlow, III sits on eight boards and serves as president of a floundering company, Lomas Financial Corp.[7]

With heavy outside responsibilities, the only time some directors focus on the company on whose board they serve is during the plane ride to a directors' meeting, which makes it difficult to ask probing questions once they arrive. The number of hours spent by outside board members on their director responsibilities has consistently declined in recent years. According to Korn Ferry, in 1983 directors spent 125 hours on board duties; in 1985, they spent 114 hours; in 1988, 108 hours; and in 1990, only 94 hours. Since the average number of board meetings is nine a year, 10 hours per meeting does not leave a lot of time for preparation.

Since nearly 80 percent of the chief executives of U.S. companies also serve as chairman of the board, it is particularly important to have strong, independent directors to promote candor in boardroom discussions. A CEO/chairman is both the principal employee and the chief overseer at the same time. This practice is used by only 30 percent of British firms, 11 percent of Japanese companies, and never in Germany. Compounding this problem is the fact that the retired chairman often remains on the board, making it difficult for directors to criticize previous decisions and change the direction of the company. When Institutional Shareholder Services surveyed present board chairmen about this practice, they overwhelmingly expressed concern that retaining retired executives on the board undermines their ability to initiate change.

Compensation

If the board's principal responsibility is to maximize the value of the company, some shareholders believe that director compensation should be structured to motivate board members to do just that. In fact, many directors agree. In a 1989 survey by Egon Zehnder International, 81 percent of directors said they believed board members should be required to hold stock in companies on whose boards they serve, yet only 37 percent stated that their compensation included stock. This percentage has subsequently increased. Since most directors of public companies are high-paid executives from other companies, few of them rely on cash board fees for their livelihood. Companies could pay their directors largely in stock without compromising their ability to attract quality board members. Equity-based director fees would eliminate one of the most frustrating experiences for a shareholder, i.e., witnessing a director who owns only a token amount or no stock in the company vote to do something that hurts the stock price.

Shareholder Voting—The Proxy System

The corporate voting process bears little resemblance to any other form of election in the United States. There are countless regulations, restrictions, reviews, and ambiguities governing what material can and should be presented in a proxy statement. Strict rules also govern communications among shareholders. These deterrents to active dialogue between shareholders, as well as limits on shareholder input into proxy statements, frustrate collective action and make voting a perfunctory exercise in most cases.

Some institutional investors, such as the New York State Common Retirement Fund, have elaborate policies and procedures to follow when voting their shares, but they are the exception. Most do not. In fact, according to a confidential survey among certain institutional investors, about a third had no specific guidelines on how they vote proxies, and over three-fourths provide no policy guidance on voting shares to their money managers, who are frequently delegated this responsibility.

It is not uncommon for a pension fund or money manager to assign proxy voting responsibilities to a junior staff person who completes hundreds, if not thousands, of ballots each year. Professional organizations such as the Investor Responsibility Research Center (IRRC) and Institutional Shareholder Services (ISS) have emerged in recent years to provide research and advice to institutional shareholders on proxy voting. But even with the benefit of research reports, which discuss proxy issues and provide guidance to investors, it is difficult to keep up with the relevant debates at hundreds of companies and exercise independent, thoughtful judgment.

In spite of the cumbersome process of using shareholder votes to effect change, voting proxies is an issue that is receiving greater attention these days. Following the recent proliferation of antitakeover provisions, which are discussed later in this chapter, shareholders can no longer rely on outsiders to accumulate enough shares to unilaterally influence the outcome of a vote. Initiatives to effect change now have to come directly from the shareholders.

In a recent survey conducted by *Institutional Investor*, nine out of 10 institutional shareholders said they wanted to become more involved in corporate decisions. Evidence of this is reflected in the increasing number of shareholder proposals. The Investor Responsibility Research Center identified 233 shareholder proposals, a record number, that had been submitted for a vote in 1991.

In December 1990, Edward Regan, who controls the New York State Pension Fund, sent letters to 40 companies in the fund's portfolio asking them to include in the proxy a proposal to mandate that the company establish a nominating committee of the board comprised exclusively of independent, nonmanagement directors. Other large investors such as the California Public Employees Retirement System have asked companies to form shareholder advisory committees to increase dialogue between owners and managers. Much of the activism has been geared toward greater shareholder involvement in a broader array of issues. For example, an IRRC survey showed that 67 percent of institutional investors favored putting poison pills to a shareholder vote, and 66 percent favor doing the same with golden parachute plans. These initiatives have been met with some resistance in the corporate community which fears that investors will meddle in corporate affairs and attempt to micromanage the company.

Business groups correctly point out that the corporate governance system was originally designed to revolve around the board because any process of educating myriad investors and securing their consent on complex issues was thought to be inefficient and lead to uninformed decision making. But for shareholders to be content with such a system, they must have confidence in the board and a practical and affordable mechanism to replace directors if they are not pleased with the board's performance. Legitimacy disappears without accountability. Several proxy rules make replacing directors problematic.

Shareholder Communications

Better communications among shareholders, and between shareholders and corporations, should result in more patient owners and, hopefully, improved corporate performance. But many of the laws and regulations designed to protect against inaccurate or misleading information have become so restrictive that they frustrate dialogue. The legislation that created the Securities and Exchange Commission authorizes the commission to regulate shareholder communications in a manner that serves the public interest and protects the shareholders. This nebulous directive is open to a wide range of interpretations, and many argue that the SEC has gone too far.

Unlike in Germany, where the banks consolidate the voting power of shareholders, ownership in American corporations is highly fragmented. The only way for shareholders to effect change is through collective action. Several existing SEC regulations seriously deter corroboration among shareholders. For example, the SEC requires that *all* communications among shareholders that pertain to a specific proxy proposal be filed with the commission. In fact, the rule even applies to communications on issues that *may eventually* become a proxy issue. In other words, if over nine investors (there is an exemption for small groups) discuss proposing a candidate for the board, the repeal of a poison pill, or any other issue that may eventually result in a proxy vote, they must file the content of their discussions with the SEC. It does not even matter how much stock they collectively own. Failure to do so would subject them to legal liability. If a shareholder advocacy group mails a newsletter advising its subscribers on how to vote on a proxy measure at a certain company, they must file the newsletter with the SEC, which reviews the material and has the authority to mandate changes.

This level of government oversight of the activities of owners occurs nowhere else in the free world. Because pension funds, insurance companies, bank trust departments, and other institutional shareholders do not want the content of their discussions publicly disclosed for reasons discussed earlier, they avoid the onerous SEC filing requirements simply by not communicating with other owners. This lack of dialogue completely undermines the ability of a highly fragmented group of public shareholders to act collectively as true owners. In fact, people have even charged that the SEC proxy rules violate First Amendment protections of free speech.

Some people argue that shareholders should have the right to include their views in the company proxy statement. Proxy statements, in theory, disclose to the shareholders the information they need to intelligently cast their vote. Since proxy statements are prepared by company management, if a shareholder or group of shareholders oppose a board nominee or disagree with any other issue to be voted on, the burden is on them to assume the total expense of communicating their views to other shareholders in a separate mailing.

Many ask why a company should bear the expense of allowing shareholders to communicate among themselves? The obvious answer is that the money spent by the company to prepare and circulate a proxy statement comes out of the shareholders' pocket, not management's. In other words, the shareholders are already paying for the proxy statement, which exclusively represents the views of management. An increasing number of shareholders argue that if, within reasonable limits, owners were allowed to include their views on pertinent subjects, it would lead to a more balanced disclosure of issues and better informed voters.

Shareholders do have limited access to the proxy statement via an SEC rule that permits "shareholder proposals." But the list of issues that qualify for such proposals does not include the most important issue on which the shareholders are required to vote, i.e., the election of directors.[8] Instead, because shareholder proposals are limited to issues that are not "ordinary business," they frequently entail social issues—such as whether the company should conduct business in South Africa or contribute to groups that support abortion—that are often unrelated to maximizing the value of the company. These restrictions have turned many annual meetings into debates over social policy rather than the company's business plans.

A growing number of shareholder proposals are directed at repealing past corporate actions that were either taken without the shareholders' consent (such as implementing a poison pill) or on which the shareholders were unable to comment in the proxy at the time of the original vote. In fact, a shareholder proposal that "is counter to a proposal to be submitted by [company management] at the meeting" is explicitly prohibited. Furthermore, even if shareholder proposals pass, they are generally nonbinding, so their bark is worse than their bite. Management and the board can dismiss a shareholder proposal that is overwhelmingly supported by the owners with no legal consequences.

When owners do want to communicate with each other, it is not always easy to determine who the other shareholders are and how much stock they own. SEC rules provide that a company must furnish a list of its owners to a qualified existing shareholder. Alternatively, the company can opt to mail a correspondence to its shareholders on behalf of someone seeking the list, assuming that the requesting party pays the expenses for the correspondence. However, lists need not include the number of shares owned by each shareholder; this makes it difficult to contact investors who constitute a critical mass without corresponding with all of them. Also, company-provided lists frequently include shares held in "street name," which reveals nothing about the names of the real owners. In other words, a list might show that Merrill Lynch holds 2,726,421 shares for 4,376 different accounts, but not who those account holders are. In some cases companies have simply refused to provide the names of their shareholders, requiring the party seeking the information to engage in a protracted legal battle. The shareholders normally prevail, but often too late to influence the vote. When Robert Monks ran for the board at Sears, he never received a shareholder list, and management refused to send his proxy statement to employee shareholders (who owned one-fourth of the shares) unless he paid the company $300,000.

Vote Tabulation

Proxy votes are generally tabulated by the corporation, which allows management to determine how a given stockholder voted on a particular issue. This can be intimidating for certain investors, especially if their failure to support management could have negative repercussions. For example, an employee who owns stock would certainly think twice before voting against management knowing that his or her superiors can review proxies.

The pressure does not end even after votes are cast. Since management can review ballots as they are received in the weeks before the annual meeting, it has an opportunity to lobby recalcitrant shareholders to change their votes prior to the meeting date. Corporate executives do take advantage of this privilege, as illustrated by a story shared with me by the president of a large money management firm. He received a phone call at home late one evening from the chief executive of a major defense contractor, which had less than stellar performance in recent years. The following day was the company's annual meeting, and the board had put a proposal before the shareholders to install anti-takeover measures, which would have completely entrenched incumbent management. The caller made his point directly. He told the money manager, who controlled proxies representing 10 percent of the shares, that if he failed to support management, his investment firm would pay a price. The money manager politely explained that he did not favor the proposal and stated his reasons. After repeated attempts to persuade him otherwise, the money manager still refused to budge.

The chief executive responded by calling several friends who ran companies whose pension funds used the same money manager. Some of them called the money manager, threatening to fire his firm if he failed to change his mind and support management at the defense contractor. These threats quickly changed the attitude of the money manager. He vowed that in the future, if he disagreed with management proposals, his firm would sell its stock rather than confront the company.

This may have been an extreme case, but the fact that senior management tried to pressure a shareholder to support its position is not isolated. Three-fourths of the investors surveyed by the Investor Responsibility Research Center said they had been contacted by corporate officers seeking support for various proposals, and one-third said they had been solicited to change a vote already cast. After all this, if management still fails to attain a majority, the board can reschedule the annual meeting to give it more time to make its case.

A number of shareholder proposals have been introduced in recent years requesting companies to make voting confidential. Already, over 50 publicly traded companies including IBM, Exxon, General Electric, AT&T, and General Motors have proxies tabulated by an independent party. In an IRRC survey of companies with confidential voting, the respondents indicated that the cost and inconvenience of having an outside party tabulate proxies is negligible. Still, business groups resist shareholder attempts to require confidential voting.

Even after ballots are cast, there can be surprises. If 70 percent of the shareholders voted, and 70 percent of those who voted opposed management, who wins? The answer is "it all depends." In Wisconsin, this outcome is tallied as 49 percent opposed and 51 percent in favor of management. Anyone who does not vote is presumed to support management. Imagine how hard it would be to replace our political leaders if the same principle applied. Some corporations count abstentions in the total votes cast to determine whether a majority of dissenting votes have been received, others do not. Although state laws occasionally provide direction on this issue, many are not specific. At present there is no uniform set of rules to govern how ballots will be tallied at public companies.

There is no doubt that enfeebling an already atomistic group of owners reduces the accountability of corporate managers. Several groups, including the United Shareholders of America, the American Bar Association, and the California Public Employees Retirement Fund have submitted extensive proposals to the SEC requesting proxy reform. However, reform efforts have been strongly opposed by business groups, including the powerful Business Roundtable, the American Society of Corporate Secretaries, and the Business Council of New York State. These groups have written the SEC to express their views that the present proxy system works just fine. The Business Council wrote that "a review of the proxy rules at this time is neither necessary or appropriate," and the corporate secretaries group actually recommended increased SEC oversight of institutional investor voting.

Governance by Plebiscite

Proxy reform is necessary, but it has its limits. A company cannot be managed by plebiscite. It is virtually impossible to fully educate a broad spectrum of shareholders on complex issues, especially without disclosing competitive information. That is why the American system of corporate accountability was designed to revolve around the board. Even the most active institutional shareholders admit that, in most cases, the board is in a better position to review data, discuss the merits of an issue, and resolve differences of opinion than a fragmented group of owners. That is why reform of the proxy system should focus on director elections rather than on the more obscure issues in which shareholders increasingly want a say. An *Institutional Investor* survey showed that 92 percent of pension fund officials believe they should have the right to vote on other issues of substance as well. There are three issues in particular that shareholders want to vote on directly—greenmail, golden parachutes, and poison pills.

Greenmail refers to the practice of a company buying its own stock back from a threatening shareholder at an above-market price to avoid a proxy fight or takeover. This is a means of dispensing with a troublemaker. Several wealthy investors including the Bass Brothers, the Belzbergs, and Carl Icahn have made millions of dollars by acquiring substantial stakes in vulnerable companies and then cutting a deal to leave the company alone in exchange for a handsome premium for their shares.

Late in 1986, Sir James Goldsmith offered to buy Goodyear Tire and Rubber Company for $49 a share. Goodyear's management fought Goldsmith with great intensity, claiming that remaining independent was in the best interest of the shareholders. Goodyear's CEO, Robert Mercer, offered to pay Goldsmith $49.50 a share for the 12.5 million shares Sir James had already acquired if he promised to drop his bid. Goldsmith sold his stock to the company, pocketing a profit of an estimated $90 million. Meanwhile, remaining shareholders saw their share price drop instantly to $41.50.

At the same time, Ron Perelman was making a run at Gillette. He had offered to buy the company for $65 a share. After several discussions with Gillette management, Perelman withdrew his offer and promised not to seek control of Gillette for 10 years. The company had paid him $59.50 a share for his 9.2 million shares, providing Perelman with a $43-million profit. When this payoff was announced, the company's stock plummeted to about $15 a share below what Perelman was paid.

Whitemail is the flip side of greenmail. In this practice, a friendly investor agrees to purchase a large block of stock—on terms superior to other shareholders'—in exchange for a commitment, stated or assumed, to help the company preserve its independence. In both cases, management is accused of "buying off" some owners at the expense of the others, which is why investors want to put such decisions to a vote. On the surface, it seems that a transaction that offers one shareholder terms unavailable to all shareholders is patently unfair. Yet some studies show that greenmail may raise shareholder value by attracting attention to potential opportunities to improve the company. Whitemail, which also appears unfair to some, may enhance shareholder value if the outside investor is able to influence management in a more positive way than other shareholders could.

Even the venerable Warren Buffett now actively engages in transactions some categorize as whitemail. In 1987, to escape the grasp of Ron Perelman, Salomon Brothers sold Buffett $700 million of preferred stock that could be converted into a 12-percent stake in the company. In addition to a very attractive conversion premium, the preferred shares carried a 9-percent yield, most of which was tax-free because it was bought through Buffett's company, Berkshire Hathaway (corporations are not fully taxed on dividend income). Buffett engaged in similar transactions with Gillette, USAir, and Champion International. Will his investments help or hurt the other shareholders? Many argue the board is in the best position to answer this question, others that the shareholders have a right to decide. The more relevant question, however, is this: If the board thought it could be replaced by making the wrong decision, would this influence the outcome?

Golden parachutes are another target of shareholder activism. A golden parachute is a contract with a member of senior management to pay him or her a certain sum of money upon a change in control of the company or a loss of employment. These contracts have received a great deal of public attention because of the enormous windfalls they have produced for some executives. According to *Business Week*, Stephen Ross, the top executive at Warner Communications, received more than $150 million in cash (some of which was placed in a trust) when Time merged with Warner in 1989, even though he preserved his job and received a raise in the process. Several other examples of highly publicized golden parachutes are given in Chapter 7.

Some argue that it would be nice to outlaw egregious payouts to executives. Congress already imposes a nondeductible excise tax of 20 percent on golden parachutes more than three times an executive's annual compensation. However, others argue that an independently functioning compensation committee of the board is in the best position to establish the proper remuneration for top management. Shareholders cannot be aware of all the circumstances surrounding the hiring of executives or what agreements are appropriate to keep top managers and encourage proper risk-taking. Once again, the shareholders would probably be less concerned about excessive golden parachute contracts if they believed that the directors on the compensation committee were accountable for paying executives in a manner that promoted the shareholders' interests.

Poison pills have attracted the greatest number of shareholder resolutions in recent years. A poison pill is an anti-takeover device that makes a change in control without the board's approval virtually impossible. These devices are usually triggered by someone acquiring a meaningful stake in the company or initiating a tender offer. Poison pills can be structured in a variety of ways. For example, suppose a bidder offered to buy all of the shares of a company for $50 a share. Once the potential buyer "triggered" the pill by accumulating a designated percentage of the shares, say 15 percent, the other shareholders would be granted the right to purchase additional shares in the company at a price far below the offer price. The company might then be selling new shares for $25, which the bidder would have to turn around and buy for $50, making the transaction prohibitively expensive. Well over 1,000 companies have implemented poison pills.

Poison pills are extremely effective deterrents against hostile takeover attempts and they can be implemented without shareholder approval. In the event they are triggered, poison pills must be repealed by the board, which prevents the potential buyer from making a case directly to the shareholders. In other words, with a poison pill, a fully financed takeover offer can be rejected by the board and never presented to the shareholders for their consideration. Since at most public companies less than half the directors stand for election each year, there is little recourse if the shareholders disagree with the board. In Orwellian fashion these measures, which effectively take away the right of an owner to sell his or her shares to someone offering a substantial premium, are referred to by corporations as "shareholders rights plans."

It is because of their effectiveness, and the Delaware Supreme Court's decision in 1985 that allows this defense to be adopted without shareholder approval, that owners are concerned that they be consulted before a poison pill is implemented. Repealing them after the fact can be problematic. In 1988, when 59 percent of the shareholders voting at Santa Fe Southern Pacific Corp.'s annual meeting supported repeal of a poison pill, the management ignored their wishes. The company's chief executive simply asserted that shareholder proposals are nonbinding. At USAir Group Inc. an antipoison pill measure considered in 1988 received a majority of the votes cast but was defeated because it received only 48 percent of the shares *outstanding*.

The debate over poison pills and their impact on shareholder wealth is not without controversy, and there are pluses and minuses. It is clear that poison pills make a company more difficult to acquire, which tends to depress stock prices when they are implemented. However, they also force buyers to negotiate with the board, which increases the likelihood that the price will be bid up if someone makes a run at the company.

As with greenmail and golden parachutes, if the board was accountable to the shareholders on an annual basis, poison pills would not be as threatening to the owners. Directors who refused to negotiate in good faith with a potential buyer could be replaced. But with the present difficulties in using the proxy system to hold directors accountable for their decisions, this is yet another issue that will continue to be a source of acrimony between owners and managers.

Changes in Control

Given all of the difficulties shareholders encounter when trying to influence corporate behavior, it is commonly accepted among institutional investors and economists that the only effective mechanism for accountability is the market for corporate control, i.e., takeovers. Even the threat of a potential takeover has served as a powerful discipline to ensure that corporations did not stray too far from value-maximizing behavior. However, in the 1980s, countless corporations systematically immunized themselves from the takeover market. There are now sufficient defenses available through state law, legal protections, and market devices such as employee stock ownership plans (ESOPs) that the costs involved in trying to acquire a company have risen and the probability of success has fallen dramatically. Forty state legislatures have enacted protective statutes at the behest of corporations either headquartered or chartered in their state. Today only the most mismanaged companies are subject to the discipline of a takeover by a financial buyer not making a strategic acquisition.

Most companies use at least some protective measures. Boise Cascade is an example (but not the most extreme one) of a company that has implemented several available takeover defenses. If someone determined that Boise Cascade was not being optimally managed and wished to acquire control of the company by offering the shareholders a premium for their stock, he or she would have to contend with the laundry list of impediments detailed in Exhibit 3.1. Many of these measures not only protect management from a hostile bidder, they make it more difficult for the existing shareholders to replace directors, thus hold the company accountable for its performance.

Exhibit 3.1

Boise Cascade Takeover Defenses

Charter Provisions

Classified board	Directors divided into three classes with overlapping three-year terms. Thus, it would take two years to win control, even if someone owned a majority of the shares.
Fair price provision	Requires a bidder to pay all shareholders a "fair price" (the highest price it paid for any shares acquired during a certain period before it commenced its offer) unless the offer is approved by a majority of the board not affiliated with the acquirer or of the disinterested outstanding shares. A vote of 80 percent of the outstanding shares is required to amend or repeal this provision.
No shareholder action by written consent	Prevents shareholders from taking action without a meeting, and only the board may call a meeting (see Bylaw Provisions below).
Eliminated cumulative voting in 1984	Cumulative voting enables minority shareholders to win token board representation by cumulating their votes for one or two candidates rather than spreading votes across the entire slate.
Blank check preferred stock	Preferred stock for which the board has broad authority to set voting, dividend, conversion and other rights. May be used for ordinary business purposes such as acquisitions, but may be used in connection with a shareholder rights plan (poison pill) or issued to a friendly party to block a takeover.

Bylaw Provisions

Shareholders prohibited from calling a meeting	Guarantees that only the board can call a meeting of the shareholders, even if a majority of the shares seek a meeting to oust the board, consider an offer or for any other reason.

Board-Adopted Protections

"Shareholder rights plan" (poison pill)	If triggered by the board during a hostile bid, allows shareholders (except for the bidder) to double their holdings at a bargain rate, causing such dilution of the bidder's equity and voting power that to continue with the takeover would be economically unviable.

Other Corporate Governance Features

Golden parachutes	Twenty-six executives have severance agreements contingent on a change in control, as of the 1990 annual meeting. The value of the top five was $10 million, if they were fired, demoted or resigned within a certain period after the change in control. While cushioning executives against job loss, parachutes also make a takeover more expensive.
Pension parachute	Provides that surplus pension assets be distributed to employees and retirees if an attempt is made to terminate or merge the pension plan or transfer its assets within a specified period after a change in control. This prevents an acquirer from using the money to help finance the acquisition even though *excess* assets legally belong to the company.
Limited director liability	Charter amendment eliminates personal financial liability of directors for breaches of the fiduciary duty of care.
Director indemnification	Charter amendment indemnifies officers and directors against legal expenses and/or judgments incurred as a result of actual or threatened lawsuits relating to their conduct. In addition, the company has indemnification contracts with certain officers and directors.
Employee stock ownership plan	The company's ESOP holds 15 percent of the voting power, sufficient to block a takeover under Delaware's anti-takeover law.

State Anti-takeover Law

Delaware three-year business combination (freeze out)	Bars a business combination with a shareholder owning more than 15 percent of the company for three years after the 15-percent acquisition unless the acquirer had board approval, acquires at least 85 percent of the shares or the combination is approved by the board and two-thirds of the outstanding disinterested shares at a special meeting (which cannot be called by the shareholders). This prevents someone from being able to finance a transaction, because lenders will not fund a buyout in which the bidder cannot secure title to the company's assets.

Source: Investor Responsibility Research Center.

The Federalism Debate

The main reason that powers historically granted to shareholders in America have been stripped away without a national debate is that most of this activity has occurred at the state level, which favors corporate management. Corporations have more influence over their local state legislatures than they do in Washington. A corporation can threaten to move facilities or charters out of the state. Either action would affect the tax revenues of the state. Shareholders, on the other hand, are often not residents of the state in which a corporation is chartered (almost half the major public companies are incorporated in Delaware) so they have virtually no political power at the state level.

Federal legislation in the form of the Williams Act of 1968 was designed to promote a level playing field in the battle for corporate control, to ensure that neither a potential buyer nor the target company is taken advantage of in the process. However, subsequent actions taken by the states superseded federal efforts to prevent favoritism. Rather than evaluating the economic merits of these measures, judges have been forced to decide debates over state anti-takeover laws in the context of federalism. One of the first lessons aspiring lawyers are taught is that corporate governance is a state, not a federal issue. With the United States now operating in a global economy, some people suggest that we should rethink this view.

Today, disparate nations in the European Community (EC) are developing uniform policies and regulations governing securities and takeovers. Yet more than 50 heterogeneous statutes regulate securities transactions and the governance of publicly traded corporations in the United States. The French and Germans will soon operate under more uniform laws than companies in California and Massachusetts.

Many of the U.S. companies regulated by the states operate on a global basis. Many do not even conduct business in the state whose laws they are governed by—where a company is incorporated has nothing to do with where its business is located. The federalism debate pits those who believe our present balkanized corporate governance system is anachronistic against those who contend that federal intervention would only make matters worse given Washington's track record in financial regulation. What makes the debate interesting is the fact that many policy makers, including most top officials in both the Reagan and Bush administrations, support both free markets and states' rights. When it comes to state anti-takeover laws, these views are mutually exclusive. Under Reagan the states' righters won out; it is not clear if this will continue in the Bush administration.

In many ways the debate over federalism is rife with inconsistencies. The same corporations that defend the status quo in takeover law vehemently oppose the states' control over issues such as product liability and securities registration. I once attended a meeting of a major business organization where the primary topic was the need to lobby *against* state securities laws because they raise the cost of capital, and *for* state anti-takeover laws, which also raise the cost of capital. The transparency of the members' motives was quite obvious. These firms felt they had more control over their local legislatures than over Congress on takeover laws, and they knew they would receive greater protection at the state level. Protection was more important than the cost of capital.

As mentioned, approximately half of all New York Stock Exchange and *Fortune* 500 companies are incorporated in Delaware, yet virtually none of these companies has significant operations or shareholdings within that state. At the same time, California, which contributes more to our national economy than any other state, is the site of incorporation for less than 4 percent of NYSE companies and less than 1 percent of *Fortune* 500 companies. In many regards we already have federal corporate law; it just happens to be made in Delaware rather than in Washington, DC.

The most popular defense for leaving corporate governance with the states is that they serve as laboratories for ideas. One state can try something, and the others can learn from the results. But for this argument to be valid, there would have to be no biases for the states to favor either management or the shareholders. Under the present system, however, the states have an economic incentive to establish laws that favor corporate management. In 1987, Delaware received 17 percent of its total revenues, or $170 million, from state franchise fees collected from 184,000 corporations. It seems logical that the Delaware legislature would want to avoid passing laws that would drive companies to reincorporate elsewhere. Instead, it seems it would be inclined to pass laws that keep pace with other states that may be more protective of management and labor. This same principle applies to every state, not just Delaware, which is why the battle among states to attract corporate charters is commonly referred to as the "race to the bottom" in corporate governance.

The fact that states have little incentive to seriously consider the interests of the owners was highlighted in 1990 with the passage of Pennsylvania's extremely restrictive anti-takeover law. A study by Wilshire Associates shows that the market value of a sample group of companies covered by the new Pennsylvania statute dropped by $3.6 billion dollars relative to the market overall, following announcement of the law. This represented 4 percent of the equity value of these companies. Another study performed by Drexel University professors in Philadelphia showed an even greater drop.[9] Yet the law passed overwhelmingly in both Pennsylvania chambers and was immediately signed by the governor. Both business groups and labor unions had sponsored the legislation.

State Anti-takeover Laws

Forty states have adopted or strengthened anti-takeover provisions in recent years. Many of these laws were enacted subsequent to a 1987 Supreme Court decision upholding Indiana's control share law; and several are more protective of management than Delaware's. Without reciting the litany of ways in which states have insulated companies from a potential change in ownership, it is useful to look at some of the provisions of a few states to get an idea of how far-reaching they have become and how they affect every owner, not just hostile bidders.

Among other restrictions, Wisconsin's anti-takeover law limits an individual's voting strength beyond 20 percent to one-tenth of the additional shares acquired. This means that if someone owned 90 percent of the stock in a company, they could vote only 27 percent (20 percent plus one-tenth of the other 70 percent) of the shares.

In 1989, an investor group known as Hyde Park Holdings attempted to purchase Wisconsin-based Universal Foods by offering a premium to the shareholders for their stock. But given the Wisconsin law, if Hyde Park's ownership exceeded 20 percent, the remaining shares were virtually worthless. Consequently, the buyer could not get a sufficient number of owners to tender their shares unless the courts struck down the Wisconsin law. After spending millions of dollars in legal fees, Hyde Park lost in court. In upholding the Wisconsin law, the Seventh Circuit Court of Appeals described it as "economic folly."[10] Although the court concluded that the law was bad for the state and bad for the economy, it was powerless to overturn it because states are free to pass whatever corporate governance provisions they wish.

In Massachusetts, the state legislature came to the rescue of Norton Company, a local company being pursued by BTR, a British-based company. Norton had already adopted adequate defenses to preempt a direct purchase of a majority of its shares by an outsider seeking control. With this avenue blocked, BTR decided to appeal to the Norton shareholders to replace the existing board, which had refused to negotiate with them. Not trusting its shareholders to know what was in their own best interests, Norton petitioned the Massachusetts legislature to alter state law in a way that would prevent the shareholders from being able to replace a majority of the board in a single year.

Norton employees were concerned about a potential loss of jobs if BTR took control of the company; during an emotionally charged protest they burned the Union Jack on the steps of the

Massachusetts state house. Only days before Norton's annual meeting, Gov. Michael Dukakis signed into law a bill *mandating* that all companies chartered in Massachusetts have a "classified" board—so-called because the board would be broken into three classes of directors, with one-third elected each year to three-year terms. The shareholders, according to the new law, could not vote to override this provision, even if 100 percent of them were in favor of having annual director elections for the entire board. Consequently, BTR failed in its bid to replace the board, regardless of the shareholders' desires. Safe from the grasp of BTR, Norton confounded many one-time supporters by selling out to a French company only weeks later.

It has become commonplace for states to modify laws at the behest of a single company. The Pennsylvania law enacted in 1990, mentioned earlier, is perhaps the most far-reaching. As in Massachusetts, the Pennsylvania bill was precipitated by an unwelcomed takeover battle involving a single local company. Armstrong World Industries, a home products manufacturer based in Lancaster, was approached by the Belzbergs, a Canadian family not known for its eleemosynary behavior after acquiring companies. Pennsylvania's corporate law was already among the most restrictive in the nation—prohibiting a majority shareholder from merging with a Pennsylvania corporation for five years without board approval, which makes securing financing for a buyout virtually impossible. It also restricted shareholders from calling a special meeting or proposing amendments to their company's articles of incorporation, rights which many consider fundamental to ownership.

However, the top executives of Armstrong still felt vulnerable, so they sponsored a new law to make certain that Armstrong remained independent. The 1990 Pennsylvania law stripped the shareholders of virtually all remaining power to replace management, regardless of its performance. The Pennsylvania law had four major provisions:

1. Boards could subordinate the interests of shareholders to other constituencies. Directors were determined not to be liable for failing to take measures that would allow the shareholders to receive the optimal value for their stock.
2. Takeovers were made more expensive by a disgorgement provision that allowed companies to confiscate the profits made by someone in a failed takeover attempt if they sold their stock within 18 months.
3. Shareholders who exceed certain ownership thresholds (20, 33-1/2, or 50 percent) would be stripped of the right to vote their shares unless the other shareholders voted to reinstate their voting rights.
4. Anyone laid off within two years following a change in control would be eligible for a significant severance package, based on their tenure. Also, acquirers would be forced to honor labor contracts in place at the time of the buyout for up to five years. (This provision was added to secure the support of organized labor.)

In a scathing editorial *Business Week* declared, "The bill undermines a key concept of capitalism: a board's fiduciary duty to shareholders."[11] A *Forbes* article on the subject was titled "Socialism, Pennsylvania Style."[12] Richard Breeden, chairman of the Securities and Exchange Commission, in a letter to Pennsylvania State Senator Vincent Fumo, wrote, "Among other things, [this bill] could do enormous damage to a fundamental shareholder right, the right of shareholders to use the proxy machinery to replace a board of directors that does not act in the shareholders' best interest." As mentioned earlier, the individual who managed the retirement funds for Pennsylvania's state employees testified that he would not be inclined to buy any shares in Pennsylvania companies if the bill was enacted. Nevertheless, with an unlikely alliance of business and labor, the bill passed the House 182–10, and there were only four dissensions in the Senate.

Clearly, part of the reason corporate boards and state legislatures are hostile to today's investors is that they seldom behave as owners. Chapter 2 examined how existing regulations, the norms of Wall Street, new technologies in the stock market, and pressures from outside parties not to become involved in corporate affairs have turned investing into a very impersonal process. But further freezing out the shareholders by stripping them of many of their traditional rights has only widened the void between capital providers and capital users, forcing up the cost of capital and encouraging both parties to focus on their parochial short-run interests rather than working together to maximize the competitiveness of American business.

Many who criticize these laws are not necessarily endorsing takeovers as an efficient means to achieve corporate accountability. The next chapter will elaborate on why takeovers are, in fact, an inefficient mechanism to redirect poorly run companies and should serve only as a backup when all other corporate governance measures fail. But in an attempt to make corporations takeover-resistant, we have virtually eliminated all accountability for corporate boards and managers, which could have some dire consequences.

Our competitors in Japan and Germany have very rigorous methods for ensuring that corporate managers are accountable for their long-term economic performance. This interaction not only reassures the owners and lenders that their interests are being looked after, but also serves as a way to educate the financial community about corporate strategies and industry trends, which helps them to know where to allocate their capital. With ongoing dialogue, business and financial leaders can define common objectives and work together to see that they are realized. Unfortunately, the present U.S. corporate governance system is not at all conducive to dialogue.

4

The Truth about Takeovers

No discussion of short-termism is complete without a debate over takeovers and leveraged buyouts. This is one subject in which the popular press has generated far more heat than light. There are generally two camps in the takeover debate—those who think LBOs have ruined our country and are the pinnacle of shortsightedness, and those who believe leveraged takeovers are an ideal way to restore a sense of accountability to our corporate governance system. The purpose of this chapter is to prove that they are neither. I will show that while many of the criticisms of leveraged buyouts are unfounded, takeovers are still too blunt an instrument to be relied upon as the primary source of accountability.

The leveraged buyout craze of the 1980s is frequently characterized as an era of meaningless financial manipulations. However, much of the "financial engineering" that occurred during the decade was precipitated by the need to restructure poorly performing companies that had been combined for purely financial reasons in the 1960s and early 1970s. How quickly we forget the likes of Harold Geneen, the former accountant who transformed ITT from a telephone company into one of the most diversified businesses in the world. Royal Little parlayed a small textile company into a billion-dollar corporation called Textron by buying and selling hundreds of businesses. And Gulf+Western was nicknamed "Engulf and Devour" because of its aggressive acquisition strategy. Perhaps the most famous financial manipulator was Jimmy Ling, the founder and chairman of LTV Industries. Ling turned a $2,000 investment into the fourteenth-largest company in the United States with revenues of almost $4 billion.[1] Unfortunately, virtually none of these conglomerates worked out. In fact, by 1991, LTV ranked among the 10 least-admired U.S. companies in a *Fortune* survey.

The purpose of creating conglomerates in the 1960s and 1970s was to perpetuate the existence of corporations. By combining enough diverse businesses, the theory went, a company could survive any seasonal or cyclical downturn. Companies could blend cash-generating, mature businesses with rapidly growing capital-starved businesses. The premise that made this theory tenable was that corporations could allocate capital more efficiently than the markets.

The problem is that this concept did not work, as evidenced by the fact that in real terms the value of U.S. companies declined considerably during the conglomerate era. As mentioned earlier, the more diversified and less focused businesses became, the more their productivity suffered. This changed during the LBO era. Output per worker grew at a remarkable 3.6 percent annual clip, three times faster than in the 1970s. Manufacturing grew from 20 percent of GNP in 1982 to over 23 percent in 1990, hardly the de-industrialization claimed by LBO critics.

Often the greatest critics of LBOs are corporate executives, some from the same companies that have engaged in financial engineering for years. Rand Araskog, chief executive of ITT, is one of the most outspoken critics of the deal mania that swept Wall Street in the 1980s. But few deal makers have ever bought and sold the number of companies that ITT did during the previous 25 years. ITT has been continuously undergoing "diversification," "restructuring," "refocusing," and any other euphemism for deal making for decades. In corporate America it seems to be acceptable for managers to become traders, but not for traders to become managers.

The takeover era of the 1980s was not about putting companies together, but taking them apart and using debt as a discipline to force managers to optimize cash flows. The theory behind the takeover wave, which was led by independent financial buyers rather than corporations, was that deploying assets and people efficiently is more important than preserving a company's existence. Naturally, many in corporate America whose jobs were at risk were not receptive to this objective.

Takeovers have their place in the American system of corporate accountability, much as the wolf provides a useful role in the Northwest Territories. Wolves feed on the frail members of the caribou pack—the sick, the lame, and the genetically weak. By doing so, the wolves strengthen the entire caribou herd. The native people of Alaska and Canada call the wolf "the friend of the caribou," but naive and uninformed observers regard wolves as cruel, avaricious, and ill-spirited creatures. If there were no wolves, the entire caribou herd would be dragged down by the underperformers, and the others would become less healthy.

Unfortunately, the LBO wave became so powerful that numerous companies eventually drowned in their debts. The wolves started preying on healthy caribou, making it easy to dismiss this era as an aberration, a trend with no logic. But there are many valuable lessons to be learned from the decade of buyouts which are often overlooked in the emotional responses of people who were negatively affected by them and the superficial news coverage of what the effects of this phenomenon have been. To understand why the financial takeovers of the 1980s were so prevalent it is essential to appreciate the economics that motivated these transactions.

Takeover Economics

Virtually every article about takeovers expounds on how a buyout group intends to sell off assets, close plants, or slash research and development to make a company worth more in the short term than it would be worth if it were managed for the long term. There is scant evidence to indicate that over a protracted period the stock market improperly values companies to the extent reflected in takeover premiums. True, many stocks are either undervalued or overvalued for short periods because of trading activities. Certainly there is a herd mentality on Wall Street that results in various industries or companies being out of favor at one time or another. And the quality-of-information problem discussed in Chapter 2 clearly produces valuation inaccuracies. But with buyout premiums averaging 40 percent to 50 percent in the 1980s, the market would have to have been very far off for a long time for takeovers to occur only because of misvaluations of long-term strategies.

There is a popular perception that the stock market penalizes long-term investment. It may not fully appreciate long-term investment strategies, but it does not ignore them. In fact, a 1985 study by McConnell and Muscarella concluded that in the early 1980s share prices *rose* when major capital expenditures were announced in every industry except oil and gas.[2] Similarly, another study completed that year showed that share prices also rise when major research and development projects are announced.[3] One study even showed that following the installation of takeover defenses that protect corporations from market forces, companies actually reduce their research spending rather than increase it as one might expect if companies shunned investments to boost short-term share prices.[4]

When takeover candidates complain that they are vulnerable simply because their stocks are undervalued, that their assets are really worth more, they may well be ignoring the fundamental concept behind equity valuation: shareholders pay for the returns they expect to receive on those assets given *current* management and strategies. Investors do not pay for the *potential* values of assets or cash flows unless they expect them to be managed differently in the future. An illustration will help prove this point.

Suppose a company has a manufacturing plant that operates on a breakeven basis. The plant might be worth $50 million if it were auctioned off to the highest bidder. (The reason a plant not producing a profit might be worth $50 million is that another owner might use it to produce a different product or might have a greater need for the capacity.) Finally, suppose management has no plan to improve the performance of the plant, yet is unwilling to sell it. In trying to value the company, should shareholders value the plant at $50 million, or zero? If they do not expect the plant to be sold in the foreseeable future, and if there is no reasonable prospect that its performance will improve, the plant should be valued at close to nothing.

Does this mean the stock is undervalued? Not if shareholders pay for what they receive, rather than what they *could* receive. What it does mean is that the company's resources are not deployed to their highest and best use, not that the market is wrong. If the company were taken over and the plant sold, some might claim that such a decision was precipitated by a corporate raider focusing only on its short-run value. But if the plant were worth substantially more to another owner, would not the country's competitiveness interests be served if the plant were sold to whoever could create the greatest value from it? Surely the shareholders would prefer $50 million in cash to an unprofitable plant! Yet we readily accuse takeover artists of taking advantage of the shareholders and ruining the economy when they sell off corporate assets. These assets do not disappear just because they have new owners.

As discussed in Chapter 2, much of the reason that investors fail to value companies properly results from an information gap. They may not fully understand the market potential or merits of a company's strategy. However, when a bidder offers to acquire a company, the market focuses much greater attention on determining its true worth. While it still may not value the business as precisely as if the owners were intimately familiar with it, the collective wisdom of the market is not likely to be off by a wide margin. The view that the entire universe of investors is unable to appreciate the economic value of a company, even when management presents its case for why the firm is worth more if it remains independent, belies the market economy our country has relied upon since its inception.

In fact, we have incorporated this perverse notion into the American judicial system. In one of the most celebrated takeover cases of the 1980s, *Paramount* v. *Time,* the Delaware Supreme Court permitted Time Inc. to avoid being taken over by Paramount Communications by allowing the company to merge with Warner Communications. The rationale used by the court was that Time's board had a plan to make the company worth more to its shareholders in the long run than it was worth to Paramount or anyone else in the short run.

Paramount had offered $200 a share for Time, and Time's board refused to allow the shareholders to vote on whether to accept the offer. When the court upheld the board's right to make this decision, Time stock plummeted to $125 a share. If Time's long-term strategy represented a superior value for the shareholders, then why could its board not convince sophisticated investors that their shares were already worth at least $200? By this point, no one was focusing on the latest quarter's earnings; all the major shareholders were carefully examining the long-run prospects of the company under various scenarios to assess the true value of the company.

There is only one plausible explanation for the court's action: no one in the marketplace except Time's board was capable of appreciating the long-run merits of Time's strategy, a strategy that presumably had a net present value in excess of $200 a share. In its opinion, the court basically said that it was the board's job to protect Time's owners from their own ignorance. Interestingly, in the eight months that it took the Delaware Supreme Court to release its written opinion, the market remained in the dark, because, in spite of a higher overall stock market in February 1990, Time's shares were trading at less than half the Paramount offer.

By then the combined market capitalization of the new Time Warner was actually lower than the capitalization of *either* company before the merger. The market clearly rejected the notion that Time's board knew something no one else could figure out.

What drives buyouts is not a mythical gap between a company's short-term value and its long-term value, it is the gap between a company's *market* value and its *intrinsic* value. The intrinsic value of a company is what its stock would be worth if all of the corporation's resources were being deployed to their highest and best use. If all employees, technologies, facilities, and financial resources were being optimally managed, the company would achieve its intrinsic value. Obviously, no company can achieve perfection, so intrinsic value is merely theoretical.

Stocks generally trade at a discount to their intrinsic value. On rare occasions, overaggressive investors bid the price of a stock beyond the level of returns that it will ever provide to shareholders no matter how well the company is run. Obviously, factors beyond the control of management affect both the intrinsic value of a company and its present market value. For example, if the economy improves, the intrinsic value will go up, but since investors are aware of the changing economy, so will the market value of the company.

However, when there is a gap between the market value of a company and its intrinsic value, the only way to close the gap is to utilize the company's resources more effectively. This "value gap" can exist for many reasons. Perhaps the firm spends too much on a corporate jet fleet or overcompensates its executives. Perhaps it undercompensates its executives or workers and cannot retain competent people. Perhaps the company is investing too much money in the development of a product that is unlikely to pan out, like RJR Nabisco's smokeless cigarette. Alternatively, the company might not be investing enough in new product development to keep up with more aggressive competitors. Basically, any difference between the way management runs the company and the way the company could be run to achieve higher returns to its shareholders produces a value gap.

This concept explains what is commonly referred to in Wall Street jargon as a "control premium." If outsiders could gain control, they would run the company in a manner that reduces the value gap because the benefits would accrue to them rather than to a dispersed group of shareholders. In other words, passive public shareholders are unwilling to pay the same price for a share that someone with greater influence would pay because they can do little to ensure that the intrinsic value is achieved. The closer managers come to realizing the intrinsic value of a company, the smaller the control premium becomes. Firms that have small control premiums are usually safe from a takeover threat. That is why it is the underperformers that most often seek protection against a buyout.[5]

When discussing intrinsic value, it is important to separate "strategic" mergers and acquisitions from takeovers. In a strategic business combination, the value of a company may increase because of synergy with the acquirer—two plus two equals five. As a result, a buyer can afford to pay more than the intrinsic value of a company because the highest and best use of its resources as part of a new entity is greater than it would be on a stand-alone basis. In these cases, even well-run companies might be vulnerable, but only if there were economic efficiencies in their being owned by someone else. From a competitiveness standpoint, we want these transactions to occur.

Most of the takeovers of the 1980s were not strategic mergers between corporations; they were independent buyouts by financial buyers. They typically involved underperforming companies with large gaps between market value and intrinsic value. A study of about 200 hostile takeovers in the United States during the 1980s, conducted by the consulting firm Marakon Associates, showed that target companies had underperformed their peers by 45 percent in return on equity, by 73 percent in growth rate, and by 25 percent in market-to-book value.[6] Almost every company targeted by a hostile bidder ranked below the top quartile in its industry in at least two of these three important measures. In other words, the takeover market provided discipline to undermanaged companies.

One ratio that is seldom mentioned, but that accounts for much of the past decade's takeover activity, is the "optimal capital structure." Every company has an optimal capital structure, which is the perfect mixture of debt and equity—enough debt to take advantage of the deductibility of interest, yet not too much to inhibit its ability to pursue the most profitable operating strategy. In order to realize its intrinsic value, a firm needs to be optimally capitalized; otherwise, its cost of capital will be unduly high.

Thus, even businesses that are exquisitely run from an operating perspective but are underleveraged have a value gap. By taking on more debt, they could increase the amount of cash available to their shareholders by reducing taxes, which raises the value of the company. After Roberto Goizueta took the helm of Coca-Cola, the company relinquished its triple-A credit rating by taking on more debt. The company saw its return on equity soar from 21 percent to more than 38 percent. Naturally, its stock price soared too. In an interview with *U.S. News & World Report*, Goizueta said, "I don't think investors will pay you to have a clean balance sheet just to hang on your wall."

But because many others failed to understand this principle, LBO firms were able to take over and leverage up several well-run companies and leave management in place to operate the business in virtually the same manner. They were creating value by lowering the cost of capital. Of course, as we will see later in this chapter, an *over*leveraged company also produces a value gap because its loan covenants and debt schedule inhibit its ability to pursue the optimal operating strategy.

The economic motivation for a takeover, therefore, stems from the perception that if a company's assets were managed differently they would create more shareholder value. Sometimes that means that individual business units need to be managed independently to achieve greater focus, which is why assets are frequently sold after a takeover. Other times it simply means that the company needs to be capitalized differently. And, unfortunately, sometimes it means that potential new owners see a mirage—the value they perceive is not really there. Only after buying the company do they discover that they have overpaid. This appears to have been the case in many instances in the late 1980s.

LBOs and Corporate Accountability

Leveraged buyouts were billed by many academics and practitioners as a cure-all for our nation's high cost of capital and inept corporate governance system. In a highly publicized article, "Eclipse of the Public Corporation," Michael Jensen of the Harvard Business School argued, in effect, that equity ownership by executives and a significant debt burden would force managers to focus on performance maximization.[7] This carrot-and-stick approach to corporate governance, however, has proven to be an inflexible way to hold managers accountable, as evidenced by recent difficulties experienced at many companies taken private through an LBO. If events change or expectations are unrealized, the burden of an enormous fixed-debt payment can force companies to take actions that are not in the long-run interests of its shareholders or of our nation's economy.

Relying on the market for corporate control (a euphemism for takeovers) to marry the interests of investors and managers is not the ideal solution. Takeovers, like tourniquets, have a valid purpose, but to rely upon them as the only way to cure a problem can produce unnecessary damage. Takeovers were intended as a backstop when the normal corporate governance process breaks down. In baseball, if the backstop comes into play too often, it means either the catcher or the pitcher is not doing his job. The fact that so many takeovers occurred means that too many owners and managers were not doing their jobs. Continuing to rely heavily on the backstop would be inefficient, but removing it altogether could be disastrous. The underlying problem needs to be resolved.

There are several inefficiencies involved with using takeovers as a substitute for the traditional system of corporate accountability. First, takeovers involve enormous transaction costs. In a typical leveraged buyout in the 1980s, the legal, advisory, and financing fees averaged approximately 4 percent of the purchase price of the company, and more than 5 percent of the prevailing market value at the time of the offer. There are also nonquantifiable expenses resulting from disruptions to the ongoing business in a change of control. Add to that the dislocations that arise from bankruptcies caused by overaggressive bidding in some cases, especially when target companies are "auctioned."

But these costs are minor compared to the major inefficiency in this approach, one that is typically overlooked. There is a massive *opportunity cost* of underperformance for all companies not realizing the intrinsic value of their assets, yet whose stock price is not depressed enough to warrant a takeover. In other words, an accountability system that is not fully effective except in extreme cases of underperformance fails to optimize the value of most corporations. Takeovers allow managers a wide margin for error. With an average takeover premium in the past decade of approximately 40 percent, it appears that most companies that perform above 60 percent of their potential are secure. The passing grade for some is even lower.

If a company is being poorly run and the shareholders lack the willingness or ability to rectify the situation, a company should be taken over. This concept undergirds capitalism. However, the fact that the American system relies so heavily on takeovers to achieve corporate accountability proves that the primary accountability mechanisms of our corporate governance system are dysfunctional.

Takeovers almost never occur in Japan and Germany because they are seldom needed. Owners and managers disagree, but they do so in the boardroom and in private meetings. However, because the owners of American companies have been effectively shut out of the boardroom, our battles take place in the newspapers and in the markets.

As discussed in Chapter 3, following the surge in leveraged buyouts in the 1980s, state legislatures and corporate boards have systematically undermined the market for corporate control. Federal policy makers have taken no action out of fear of offending those who support states' rights. Corporations have insulated themselves from the accountability provided by the threat of a takeover through poison pills, staggered boards, supermajority provisions, and several other anti-takeover devices. Even ESOPs, ignored by most companies when initially viewed as an instrument for employee participation, have become a popular anti-takeover tool since Polaroid put a large number of shares in employee hands to rebuff Shamrock Holdings.[8]

Since the "victims" of takeovers are overwhelmingly underperformers, these entrenchment policies could eventually incur enormous economic costs for our society. Insulated companies are free to pursue activities that fail to realize their intrinsic value, and the shareholders have no recourse. Meanwhile, the underlying problems that made takeovers necessary have gone unaddressed.

A careful examination of what happened in the 1980s' LBO wave and what its consequences have been supports the view that takeovers are not as efficient as their defenders claim nor as despicable as critics suggest. When I joined Treasury, it was at the height of the LBO fever. My first assignment was to explore what the administration's policy ought to be regarding highly leveraged transactions given the many congressional efforts underway at the time to curtail buyouts. The House Ways and Means Committee had given Treasury a list of more than 30 tax proposals aimed at curbing LBOs and asked for our views.

At the time I had mixed emotions. Having been involved with several buyout transactions firsthand, I appreciated the many benefits of emancipating unwanted or unappreciated stepchildren from corporate bureaucracies. I had personally witnessed how the performance of businesses and the morale of employees could be enhanced through stock ownership and the challenge of maximizing cash flows.

But I had also experienced the perils of excessive leverage. As a board member of a small manufacturing company, which had been spun off by a major conglomerate through a leveraged buyout, I witnessed a painful bankruptcy. The company had been taken private in 1984 in one of the earlier LBOs, and the bank that financed the spinoff had little experience in funding highly leveraged transactions. The loan payments were scheduled far too aggressively, and the company was unable to repay 50 percent of the purchase price in the first two years as the loan agreement called for.

Instead of working with the company to restructure its debt, the bank forced it into bankruptcy. The company was too small for one of the world's largest banks to bother with. So the bank put the leading employer in a small North Carolina town out of business. I had come to know many of the employees well, and it was painful to see them laid off, especially since I knew the business would have survived with a more reasonable lender and a more conservative capital structure.

Given my mixed emotions toward LBOs, I approached my task at Treasury with a keen interest in finding out the facts about what was going on at a macro level. After collecting as much data as possible, and talking to academics as well as industry experts who had been involved in these transactions from a variety of angles, I concluded that there was more misinformation than accurate characterizations when it came to assessing the causes and effects of leveraged buyouts.

The Causes of LBOs

The takeover boom of the 1980s did not just *happen*. It was no accident. Nor was it solely the manifestation of unbridled greed as the popular press and Hollywood would have us believe. Instead, it was a totally predictable phenomenon resulting from the high cost of capital in the United States, the abdication of responsibility by owners, and the failure of managers for more than 15 years to create shareholder wealth.

Consider the American business scene of the early 1980s. U.S. companies, particularly mature businesses whose high cost of capital was a severe competitive disadvantage, were losing global market share. Unlike their foreign rivals, the typical U.S. company carried very little tax-deductible debt. Many public companies were massive conglomerates which were failing to produce the promised financial synergies. Shareholders were frustrated. The Dow Jones industrial average was floundering around the 900 level, having gone nowhere since 1966. A few vocal investors pushed corporations to restructure, but met stiff resistance and had little power to effect change. Institutional investors were preoccupied with new automated trading techniques and stock indexing, rather than with fulfilling their role as owners. Private pension funds were under pressure to keep up with quarterly market bogeys because their corporate sponsors were committing roughly 20 percent of pretax profits to fund pension liabilities. If institutional investors were offered a premium for their stock, they were prepared to sell in a heartbeat.

It is easy to say with the benefit of 20/20 hindsight that the scene was clearly set for a rash of takeovers and restructurings. But, for the LBO wave to be as dramatic as it was, there had to be other factors involved, including those discussed below.

Cash Flow Valuation Techniques

The yardstick used by investors to measure the value of a company shifted from accounting earnings to cash flow as the concept of intrinsic value became more widely understood. Accounting profits are merely a proxy for cash flow, and a murky one at that. In the 1980s, sophisticated investors began to focus on cash flow as the real measure of value, and as they did, the extent to which some companies were undermanaged became apparent. Carl Icahn, a prototypical takeover specialist, summed up the way he selects LBO candidates, "I look for disparity between stock price and true value. I won't go near the ones where the stock is close to the true value."[9] By true value, Icahn was referring to intrinsic value, which is judged by cash flows.

In recent years banks also have begun to focus more attention on cash flow in making lending decisions, rather than simply considering asset values. Meanwhile, over at the stock market, many investors continued pricing stocks using multiples of reported earnings or net asset values, leaving executives confused as to which objective to pursue. A 1988 Harris poll showed that 54 percent of executives believed earnings per share to be the most important gauge of corporate performance; 44 percent viewed cash flow as more important; and the other 2 percent were not sure what their financial goal was. For many companies there was a disparity between the amount one could borrow against its cash flow and the value the market placed on its stock, especially when management refused to dividend excess cash to the shareholders. This allowed financial buyers to acquire companies with little cash of their own, especially if they had a plan to improve the company's cash flows.

Junk Bonds

The explosion in the market for high-yield bonds—more commonly known as junk bonds—greatly expanded the field of potential buyers of companies. One no longer needed vast personal wealth or corporate resources to purchase a company—the money could be raised from institutional investors and savings and loan associations. The largest of the new "financial buyers" was the firm of Kohlberg Kravis Roberts. Starting with a mere $3 million in 1976, KKR had purchased 35 companies by 1989 for more than $62 *billion*.

Prior to 1980, junk bonds were typically debt securities of companies that had encountered hard times (fallen angels), or smaller and less creditworthy corporations. But led by the firm of Drexel Burnham Lambert and its junk bond king Michael Milken, Wall Street expanded the high-yield bond market from obscurity to approximately $60 billion by 1985 and more than $200 billion in 1989. Junk bonds were popularized by the notion that they combined the return characteristics of an equity security with the tax advantages of debt. These features made junk bonds a major tool in re-capitalizing a number of American companies in the 1980s.

However, the risks of junk bonds were not well understood in the marketplace. They appeared to be far more attractive than they actually were. In 1988, Paul Asquith, David Mullins, and Eric Wolff of the Harvard Business School published a paper that showed that defaults on junk bonds were exponentially higher than investors had been led to believe.[10] Because Milken and Drexel had been able to restructure defaulted bonds without bringing to light the problems companies had in meeting their payment schedules, the market dismissed the Asquith/Mullins/Wolff study. Only after other investment banks jumped into the junk bond market and an increasing number of Drexel deals began to unravel did these risks become evident. By the early 1990s, the interest rate spread between junk bonds and Treasury securities had skyrocketed from 3 percent to about 12 percent, which put an end to many junk-financed deals.

Availability of Money

The returns from early LBOs were phenomenal. Not surprisingly, money poured into buyout funds. Wilshire Associates evaluated the returns on 72 LBOs that had gone private and then either taken public again or sold. The average return to equity investors was 81 percent annually, and the median return was 43 percent. Compared to typical equity returns of 18 percent during the previous decade and bond returns of less than 10 percent, it should come as little surprise that institutional investors clamored to invest in buyout groups.

Buyout funds also proved to be a convenient way to acquire private equities free from the apparent vagaries of public markets. Market innovations such as program trading, index futures, and portfolio insurance confused and intimidated investors who wanted to make long-term equity investments.

Coupled with a surge in capital allocated to buyout funds was a shift in the focus of many venture capital firms. Rather than fund startup companies and risky technologies, venture capitalists began to finance leveraged buyouts. In the early 1980s, venture capital firms had grown rapidly; they were staffed largely by MBAs with finance rather than technology or operating backgrounds. These firms discovered that focusing on transactions with financial risk, i.e., high leverage, rather than on deals involving business risk and often complex technologies better utilized their skills. Returns on traditional venture capital deals declined considerably throughout the 1980s. Meanwhile, venture capital funds had become so bloated with dollars to be invested that they had to find larger deals. And leveraged buyouts could absorb far greater amounts of capital than startup companies.

The money invested in leveraged buyout funds and venture capital funds had to be put to work to show the returns these firms had promised their investors. By the peak of the LBO frenzy in the late 1980s, these partnerships were bursting with $30 billion in uninvested equity capital looking for a home. Leveraged at a capital ratio typical for an LBO at the time (10 percent equity and 90 percent debt), this sum represented enough money to acquire 10 percent of all publicly traded companies in the United States. Fund sponsors scoured the market for viable candidates. Since the supply of capital to fund LBOs had outgrown the pool of likely targets, prices were driven up. At the same time, bankers aggressively sought opportunities to finance these transactions, hopeful of making up for eroding profits within their traditional business lines. The eagerness of LBO funds, venture capitalists, and bankers to finance transactions, coupled with a favorable economic climate and a rising stock market, kept the boom going.

Obvious Candidates

As mentioned earlier, in the early 1980s there were a number of companies that clearly were not maximizing the returns they provided to their owners. Companies such as Wilson Sporting Goods, which had been acquired by Pepsi, were thought to be worth more if operated independently by managers who truly understood the business rather than by the management trainees of a large parent. Compounding the problems of poor performance was Wall Street's confusion as to how to value confederated businesses that operated in a host of unrelated industries. Some companies were undervalued simply because outsiders could not figure out what they did.

In 1982, the market value of the shares of nonfinancial companies was a paltry 44 percent of the replacement value of corporate assets. A lot of money was being left on the table, not only by conglomerates, but by mature businesses with steady cash flows that failed to take advantage of tax-deductible debt. Because these firms operated with remarkably low levels of debt, their return on equity suffered. As companies mature and produce more consistent cash flows, their capital structures should be adjusted to match declining business risk with greater financial risk to preserve the returns provided to owners. This concept escaped many corporate financial officers. It did not, however, escape the notice of corporate raiders.

Through leveraged buyouts, investors were able to redeploy assets to increase their value. By 1988, the market value of nonfinancial businesses had risen to 70 percent of the replacement cost of corporate assets, and by the end of 1989 exceeded 84 percent. The market obviously perceived that there were efficiencies to be derived from restructurings precipitated by LBOs.

Defensive Buyouts

While junk bonds gave independent investors new power to take over companies, the spectrum of potential corporate buyers also expanded in the 1980s. The relaxed antitrust environment of the Reagan years allowed companies to be acquired more easily by competitors. The number of foreign buyers also grew. During the 1980s, foreign investment in the United States increased fourfold. Because of their lower cost of capital, foreign companies could afford to pay higher prices to acquire an American business than could domestic buyers. In 1983, the value of U.S. acquisitions of foreign companies and foreign acquisitions of U.S. companies were both approximately $5 billion. By 1988, foreign buyers were spending $60 billion a year to purchase American companies, over six times the amount U.S. companies spent on overseas acquisitions.

Wary of a potential bid from a foreign company or a competitor, some companies went private or restructured voluntarily as a defensive maneuver to avoid being acquired. For example, FMC Corporation, Multimedia, and others borrowed large sums of money and exchanged their existing stock for cash, subordinated debentures, and new shares. An unpublished SEC study of going-private transactions revealed that approximately half of the companies that went private from 1985–1987 were the subject of competing bids or takeover speculation during the year preceding the announcement of their going private.

Management Incentives

Corporate managers had an opportunity to greatly increase their personal wealth through management-led buyout transactions. LBO sponsors typically offered top management a sizable equity stake in the company both to gain their support for a friendly transaction and as an incentive to make the company successful after the buyout. Private companies did not face the pressures to limit management compensation that exist in a public company where compensation is disclosed in proxy statements and published in major business magazines. Also, executives' salaries and bonuses were less likely to be limited by the size of the company and were more dependent on performance following an LBO.

The Wall Street Gold Rush

Investment bankers actively promoted leveraged buyouts because of the enormous fees involved. In the RJR Nabisco transaction alone, more than $1 billion in fees were distributed to bankers and lawyers. With their traditional brokerage, public finance, and equity underwriting businesses in the doldrums, Wall Street firms relied increasingly on merger and acquisition work to produce profits. According to the Securities Industry Association, from 1980 to 1989 securities industry revenues from brokerage commissions doubled from $5 billion to $10 billion. Meanwhile, revenues from mergers, acquisitions, and similar transactions exploded tenfold from about $2 billion to $20 billion. Thousands of young MBAs were hired to scout for and execute transactions.

Commercial banks also encouraged leveraged buyouts. LBO loans generated significant fee and interest income in an era when third-world debt and real estate losses, coupled with declining lending spreads, were eroding bank profits.

The Impact of Buyouts

Appreciating the root causes of the leveraged buyout wave helps us to better understand its effects. It is often difficult to separate the two. Emotions run high on this issue and sometimes obscure the facts. Critics of leveraged buyouts blame them for everything from forcing American businesses to concentrate on short-term performance to raising the price of Oreo cookies. Defenders of LBOs credit the buyout wave with the surge in the U.S. stock market and a rebirth of U.S. competitiveness in the 1980s.

Unfortunately, because the LBO phenomenon occurred so recently, much of the data needed to form definitive conclusions about its real effects do not yet exist. Also, comprehensive data are difficult to come by. Because many leveraged buyouts were financed without issuing publicly traded debt, the results of many privately owned companies are not known. And the story has not ended for many LBO companies. The deals completed at the end of the 1980s involved riskier companies and higher prices, so the data accumulated so far may reflect more optimistic results than can be expected in the future.

Most of the "evidence" put forth in praise or condemnation of LBOs has, to date, been anecdotal. Anecdotal evidence can be used to prove just about anything, and the media has often used incomplete and biased information to create misperceptions about the impact of LBOs. For example, one of the most publicly criticized buyouts at the time it was announced was the 1988 purchase by Kohlberg Kravis Roberts of Duracell, the battery company. Skeptics cried: "Too much leverage; expect layoffs; they overspent; asset sales are a must to meet debt obligations." Instead Duracell flourished. The company increased market share, boosted research and development spending by 20 percent, and improved its products. Duracell accomplished this without laying off workers and while paying off debt ahead of schedule.

It is just as easy to find examples of LBO disasters. Perhaps the most celebrated was Campeau Corporation. On Halloween 1986, Canadian real estate mogul Robert Campeau acquired Allied Stores in an unfriendly $3.6-billion leveraged buyout. On April Fool's Day a year and a half later he purchased another retailing giant, Federated Department Stores, for $6.5 billion. Within two years Campeau's massive retailing empire, suffocating under the burden of enormous interest and debt payments, declared bankruptcy. Many of the stores' 300,000 creditors received bad checks. More than 100,000 employees nervously wondered about the future of their jobs. And retired executives failed to receive benefits the company owed them. *Fortune* chronicled this transaction under the headline "The Biggest, Looniest Deal Ever," in which it presented a mind-boggling tale of egos gone wild and sophisticated financiers making blatant errors of judgment.[11]

Which deal is truly representative of the leveraged buyout phenomenon? The evidence indicates that neither is the norm. In fact, it is difficult to generalize about LBOs except to say that there are enough success stories to prove that the concept is often a valid way to achieve accountability when the corporate governance system fails, and there are enough failures to show that fixing the underlying problems in owner/manager relationships would be a preferable solution.

Since the common perception is that LBOs have hurt America's ability to compete and have fostered business myopia, it is useful to take a close look at the evidence as it relates to the major criticisms of leveraged buyout transactions. Here is what the critics say:

> LBOs force managers to ignore long-run considerations.
> LBOs result in major layoffs and higher unemployment.
> LBOs produce cutbacks in spending for the future such as in research and development.
> LBOs imperil the U.S. banking system.
> LBOs deprive the government of tax revenues.
> LBOs will exacerbate an economic downturn.
> LBOs enrich deal makers at the expense of the original shareholders.

Managerial Decision Making

There has been a great deal of debate over whether the debt incurred in a leveraged buyout forces managers to ignore long-term competitiveness in favor of immediate attention to the cash flows required to repay debt. The answer to this debate seems to depend on whether the debt load is manageable. There is a fine line between the benefits of becoming lean and mean to meet debt schedules and becoming preoccupied with near-term cash needs at the expense of the future of the company.

My observation is that most LBOs completed in the halcyon days of the early and mid-1980s fell into the former category, and many of those consummated in the feverish late 1980s belong in the latter category. It will be many years before there is sufficient data to form a concrete opinion. One obvious cause for greater attention to short-term issues in deals completed in later years is that prices were bid continually higher throughout the decade.

Many of the prices paid in the more recent deals stretched the ability of the company to service its debt. From 1985 to 1987 alone, the average price/earnings multiple paid in a leveraged buyout soared from 12 to 23.

Properly structured LBOs, with tight but adequate principal and interest coverage, can perform quite nicely. In fact, most studies, such as one conducted by Frank Lichtenberg and Donald Siegel for the National Bureau of Economic Research, conclude that LBOs produce efficiencies and productivity gains.[12] This study compared the "total factor productivity" growth at 1,100 manufacturing plants involved in LBOs to productivity growth at non-LBO companies. It found that over a five-year period the newly leveraged plants showed a 14-percent greater increase than plants in the same industries not involved in an LBO. One possible reason is that managers who operate under the carrot of significant equity ownership and the stick of substantial leverage focus more attention on maximizing cash flows and minimizing expenses. (The Lichtenberg/Siegel study only covered companies purchased prior to 1987, before the prices paid were much steeper.) Reasons why management decision making might improve following a leveraged buyout include the following:

- Businesses are more focused; unrelated units or underperforming assets are typically sold off. This allows managers to concentrate on a core business.
- Entrepreneurial action is enhanced. The ability to be more creative and take bold initiatives is greater in a private company where it is not necessary to convince bureaucratic staffs, stock analysts, diffused owners, and a large board of directors of the merits of a strategy.
- Managers become owners and act like owners. Top managers in most large public companies own less than 1 percent of their company's stock. In most buyout companies, the senior executive owns several percent, and the management group as a whole

frequently owns about 20 percent of the company. Maximizing shareholder value is clearly more important if the executives are themselves significant shareholders.

- Current compensation is more closely tied to performance. Consequently, managers are less prone to make acquisitions simply to increase the size of the company. Managers are also more frugal since bonuses are usually pegged to cash flow rather than to revenues.
- LBO debt disciplines managers to make careful investment decisions. The new owners are in a stronger position to discourage investment in projects whose returns do not exceed their cost of capital than fragmented public shareholders.
- Smaller, more involved boards are more effective. Directors are more likely to be able to add value when they are chosen for their business expertise rather than their appeal to various constituencies or are handpicked by the CEO. The chairman of the board is likely to be a large outside shareholder, rather than the chief executive, which encourages debate in the boardroom. And directors are less exposed to shareholder lawsuits and more likely to make tough decisions in private companies.
- A renewed focus on cash flow requires closer working relationships with customers and suppliers to minimize working capital. The side effect is often better operating relationships.
- There are fewer diversions for senior management. The typical CEO or CFO of a large public company spends a significant amount of time with stock analysts, investor relations activities, filing SEC reports, and other tasks not required in a private company to nearly the same extent.

Although each of these benefits sounds appealing, they can quickly vanish if a company is overleveraged. A preoccupation with rigid and overly aggressive debt-repayment schedules can dilute the best of intentions. When a company has to come up with a pile of cash at the end of each month or each quarter to remain solvent, short-term cash flow can become the company's overriding objective. With the exception of the final point regarding some of the diversions of being publicly owned, each of the managerial benefits of an LBO could be achieved without incurring the risks inherently involved with high leverage by reforming the corporate governance process and modifying the behavior of institutional investors.

Employment Levels

One of the main reasons that leveraged buyouts have such a bad reputation is the belief that there is a significant displacement of workers in acquired companies. Although it is not uncommon for a leveraged buyout transaction to be accompanied by some layoffs, the empirical evidence is mixed. In addition to the layoffs that do occur, it is also important to consider the increased hiring in other business units or departments.

Occasionally loyal, competent employees are the innocent victims of plant shutdowns or asset sales caused by an LBO; this is what the media tends to focus on. However, a 1989 Bureau of Labor Statistics study of plant closings and wholesale layoffs showed that less than 5 percent of major layoffs were a consequence of a change in business ownership.[13]

Perhaps too much attention has been paid to aggregate employment levels at LBO companies in general. For a nation to be competitive, it is vital that labor—like capital—is deployed efficiently. Some layoffs may be appropriate if they involve nonproductive workers, or workers in nonproductive business units. In this sense, LBOs may expedite the painful but necessary process of restructuring noncompetitive or declining businesses by laying off unnecessary workers. And if this means that more employees will be available for other companies that are experiencing labor shortages, the impact on the economy—and on many of these employees—may end up being positive in the long run.

It would be premature to conclude, however, that unnecessary layoffs will not result from LBOs. Many of the companies bought in the latter part of the decade took on some potentially explosive debt, called "payment-in-kind" debt. With PIK debt, interest is paid with more securities in lieu of cash. Eventually these securities will have to be redeemed with real cash instead of more funny money. If the companies with PIK debt are not in strong shape when the cash payout comes due, they will be looking for any way they can to reduce expenses and improve cash flow. Furthermore, economic slowdowns—which did not occur during the second half of the 1980s—would clearly aggravate the need to cut workers. Consequently, there may be some layoffs that trim a little of the bone along with any remaining fat. One of the early LBO bankruptcies, Revco, was initially able to restructure its debt without any material layoffs or store closings. As time went on, however, the prospect for layoffs grew. Another likely scenario in the 1990s is that some companies will simply have to shut down as Fruehauf did after taking on an exorbitant debt load to rebuff a hostile bidder. When it became insolvent, the company put 10,000 people out of work.

Research and Development Spending

There is a great deal of concern over whether LBO debt forces cutbacks on investing for the future. The preponderance of studies indicates that companies do spend less on research and development and capital expenditures after a buyout; however, a couple of mitigating factors make this less of a threat to competitiveness than meets the eye.

The vast majority of LBOs occurred in nontechnology industries. The industries where more than one-fourth of the assets were taken private from 1980 to 1988 included textiles, apparel, furniture, food stores, and health services. None of these are major spenders on research. Prior to the buyout, the average R&D expenditures for a typical LBO company were less than 1 percent of revenues. In fact, the SEC found that 77 percent of the going-private transactions in the 1980s involved companies reporting *no* R&D expenditures in the year preceding the buyout. The aggregate R&D budget of every company that was acquired through an LBO during the 1980s was less than half the amount spent each year by IBM on research, and less than 2 percent of total U.S. industrial spending on research and development. So even if LBO companies slashed research expenditures in half, it would lower our national investment in the future by less than 1 percent a year. Companies such as Safeway, Macy's, and Nabisco never have spent much money on research and probably never will.

Another reason the concern about investment cutbacks in research by LBO companies is overblown is an implicit assumption that all research expenditures are well spent. The true measure for competitiveness ought not to be the relative amounts spent on R&D before and after a transaction, but the amount spent on *useful* R&D. For example, at Reliance Electric, one of the few technology-based companies to undergo an LBO, R&D expenditures declined from $30 million to $25 million in 1989 because of the elimination of redundant and nonproductive research. Now that research funds are more efficiently used than they were at prebuyout levels, the company believes it is more competitive. And at Revlon, which has been criticized for disposing of unrelated and unprofitable businesses, the company doubled the R&D budget of the remaining core businesses and invested heavily in factory automation following its LBO.

Still, this is another area where the past may not foreshadow the future. Research and development expenditures are discretionary. It is hard to imagine that in a weak economy investments with distant payoffs would not suffer more than they did in the vibrant economy of the 1980s. The capital budgets at many companies involved in highly leveraged transactions in the late 1980s were thin to begin with. Because prices for leveraged buyouts in the latter part of the decade were so high, many LBO financing proposals budgeted little growth in R&D investment in order to produce the pro forma cash flows needed to justify their valuations. If a little more cash was needed to defend a higher price, the next computer run generally sliced discretionary expenditures such as research. Consequently, if these companies experience difficulties and have to pare back expenditures from already tight budgets, some useful spending on research may very well be curtailed.

Risks to the Banking Industry

The most common concerns expressed about the impact of LBO lending on the credit markets are that 1) legitimate credit needs such as new investment are going unfulfilled because banks allocated such large sums to LBOs, and 2) defaults on LBO loans could severely damage the banking system. Both of these concerns appear to be overstated.

Banks will clearly suffer substantial losses from failed LBOs. But they have also made a lot of money on LBOs. Regardless of the impact of leveraged buyouts on the U.S. banking system, it will be dwarfed by bad real estate loans and unpaid debts incurred by third-world countries. Highly leveraged transactions accounted for less than 4 percent of the problem loans at the 10 largest banks as of year-end 1989; and these banks owned almost half of all LBO bank loans. The percentage of commercial bank loans attributable to LBOs rose dramatically in the mid-1980s; however, much of this debt was repaid ahead of schedule and new LBO loans declined considerably in 1990. So although defaults may increase, LBO loans will not unilaterally bring down the banks.

Most bankers will admit that they got carried away with LBO lending. To be a "player" in the 1980s, a commercial bank had to fund buyouts. The enormous fees and attractive loan spreads covered up other problems. Unfortunately, the herd mentality led banks down paths that were not prudent. But by early 1989, several prominent bank executives had privately contacted federal regulators asking them to clamp down on LBO lending to save the banking industry from itself. The Federal Reserve Board and Office of the Comptroller of the Currency responded by issuing new guidelines for categorizing "highly leveraged transactions" that highlighted a bank's exposure to LBOs. This heightened disclosure on the heels of a few celebrated LBO failures prompted shareholders to pressure banks to withdraw from this market. If anything, perhaps the pendulum swung too far the other way. Many middle-market companies and industries that have always used significant leverage, such as cable television, fall under the regulators' definition of highly leveraged transactions. These companies experienced a severe tightening of credit when the new bank-reporting requirements were imposed.

The risk to our banking system from leveraged buyout lending has never been as serious as many people believe, for the following reasons:

- Unlike the real estate loans made by the S&Ls, there is a substantial equity cushion for senior lenders in most LBOs. Even the transactions in which little equity was involved had a layer of subordinated debt that is junior to the banks in a liquidation. (Some bank-holding companies also underwrote mezzanine debt in later deals, but not in their insured banking subsidiary.)
- The most popular game in buyout lending became "pass the trash." The vast majority of LBO loans were sold off by the originating bank on a nonrecourse basis. Federal Reserve Board statistics for 1988, the peak of the LBO era, indicate that two-thirds of merger-related loans were sold either to nonbanks or to foreign banks. Thus, the credit exposure from buyouts has been dispersed throughout the entire banking system worldwide and not concentrated in a small group of domestic institu-

tions. At their peak, LBO loans accounted for less than 10 percent of total loans at most banks.

- LBO bank loans are not as interest-rate sensitive as commonly believed. The large majority of floating-rate LBO debt is either swapped into a fixed rate or capped so that its rate will not exceed a certain level. One of the major LBO lenders, for example, required that all debt-covering assets that were not expected to be sold in the first 6–12 months following a transaction be either fixed or capped.
- In the early years the risk/return trade-offs on buyout lending were quite attractive. The returns realized by banks in terms of fees and equity kickers built substantial capital at banks, which provided them with a greater margin for error in the underwriting of higher-risk loans than in traditional lending.

In general, the larger commercial banking institutions are adequately prepared to deal with the risks involved in buyout lending and supervised closely enough so that a crisis on the level of the S&L debacle is highly unlikely solely because of LBOs. The one potential area of concern is with the smaller, less sophisticated institutions which purchased LBO loans, referred to as the "stuffees" by Drexel. The superregional and regional banks and S&Ls that purchased LBO participations will probably fare worse on these investments than the larger institutions that originated LBO loans, for the following reasons:

- Loan purchasers do not perform the same level of examination of the credit risks as the lead institution, thus do not understand the business risks as well as the original underwriter. Consequently, many of the loans with "warts" have been sold to unknowing institutions.
- Loan purchasers take on most of the risk, yet they receive less of the return than the originator. They

typically do not participate fully in the equity kickers, fee income, and interest spreads.

- Smaller banks lack specialized lending expertise in highly leveraged transactions and are not as well prepared to work with borrowers through periods of tight cash flow. Defaults that are the product of a poor loan structure may be misinterpreted by less sophisticated lenders as a sign of decaying business prospects, which would encourage them to force a customer into bankruptcy rather than restructuring the loan.

One of the primary reasons banks were so enamored with LBO lending was their lack of other profitable commercial lending opportunities. As will be described in Chapter 5, disintermediation and securitization eroded the commercial lending business—the mainstay of most banks. In the 1980s, borrowers increasingly accessed the public and private debt markets at rates often below a bank's cost of funds. Having experienced the perils of third-world, oil patch, and other noncorporate lending, banks turned to high-yield corporate restructuring loans as a way to regain lost commercial customers.

The leveraged buyout phenomenon had the potential to help reinvigorate America's declining banking industry by affording banks a chance to forge new relationships with many of the corporate customers that had abandoned them in recent years. Banks could charge higher fees and more attractive rates on LBO loans. And because these loans involved substantial risks, the borrower would have benefited from having a financial intermediary working closely with them to detect potential problems early and rework agreements to allow for some flexibility to deal with unforeseen circumstances.

As a matter of course, most German and Japanese companies operate with more leverage than the typical U.S. industrial firm, but they have close ties to a lead bank that mitigate some of the risks inherent with leverage. However, instead of maintaining close relationships with LBO borrowers, the U.S. banks chose to "diversify" their risk and sell off pieces of LBO loans to smaller banks and foreign lenders. By dispersing loans to a fragmented group of lenders, the banks made it more difficult for borrowers facing the likelihood of defaults to avoid bankruptcy, because it is difficult to achieve consensus among a large number of lenders when renegotiating loan documents, especially if creditors are spread all across the world.

Tax Revenues

There is no doubt that many leveraged buyouts and restructurings were facilitated by the fact that interest is tax deductible and dividends are not. Consequently, one of the more common criticisms of leveraged buyouts on Capitol Hill is that they are simply short-term efforts to deprive the government of tax revenues. In a period of budget deficits, this complaint receives plenty of attention.

Critics of LBOs are quick to point out that a corporation pays less tax after a buyout because of the enormous interest deductions produced by adding so much debt. But the question policy makers should be asking is what happens to *total* tax revenues as a result of LBOs. Someone is on the receiving end of those interest payments. Should the Treasury really care whether a dollar of income tax is received from the corporation whose tax bill has declined or from the bondholders whose tax bill has increased?

It is important to follow the tax impact of a transaction all the way through to assess the deal's influence on national tax revenues. Clearly, corporate receipts decline following an LBO. But the corporation's tax payments are only one variable in the equation. At the same time, a significant amount of new tax revenues are generated by:

- capital gains taxes paid by the shareholders who sold their stock;
- interest income earned by the banks and insurance companies that underwrite LBO loans;

- fees earned by investment bankers, lawyers, LBO firms, and lenders;
- gains recognized by the company on the sale of assets or divisions that are split off; and
- capital gains when the company is taken public or resold in the future.

Theoretically, if the underlying operating profits are not influenced by a leveraged buyout, the taxes paid by the above parties should, more or less, offset the taxes not paid by the corporation. However, studies indicate that operating profits actually *increase* after a buyout,[14] which makes it unlikely that the Treasury Department has suffered from the LBO binge. In fact, one study of the effects of LBOs on federal tax revenues showed a 61 percent increase over prebuyout payments.[15]

Threat to the Economy

Loading a company with debt is like loading a sailboat with so much cargo that it rides low in the water. In calm seas the boat may sail fine, but rough waters can sink her. Clearly, in a downturn, there will be more stress on highly leveraged companies than conservatively capitalized businesses. One highly publicized study made in 1989 indicated that up to 10 percent of U.S. companies would experience serious financial difficulties in a recession as severe as the one in 1973–1974, largely because of the increased financial risk incurred in LBOs.[16]

With some LBOs, the economy did not have to get too bad for things to unravel. Interco is a classic example of how small changes in the economy produced large problems. To avoid a takeover threat by two young men who faxed an offer to the company, Interco hired a well-known investment banking firm to plan a defense. The banker designed an aggressive recapitalization plan that left the company shouldering a weighty debt load of $1.8 billion. After selling Ethan Allen, Central Hardware, and the company's apparel group (each for substantially less than projected), the maker of Converse tennis shoes had insufficient cash flow to pay its debts. This occurred in 1989 and early 1990, when the economy was flat, but not yet in a recession.

There is a flip side to this, which none of the studies evaluate, i.e., the impact the LBO phenomenon had on companies that were not involved in a transaction. Countless companies restructured, slimmed down, and refocused in order to avoid being bought out. In many ways that will never be measured, the economy has been boosted by LBOs. It may not be a total coincidence that economic growth and LBO activity paralleled each other in the United States during much of the 1980s.

Economists are quick to point out that leverage in America skyrocketed in the 1980s. But a careful look at the numbers shows this to be somewhat misleading. On a market-value basis, which is far more relevant than book value, leverage did not increase substantially. Furthermore, while post-interest profits at U.S. companies declined, it was not solely because of more debt. The drop in corporate profits would have occurred regardless of the gradually increasing interest burden.

More relevant is what amount of debt is appropriate, not how current aggregate numbers compare on an historical basis. Much of the expansion in debt occurred in industries that were underleveraged by international standards. Stephen Roach, a senior economist at Morgan Stanley, broke down U.S. industry into two categories: stable and cyclical. What he found was that from 1982 to 1989, interest expense as a percentage of total cash flow rose from 21 percent to 25 percent in stable industries, which are less sensitive to economic downturns. But during this period interest expenditures *declined* from 21 percent to 17 percent in cyclical industries. He determined that 70 percent of the debt accumulated in the 1980s was added to the balance sheets of noncyclical companies.[17] This fact is lost in the averages when the numbers are aggregated.

The major feature of leveraged buyouts that poses an economic threat is the sudden, enormous increase in leverage at specific companies. Rather than systematically and gradually gearing a company's balance sheet to achieve an ideal capital structure—which could be accomplished through effective corporate governance—LBOs tend to first overleverage the companies and then pay down debt to achieve an optimal capital structure, which is a risky way to take advantage of the benefits of debt.

At present, there is a small group of companies that have undergone LBOs and taken on staggering amounts of debt, arguably too much; these are the ones that appear in the headlines. But the remainder operate with very little debt relative to international standards, arguably not enough. Yet when underleveraged companies gradually lose competitiveness because of a high cost of capital, no one notices. There is no "event" to report in the papers. So the perception is that the use of greater leverage has been bad for the U.S. economy. Chapter 5 will show that the amount of leverage in America is not the source of potential economic disruptions. Rather, how the U.S. financial system makes leverage riskier than in Germany or Japan is the problem.

Fairness to Shareholders

A common complaint of leveraged buyouts, in particular those led by management, is that deal sponsors and insiders have access to confidential information, which they use to acquire a company at less than its true value. If true, this would be unfair to other shareholders. However, the data collected thus far fail to support this charge. The average premium paid in going-private transactions during the 1980s was approximately 40 percent; it exceeded 50 percent in 1988. By most standards this provides a pretty handsome return to selling shareholders.

Evidence gathered by the SEC indicates that transactions led by management actually provided slightly higher premiums than the average buyout. Also, according to the SEC, there is no evidence that insiders artificially depress their stock price prior to a buyout to make the company cheaper to acquire. Some data suggest, however, that management accumulates more than the usual amount of stock in the year preceding a management buyout, presumably to cash in when the deal is announced. But on balance, in today's market where most buyouts occur only after a public, and often extended bidding process, it is hard to argue that selling shareholders fail to get a fair deal.

The Future of LBOs

The 1980s' takeover wave would not have occurred if the United States had an effective system of corporate governance, and if investors had behaved as owners rather than as speculators. The efficiencies achieved through buyouts could have been achieved by internally driven changes. Shareholders and managers could have worked together to maximize the value of their companies by redeploying assets more efficiently and making greater use of low-cost debt. If this had occurred, less money would have been left on the table to enrich an industry of corporate raiders and arbitrageurs.

As we begin the 1990s, the takeover era appears to be on the decline, but not because we have addressed the problems that precipitated buyouts. Most observers attribute the dramatic drop in the value of leveraged buyouts to the fallout of the junk bond market. With LBO king Michael Milken sentenced to a lengthy prison term and his former employer Drexel Burnham Lambert bankrupt, the junk bond market has been dealt a dramatic setback. Junk bond investors now realize that high yields are not as attractive if they are accompanied by losses in principal.

There are also other reasons cited for the drop in buyouts. Bank financing for takeovers dried up considerably following the regulators' stricter reporting guidelines for highly leveraged transactions. With the sentiment turning against LBOs, banks feared that stock analysts would penalize them if they continued to report growth in highly leveraged transactions. Meanwhile, sellers' expectations remained inflated, so investment bankers were reporting that many negotiations were breaking down over price.

But there is a more lasting and profound reason that buyout activity has declined. Hostile takeovers initiated by anyone without deep pockets, for all intents and purposes, are dead. The multitude of takeover defenses installed by corporations in the 1980s and the highly restrictive anti-takeover laws passed by the states in recent years will not disappear with an improving economy or greater bank liquidity. About 1,500 companies have now installed poison pills. The vast majority of U.S. public companies are chartered in one of the 40 states that enacted or strengthened anti-takeover laws in the 1980s. These defensive mechanisms substantially raise the cost of engaging in a buyout, reduce the likelihood of success, and discourage many potential bidders from even attempting to take over a company unless they can do so in a friendly manner.

One buyout group that successfully acquired a poorly performing company and turned it around—dramatically improving its performance—spent almost a year and over $15 million trying to acquire another company two years later. Rebuffed by a poison pill, a supermajority provision, and a new state law that would have stripped its voting power had they taken title to the shares offered to them, the buyout group gave up and is no longer searching for underperforming companies to acquire.

The legal measures taken to insulate corporate boards and managers will have a profound impact on the relationship between owners and corporations. The one positive outcome is that these measures are forcing shareholders to be more attentive to their role as owners. They can no longer rely on takeover artists to do their jobs for them. But in the process of protecting themselves from hostile bidders, corporations have stripped owners of many of their traditional rights. Attempting to effect change through the corporate governance system today is more futile than ever. The only reason that some progress is being made is that shareholders have no choice but to try much harder. But we should not be misled into believing that because the proxy system is being used more often that it works; if it did, we would never have had to rely so heavily on takeovers in the first place.

5

The Demise of Relationship Banking

Untermyer: Is not commercial credit based primar-
ily upon money or property?
Morgan: No, sir, the first thing is character.
Untermyer: Before money or property?
Morgan: Before money or anything else. Money
cannot buy it. . . . Because a man I do
not trust could not get money from me
on all the bonds in Christendom.
　　　　　　　　—Ron Chernow,
　　　　　　　　The House of Morgan

A lot has changed since the days of J.P. Morgan. The same
phenomenon that has occurred in the equity markets—an erosion
of the relationship between capital providers and corporate managers—has been taking place in the debt markets. Relationship
banking in the United States is a thing of the past.

Before the Great Depression, U.S. banks were extremely close
to their customers. Bankers typically sat on their customers'
boards, owned their stock, and consulted regularly with senior
management about long-term strategies and short-term operating
plans—practices that remain the norm in Japan and Germany
today. There was a great deal of mutual trust and respect. And
there is evidence that equity investors felt a sense of confidence

143

knowing that sophisticated financiers such as J.P. Morgan and his partners were looking out to ensure that companies were well run and that the investors' capital was being used efficiently. In fact, just the presence of a Morgan banker on a company's board was associated with a substantial increase in the value of a company's stock.[1]

However, U.S. banking and securities laws during the pre-depression era were lax, providing some of the more aggressive banks opportunities to engage in unseemly behavior. Self-serving bank practices at the time contributed to—some say caused—the Great Depression. Because of their enormous influence over corporations, banks were able to manipulate certain companies. Bankers loaned money to customers to purchase equities sold by the bank's own securities departments, often at inflated prices. Banks purchased overvalued stocks from their securities affiliates to place in trust accounts of customers. And banks raised money for their customers by selling stock whose proceeds were used to pay off outstanding bank loans before a company went under.

A colossal number of banks failed during the depression.[2] Constituents in every district lost their life savings and, not surprisingly, Congress overreacted. Rather than simply enacting laws to close the regulatory windows that permitted unscrupulous practices, Congress banned banks from underwriting corporate securities and prohibited their owning equity in nonfinancial companies. Branching issues were returned to the states, whose fragmented regulation eliminated the opportunity for banks to operate nationwide. Banks could no longer follow their customers across the country or diversify their loan portfolios geographically, limiting their ability to offer customers service and increasing their risk.

Some banks circumvented these highly restrictive laws by forming holding companies. In the 1930s and 1940s, a number of commercial firms acquired banks via this loophole. Transamerica Corporation, the largest insurance company on the West Coast, combined manufacturing, shipping, fishing, and taxi companies with a banking franchise that included the largest banks in several Western states. But in 1956, Congress put an end to these practices as well by enacting the Bank Holding Company Act, which prohibited bank holding companies from engaging in "nonbanking" activities.

Since that time, the globalization of capital markets and modern technologies have opened up alternative ways for corporations to access capital. Lacking strong, broadly based relationships with financial intermediaries, U.S. companies rushed out the doors of their banks to tap these "cheaper" sources of loans. U.S. banks have become increasingly irrelevant to major corporations. And not surprisingly, banks have pursued other types of business in an effort to replace their traditional customer base. Most of these efforts, such as lending to third-world countries and commercial real estate developers, have gotten them in trouble.

Many of the criticisms of U.S. bankers today can be traced directly back to the legal and regulatory environment that governs America's financial services industry. Banks are often accused of taking undue risks at the taxpayers' expense. But they operate in a system where managers and shareholders reap the benefits if banks do well, and the government assumes the risk if they fail. In most of the savings and loan and bank failures, institutions have been allowed to continue to operate even though their capital was well below the regulatory minimum. With little to lose, the shareholders were willing to allow managers to roll the dice on risky loans. When you privatize success and nationalize failure, excessive risk-taking should be expected.

Banks are also accused of lacking talented, innovative people. But given the regulatory shackles placed on U.S. banks, the daily routine of American bankers is much more mundane than that of their overseas counterparts, making it difficult to attract the top talent. German, Japanese, and British banks recruit the cream of the crop from major universities. In the world of regulated deposit rates and limited portfolios of products and services that existed in the United States throughout the middle of the century, it did not take much creativity or skill to be a banker, so banks were renowned for low pay and mediocre talent. Then, by deregulating the price financial institutions paid for deposits in the mid-1970s without deregulating what they could do with that money, we imposed greater risks on the same people with the same skills and restrictions.

The savings and loan debacle and the present problems with the banking system are proof that our financial services industry is not properly structured or effectively regulated. It may be too late to resuscitate the S&L industry, but the nation cannot afford to passively observe the demise of our commercial banks. Their role in the economy is indispensable. Over the next several years, Congress, regulators, and financial services providers will give us their opinions on how the banking industry should be reconfigured. As they do, it is important to recognize the aspects of the present banking system that contribute to myopic behavior and reduced U.S. business competitiveness:

- Without cooperative relationships between borrowers and lenders, debt becomes a riskier source of capital.
- The financial system in the United States contains inefficiencies when it comes to channeling capital to ventures with long-term payoffs such as research, development, and emerging businesses.
- Banks and corporate customers who cannot work closely together will both miss opportunities to penetrate foreign markets.

Relationship Banking and the Cost of Capital

If the risks of borrowing were identical in all countries, one would expect Japanese and German companies to operate with less debt than their American counterparts for tax reasons. In the United States there is a greater disparity in the way debt and equity are taxed, which disproportionately penalizes equity investments.

German and Japanese shareholders, for example, receive tax breaks on both capital gains and dividend income; U.S. shareholders do not. Consequently, on a relative basis, equity finance should be shunned in the United States. But the exact opposite occurs—American companies use *less* debt and more high-cost equity than German and Japanese companies.

The reason for America's aversion to debt is that the risks of borrowing are greater in the United States. Japanese and German companies are able to operate with significant debt without increasing the risk of bankruptcy or compromising their long-term strategies because lenders in these countries are more willing to renegotiate debt payments in times of trouble and extend new loans if unforeseen difficulties or opportunities arise. The product of this greater willingness of banks and their customers to establish close relationships is more flexible debt, which makes leverage less threatening. As will be explained in Chapter 6, debt is cheaper than equity within a given company, so the bias against debt in the United States results in a cost-of-capital disadvantage. Even if the cost of debt and cost of equity were identical across countries, the country that used a higher proportion of the less expensive component would have a lower cost of capital.

Companies that select a loan based solely on the interest rate, without considering the risks involved, are very shortsighted. A loan with a *lower* interest rate may end up *raising* a company's overall cost of capital by limiting its ability to use a higher percentage of tax-deductible debt in its capital structure. Yet the interest rate is often the overriding criterion used to select a loan. Interest rates are easy to quantify and risk is not. Consequently, current trends in the financial services industry favor lower nominal borrowing costs, even at the expense of greater risk.

The Commoditization of Debt

Bank loans have been commoditized just as stocks have been in the United States. American banking trends such as disintermediation, securitization, and globalization are vivid illustrations that price-driven transaction banking is the norm, and relationship banking is, for all intents and purposes, over.

Disintermediation is the process of corporate borrowers accessing capital directly from the ultimate source rather than through a financial intermediary like a bank. The bread-and-butter business for banks in the past was lending to companies to fund their working capital needs. Today, creditworthy companies often issue commercial paper for these purposes. This market for short-term corporate IOUs grew from $124 billion a year in 1980 to more than a half a trillion dollars in 1990. The ratio of total commercial and industrial loans to commercial paper outstanding dropped from nearly 10 in 1960 to about 1 today. Commercial paper is generally sold to money market funds and other investors seeking significant liquidity. Some firms have even begun to disintermediate the commercial paper market. General Motors, Ford, and AT&T now offer money market accounts directly to consumers. Investors who purchase high-grade commercial paper view it as a commodity; they do not establish loyalty to a specific issuer. Even a slight decline in a borrower's credit rating can cause the market for that company's commercial paper to evaporate overnight.

Similarly, for longer-term borrowing needs the trend is also to disintermediate the banks. Many larger and mid-size companies issue bonds to the public. As with commercial paper, within the spectrum of companies with reasonably good credit ratings these bonds are essentially viewed as financial commodities by investors. Because these bonds can be readily bought and sold, investors are willing to accept a lower return than a bank would charge for a loan that had to be held to maturity.

Corporate bonds are purely contractual obligations, which makes it difficult to change the terms. In fact, the Trust Indenture Act of 1939 provides that indentures on public debt relating to the principal amount, interest rate, or maturity cannot be changed without the unanimous consent of bondholders. Bankruptcy laws also severely inhibit term modifications without the consent of an overwhelming majority of bondholders.

As a result, restructuring publicly traded debt can be problematic, as Southland Corporation discovered. Southland, the nation's largest convenience store chain, tried for more than six months to negotiate with its public bondholders to restructure its debt in order to avert bankruptcy. Even after extending its tender offer to repurchase these bonds four times, Southland was unable to satisfy all the demands of its recalcitrant bondholders and was forced to file for protection under Chapter 11 of the bankruptcy code.

In addition to selling bonds publicly, many established companies borrow on a long-term basis from large nonbanking institutions, primarily insurance companies and pension funds. These institutions take in enormous sums of money which must be invested for a long time period. Life insurance companies, for example, receive premiums over a number of years and only pay benefits upon a policy holder's death; and pension funds accumulate capital each year, which is only paid out upon an employee's retirement. Obviously, loans with lengthy maturities facilitate financial planning for these institutions.

Banks, on the other hand, are funded not with long-term obligations, but with deposits that can be easily withdrawn. The Federal Reserve's role in supporting bank liquidity reduces some of the risk of longer-term lending by banks. However, many financial institutions (especially the thrifts) have been squeezed in the past by interest rates when they borrowed short term and lent long term. Consequently, they have historically preferred short-term loans. Today that problem no longer exists. Banks can synthetically alter their interest-rate sensitivity through the trillion dollar interest-rate swap market where they can instantly convert a floating-rate obligation into a fixed-rate exposure. So, theoretically, banks should be competitive in both short-term and long-term lending. Unfortunately, their rates are often no longer competitive. Because of their declining performance and credit quality, most banks now pay more for their long-term capital than the typical insurance company does, so they have to charge higher rates.

Although pension funds and insurance companies offer competitive rates, they do not have the staffs to closely monitor loans and establish strong relationships with their borrowers. Therefore, they often structure privately negotiated loans with covenants that limit the operating flexibility of a borrower. So through the process of disintermediation, whether it be through the public bond market or the private placement market, borrowers are sacrificing flexibility in exchange for a lower rate and increased risk of borrowing.

Many of the larger Japanese companies have also begun to circumvent their banks and secure capital directly from the markets. This is often cited as proof that relationship banking does not make sense. It is important to note, however, that this trend has not gone nearly as far in Japan as it has in the United States. Furthermore, it may only indicate that some Japanese, like many Americans, are willing to take added risks that are hard to quantify—especially during favorable economic times—in exchange for a lower rate. Americans do not have a monopoly on short-term behavior. In fact, a study mentioned later indicates that Japanese companies that disintermediate their banks have much less consistent levels of investment.

The second major trend in our financial markets, *securitization*, is an activity that turns a partial interest in a loan or a pool of loans into a security that can be sold to third parties and traded among investors. Most people think of securitization as a way to take a bundle of car loans, home mortgages, or credit card receivables, package them up in a box, and then sell partial interests in the total box. However, securitization is also used with business loans. A corporate loan that a bank has underwritten can be carved up and sold off to other banks or to sophisticated investors.

Buyers of these business loans are usually foreign banks and, to a lesser extent, smaller regional banks and institutional investors in the United States. Securitized loans appeal to smaller banks that lack the capital to underwrite the credit of larger companies. Buying a piece of larger loans allows them to better diversify their portfolios by customer size and geographic location. Foreign banks purchase these loans because they are seeking an American presence but lack the network in the United States to be selected on a regular basis as the original underwriter. On the surface, securitization is particularly attractive to the bank that originally underwrites the loan and sells off pieces because it receives the fees for originating and servicing the loan, but passes the bulk of the risk on to other investors. The Basel Accord, which stipulates that all banks worldwide need to meet higher capital standards, further promotes securitization, because selling pieces of loans keeps asset levels down and capital ratios up at the institutions that originate the loans. And obviously, securitizing loans appeals to customers who receive lower interest rates.

With these many benefits, the securitization phenomenon has exploded in recent years. The total market for securitized loans in the United States is more than $1 trillion. Although most of this is in mortgage-backed securities, the growth of business loan sales is rapidly escalating. But as with disintermediation, there are risks to securitization that have been overlooked in the rush to secure lower interest rates.

The downside to securitization is similar to the pitfalls of disintermediation: securitized loans are less flexible. Imagine a company that suddenly experiences a cash crunch and has to restructure a securitized loan. Bankers from all over the world—some sophisticated, some not; some who do not even speak English—all have to agree to the same terms. In many cases, all it takes is one dissident lender to undermine the entire process.

Securitized loans, therefore, also add substantial risk to the borrower, which is only realized in the event of unforeseen circumstances, which, in turn, makes the risk easy to ignore. Ironically, many of the business loans that have been securitized in recent years are those used to fund leveraged buyouts, the deals most likely to need restructuring.

Securitization makes sense for mortgage and other loans that are similar to commodities, but not for companies that operate with substantial leverage or have uncertain cash flows. The securitization phenomenon has gotten out of hand, as evidenced by the junk bond market. Highly risky loans have been broken up and distributed across the globe so that borrowers could save a small amount on their interest expense. When these companies encounter difficulties and are unable to restructure their securitized loans, their short-term perspective in grabbing the least expensive loan will come back to haunt them.

The third major financial trend that contributes to the commoditization of loans is the *globalization* of financial services. American companies are more willing to borrow from foreign banks than ever before. A Greenwich Associates survey showed that the typical U.S. company now borrows from fewer than ten domestic banks and more than five foreign banks. In 1984, American companies used fifteen domestic banks and only three foreign banks.

These foreign banks have built their market shares largely because of competitive rates. According to First Manhattan Consulting Group, Japanese banks can receive a rate 50 basis points (one-half of 1 percent) below that of an American bank and still show the same profit margin. Partially regulated deposit rates in Japan and the capitalization of Japanese banks which have operated with less equity in the past than their American competitors, are credited with providing Japanese banks this advantage. However, with the push to fully deregulate deposit rates in Japan and the planned harmonization of bank capital standards worldwide, these advantages should dissipate.

But the fact remains that Japanese banks do not have to achieve the same level of profitability as their U.S. competitors. Federal Reserve Bank of New York economists Robert McCauley and Steven Zimmer estimate that because of differences in bank equity costs, U.S. banks require *net* interest rate spreads on corporate loans of about 70 basis points (.70 percent) versus only 24 basis points (.24 percent) required by Japanese banks.[3] So the pricing advantages of foreign banks should endure because of their lower cost of capital.

This increasing reliance on foreign banks by U.S. companies has two potential drawbacks. First, establishing a close relationship with a financial institution headquartered thousands of miles away and whose executives may not even speak the same language is problematic. Even if foreign banks have U.S. offices with English-speaking loan officers, these individuals are seldom decision makers. Second, the loss of business for U.S. financial institutions is driving down their profit margins, and a weaker financial sector will hurt all businesses that require capital.

The financial services industry in the United States is rapidly losing global market share. The U.S. share of world bank loans dropped 45 percent from 1984 to 1988, while Japanese and West German banks saw their market shares rise 66 and 30 percent, respectively, in this period. As of year-end 1989, Japanese banks alone accounted for about 14 percent of total U.S. commercial and industrial loans, and all foreign banks collectively control about one-quarter of U.S. commercial banking assets.

At the same time they were losing market share at home, U.S. banks have been pulling out of foreign markets, as I will discuss later in the chapter. Some might argue that U.S. markets are more open, giving outsiders a greater chance to compete in America than in Germany and Japan. This may be true, but the greatest hurdle to overcome in these countries is not regulation but the strong bonds between lenders and borrowers, ties that do not exist in the commoditized U.S. market where price is virtually all that matters.

Obviously, the trends of disintermediation, securitization, and globalization are not all bad. There are significant benefits to be gained from each when applied properly. But carving financial intermediaries out of the capital markets has exacerbated the risks of borrowing for many companies, raising the capital costs of some borrowers by limiting the amount of tax-deductible debt they can use without severely restricting their operating flexibility.

Sources of the Distance

Money is the most fungible commodity. Without strong relationships that allow banks to provide customers more than capital, a bank has nothing to offer but money at a price.

It is useful to understand why U.S. banks are more distant from their customers than bankers in other countries. Part of the explanation is historical. In Germany, for example, in the nineteenth-century period of industrialization, the founders of commercial banks and industrial companies were often the same people. And following devastating world wars in the twentieth century, both German and Japanese banks were intimately involved with reconstruction efforts to get commercial enterprises back on their feet. But more important, banks in both Germany and Japan have greater legal and regulatory freedom to work closely with their customers than do American banks. They can provide a broader array of products and services, and they can become partial owners of their customers. The highly fragmented U.S. financial services industry, by contrast, inhibits broad-based relationships between businesses and their financial services providers. In the United States, a company has to use four different financial intermediaries, and establish a new relationship each time, in order to secure startup capital, take out a loan, sell stock, and purchase insurance. In Germany, a single institution offers all of these services. And in Japan, a related group of financial intermediaries with close ties cooperate to offer a broad array of services as well.

In addition to our regulatory system, the U.S. legal system also contributes to the problem. U.S. banks function in an environment where loans are governed by legal documents, rather than by people. When a bank, insurance company, or other lender extends credit to a company, lawyers for both parties take over, each jockeying to protect their client against actions by the other party. Loans are often structured with restrictive operating covenants and fixed-payment schedules that can be difficult to renegotiate. Our legalistic approach to lending inhibits lender/borrower cooperation in times of difficulty, making it difficult to respond to unexpected events constructively. Borrowers in the United States rely more heavily on bankruptcy courts to insulate themselves from their creditors, and lenders rely more heavily on contracts to make sure they have legal recourse if a borrower misses a payment.

In contrast, Japanese loan documents are often a page or two, not the voluminous documents we rely on in the United States to address every possible contingency. In both Japan and Germany, bank representatives meet regularly with their clients, review strategic plans, and participate in decisions regarding capital expenditures. In many cases banks are represented on the boards of German and Japanese companies. In fact, as I described in Chapter 3, banks often control the boards of German companies. And it is not uncommon for an employee of a Japanese bank to spend a year or two working in a full-time capacity for a bank customer to learn its business better. Because they know their customers well, bankers in these countries detect potential problems much sooner and take corrective actions to prevent financial catastrophes. Greater influence leads to greater flexibility.

In his book *Japanese Takeovers,* Carl Kester describes the rescue of Akai, a Japanese consumer electronics company, in the mid-1980s.[4] Akai, a member of the Mitsubishi keiretsu, experienced difficulties following the yen's appreciation in 1985, causing its export markets to dry up. Mitsubishi Electric provided an equity infusion and sent seven top engineers to Akai to help it develop digital audio tape recorders. Mitsubishi Bank extended Akai greater credit, as Kester describes it, not simply to meet short-term creditor demands but to preserve the company's role in the group's global trading network.

In early 1991, Sumitomo Bank Ltd. rescued Itoman & Co., a major Japanese trading firm saddled with massive property-related debts. After ousting its top executive, Sumitomo arranged to transfer most of Itoman's property-related debts to other parties, including itself, better positioned to handle them.

In the United States, on the other hand, banks are often unaware of potential crises, and customers often forestall bank efforts to intervene when they become aware of problems. The result is that more U.S. companies go bankrupt, even though they operate with less leverage.[5] Knowing this to be the case, U.S. banks are more conservative in how much they are willing to lend a company. When relationship banking breaks down, the risks to lenders increase as well. The following excerpt from an article in *The Wall Street Journal* announcing the bankruptcy of Britain's Polly Peck International PLC states this point clearly:

> The collapse of [Polly Peck] is seen as a symptom of the growing cut-and-run mentality in the corporate banking world . . . [T]he failure of a company with an unblemished debt-payment record in a matter of weeks is linked in part to the breakdown in relationship banking.[6]

Bankers as Owners

German and Japanese banks have a tremendous economic incentive to ensure that their customers thrive, if not at least survive—they own part of the company. Owning equity, even a small fraction of the company, injects an entirely different perspective into a lending relationship. No longer is the goal simply to have the customer perform adequately enough to repay its debt; banks that own equity want their customers to achieve maximum success.

Equity ownership by banks encourages them to finance strategic pursuits of their customers because the bank participates in the upside rewards. This is evidenced by a recent study conducted by staff members at the Federal Reserve Board who looked at what happened to the investment patterns of companies in Japan that circumvented their bank and borrowed directly from the market.[7] The study confirmed that strategic flexibility is lost through disintermediation. Corporations that still borrowed from a bank in their keiretsu were not as dependent on the company's internal cash flow for investment. They could count on a reliable source of external financing to fund an unexpected opportunity or to make up for a seasonal or cyclical cash shortage. In contrast, the companies that accessed the markets directly may have secured slightly lower rates, but they could not rely on capital being available when they needed it. Their investment levels were more closely tied to internally generated cash.

Since banks in the United States invest solely in the debt of a customer, they have no upside potential if the company excels. In fact, in many ways U.S. banks suffer if their customers do well. Successful companies are likely to finance continued growth through the issuance of public bonds or stock, services that commercial banks typically cannot provide. Furthermore, when growing companies first begin to access the capital markets directly, they often use the proceeds of public offerings or private placements to repay their bank debt, leaving the banker with one less customer. The present lack of underwriting powers and inability to own equity both provide perverse incentives for banks to hope that their customers are not too successful.

In addition to encouraging their customers' success, banks that own equity have a greater economic incentive to help clients stay in business. When a company goes bankrupt, it is not uncommon for the secured creditors to receive most or all of their money back in a liquidation, so lenders frequently escape without significant losses. But the owners never escape unscathed. As a result, banks that are not owners are far more willing to pull the plug rather than inject additional capital to help a customer meet a competitive threat or stay afloat.

Contrary to popular belief, the reason that U.S. banking firms do not own stock in their customers is not primarily a product of banking regulations. Although the Glass-Stegall Act of 1933 prohibits national banks from owning stock in nonfinancial enterprises, the Bank Holding Company Act of 1956 does allow the parent of a national bank to own up to 5 percent of the voting shares in an unrelated business. This restriction is not significantly different from Japan's Article 65.

U.S. banks operate in a different legal environment, one in which equity ownership exposes them to potential legal liability. Banks could find their rights as secured creditors stripped by a legal doctrine called "equitable subordination." In fact, they might even be sued for amounts that far exceed their investment. The U.S. legal system allows creditors in a bankrupt company to sue a bank that has influence over its customer's business decisions; and equity ownership is considered a primary determinant of influence. The theory behind the concept of equitable subordination is that the bank can manipulate the company to ensure that its debt receives preferential treatment vis-à-vis other creditors. Through court action the other creditors can push a lender that is also an owner to the back of the line when the company's assets are liquidated. And if there is reason to believe the bank influenced decision making in the company for its own gain, the creditors can seek damages, exposing the bank to unlimited liability. Few people would argue with the intent of this doctrine, but its deterrence to equity ownership by banks is an unfortunate side effect.

Other legal concerns further inhibit equity ownership by banks. Today banks are being sued for the cost of cleaning up hazardous wastes found on the sites of companies to which they have loaned money, even if the problem existed for years before the loan was made. Owning shares would only weaken their defense; EPA regulations specifically cite this as a test of influence, thus potential liability. A commercial factoring company, Fleet Factors Corp., loaned money to a southeastern printing business and, as is customary, secured its loan against equipment and inventory. In 1982, when the borrower went bankrupt, Fleet took title to the assets and immediately sold them to repay the loan. Five years later, the Environmental Protection Agency sued Fleet to recover the cost of cleaning up hazardous waste on the site of the printing company. The 11th U.S. Circuit Court of Appeals ruled against

Fleet in what appears to be a blatant case of going after deep pockets; no one else involved had the money to repay the EPA, and the fact that Fleet did not cause or contribute to the pollution was deemed irrelevant.

A 400-year-old concept from British common law known as "fraudulent conveyance" is also being used to sue banks that loaned money to fund highly leveraged transactions if the company later goes bankrupt. The argument here is that the leverage taken on by the company made it insolvent from the beginning. The recourse is to disgorge the fees the bank earned on the transaction and unwind the deal, leaving banks that own equity open to greater losses. An Ohio federal court hired a special examiner to determine whether Revco could sue its banks for fraudulent conveyance following the bankruptcy of the drugstore chain that was purchased in a $1.25-billion leveraged buyout in 1986. Early in 1991, the court-appointed examiner concluded that the company had grounds to sue, which was expected to ignite additional fraudulent conveyance activity.[8]

Inside information rules also deter bank equity ownership. Banks whose officers serve on boards and have access to confidential information regarding their customers' plans may be obligated to share that information with other members of a loan syndicate. Knowing this, the lead bank may be disinclined to learn the type of customer information upon which German and Japanese banks rely to perform their jobs.

All these threats of lawsuits and regulatory censorship raise the cost of debt by boosting legal bills in the preparation of loan documents, defending against frivolous lawsuits, and funding expensive studies to detect hazardous wastes before closing a loan. A study conducted by an insurance consulting subsidiary of Towers, Perrin, Forster & Crosby found that in 1987 the cost to litigate torts in the United States, including lawyers' fees and awards to injured parties, equaled 2.6 percent of our GNP. The comparable figure in both Japan and Germany was below one-half of 1 percent. Banks in Japan and Germany become intimately involved with their customers' business with no legal exposure unless, of course, they engage in fraudulent or manipulative behavior. But in trying to avoid any potential for foul play, the U.S. legal system has blown a cold wind on the relationships between lenders and their customers.

Some argue that bank equity ownership has serious drawbacks, the most common being that it produces a concentration of economic power. This can be readily addressed by limiting the amount of stock a bank can own in a single company as proposed in Chapter 8. The other primary argument is that equity ownership would make a bank's earnings more volatile. Following a 40-percent drop in Japanese share prices in 1990, the large Japanese banks' profits suffered considerably. But it is important to remember that it was equity-related profits that provided much of the capital that allowed Japanese banks to become the largest and most powerful in the world. Furthermore, equity profits afforded Japanese banks the ability to charge their customers lower interest rates in the 1980s because their stock-related gains supplemented loan yields.

And there is always the question of whether we want the same people who lent billions to third-world countries, to developers who built tenantless office buildings, and to fund overpriced LBOs having greater influence over America's corporations. Obviously, U.S. commercial banks lack the skills of their German and Japanese counterparts when it comes to monitoring and directing corporations. Without the opportunity to do so, they have had no reason to develop those skills. But if foreign bankers are able to acquire such talents, there is no reason that given the opportunity, U.S. bankers could not do the same.

Furthermore, from an administrative perspective, it is more efficient for providers of capital to own both debt and equity. Responsible suppliers of capital, both lenders and shareholders, will expend time and resources to monitor the results of the company, stay abreast of industry trends, keep up with the company's plans, and provide them input and direction. There are synergies to having fewer institutions, rather than a fragmented group of creditors and owners performing essentially the same monitoring function. These efficiencies should contribute to a lower overall cost of capital.

Investment in Innovation

In addition to raising the risks of borrowing money, and thus the cost of capital, regulatory fragmentation in America has produced a financial system that lacks efficiencies in funding ventures with long-term payoffs. Investment in new ventures and technologies is a prime determinant of a country's economic future. But today many newly formed and growing U.S. companies claim that capital is not available to them at any cost. These claims are often dismissed by economists who argue that worthwhile projects will find financing. But this presumes efficient markets.

The Department of Commerce has sponsored the Advanced Manufacturing Program for several years, in part to determine why small businesses have been slow to adopt sophisticated manufacturing techniques. After an exhaustive analysis, the staff concluded that the primary impediment was a dearth of capital. The men and women who run these companies feel that because they are in small, basic businesses, their needs are not glamorous enough to appeal to venture capitalists and too risky for commercial bankers. The United States is often credited with having the most advanced venture capital market in the world. Certainly innovation in America has outpaced that in other countries, so it is hard to argue that the present system is totally ineffectual. However, it could be improved.

During the unforgettable federal budget fiasco of 1990, a proposal to offer a tax break to people who invested in small businesses was included in the package jointly proposed by the administration and the congressional leadership. The idea was quickly killed because it was billed as a tax break for the rich. In the process of debating its merits, my office contacted several successful entrepreneurs to seek their input on the proposal. Many of those who ran high-tech companies told us that they are now forced to rely on the Asians as their primary source of long-term capital since no one in the United States is addressing their needs. Money was available to get their company going, but it is the emerging business that has not yet commercialized its products that seems to be having the most difficulty finding capital.

Many companies with promising technologies are dying on the vine. Others are being sold to Asian companies willing to help them bring their products to market. For example, a Taiwanese consumer electronics company, Tatung, invested $1 million in Graph On Corp., a San Jose maker of computer-window displays. Another Taiwanese company, Hualon Microelectronics, purchased 10 percent of Seeq Technology for $5.3 million. And Massachusetts-based Edsun Laboratories raised money from Singapore's Ssangyong Cement Ltd. Entrepreneurs are finding that the professional venture capital sources they have relied on in the past are no longer interested in early-stage ventures. They lack the infrastructure to make a large number of small investments. Besides, they offer only money; corporate and foreign sources of capital frequently bring distribution channels, marketing arrangements, and managerial assistance as well.

Professional venture capital firms provide only $3 billion, or about 5 percent of the high-risk capital invested each year in the United States. Although these investors serve a useful purpose, the professional venture capital market is small, highly fragmented, and unable to address the needs that arise in many local markets. According to the National Venture Capital Association, there are only 674 venture capital firms nationwide, with an average of four employees each. In 1989, 13 states accounted for 93 percent of the venture capital investment in the country, which means companies in three-fourths of the states have few sources of high-risk capital.

The primary source of venture capital in the United States today is individuals who are referred to as "angels," i.e., the relatives and friends of entrepreneurs and other private investors willing to invest their savings to help get a new business off the ground. These informal sources account for most of the $50 billion in venture capital invested annually. Many entrepreneurs have found that because of the lack of adequate institutional sources for high-risk financing, who you know is often more important than what you know. The problem is that these individuals often lack, or are unwilling to provide, the deep pockets needed to commercialize many products and technologies emerging today. They also lack the institutional capability of providing more than money.

The entrepreneurs who have been able to get an audience with the professional venture capital funds have discovered that many of them have shifted their focus in recent years away from early-stage financings in favor of highly leveraged transactions and later-stage financings. This has occurred for two reasons. First, because venture capital firms have limited staffs, they tend to lack industry-specific knowledge. Most venture capitalists are trained in general management or finance. Rather than fund business risk that may involve technologies they do not understand, many have opted to target opportunities that involve financial risk, i.e., leverage, which is their area of expertise.

Second, the venture capital funds that were successful in the late 1970s and early 1980s raised so much new capital in the late 1980s that they have been forced to invest large sums in each transaction in order to put this capital to work. The buyout of an existing business deploys more capital than funding an emerging growth company. With a staff of three or four people, a $50-million venture fund could hardly identify 100 suitable new companies, invest a half million dollars in each, and monitor their performance.

The ideal source of venture capital would be an institution with a nationwide network of professionals capable of identifying promising business in local markets and large and sophisticated enough to afford a staff of specialists who had in-depth, industry-specific knowledge and who could review financing proposals. The specialists could provide guidance as to the viability of the technology or size of the potential market and help the loan officers structure the transaction. The most logical candidate to fill this role is our banking system. Today, however, the McFadden Act and patchwork state laws limit banks from expanding nationwide. And the present all-encompassing deposit insurance system, coupled with restrictions on bank equity ownership, deters banks from engaging in activities this risky.

Repealing the McFadden Act and allowing banks to own equity would help innovation. If Citicorp had a banking officer in Topeka who was approached by an entrepreneur wanting seed capital for a new widget, the banker could call the widget expert in New York and get advice on whether the widget technology was viable and input on how to structure an early-stage financing. As it is, Citicorp cannot open a branch in Topeka: it is not involved enough in venture capital to have a large staff of specialists, and it would not take on the risks of a startup because its ability to own equity is limited. In most European countries, including Germany, France, and Italy, a majority of venture capital is channeled through the banking industry. In Japan, the banks work so closely with their customers that they do not need their own staffs to evaluate opportunities; they ask their customers.

Without the ability to own equity, the risk/reward profile of a bank is not suitable to fund innovation. Most venture capital investments are made in the form of equity. Ownership provides investors in high-risk companies with greater control; it also allows them to secure a return commensurate with the risk involved. A loan with a 35-percent interest rate would devastate a research project on a tight budget, a small business just getting off the ground, or other projects that have little, if any, cash coming in during the first few years. Entrepreneurs are in a position to reward their investors only after the venture becomes a success, which is typically several years into the future. That is how equity works, not debt. Obviously, unless U.S. banks are allowed to own more equity, they will never regard venture capital as a viable business. Without access to equity-type returns, banks will funnel their capital into more conservative projects and mature companies where the risks are lower.

The federal government has attempted to address the problem of banks not being in the venture capital business with a Band-Aid solution. The Small Business Administration (SBA) was created to establish a program to encourage banks to fund entrepreneurial ventures. However, as is often the case, this program is fraught with onerous regulations. For example, in order to be eligible for SBA direct and guaranteed loans, a company must have been turned down by two commercial banks. In other words, the SBA program forces participants to cater to less-desirable customers. Like venture capital funds, many of the U.S. banks that participated in the SBA program have stopped investing in startup companies and chosen instead to fund leveraged buyouts.

The SBA program has had questionable success. A recent study shows the program may lose up to $800 million, which is more than half of the $1.4 billion in federal funds allocated to the project.[9] As of September 1990, there were at least 150 SBA-backed investment companies in liquidation proceedings. Apparently, using government subsidies and regulations to force-feed capital to startup companies is not working. Even if it had been more successful, the SBA program would only be a drop in the bucket since it accounts for only 5 percent of U.S. venture capital investments. A scant two-tenths of 1 percent of all small businesses receive SBA loans according to the Heritage Foundation.

The limited success of the Small Business Administration program should not be used to conclude that banks are incapable of making successful equity investments. European banks do it. And the only U.S. bank that has consistently committed substantial resources to its venture capital activities, First Chicago Corporation, generated almost half of the corporation's total profits during the period of 1985 to 1989 from its venture capital subsidiary with fewer than 30 employees and only $300 million of the firm's capital.

Cooperative Efforts to Penetrate Overseas Markets

Finally, the balkanization of the U.S. financial services industry inhibits both American financial intermediaries and corporations from working together to penetrate foreign markets. More cooperation could help both parties take a longer-term perspective when competing overseas. Japanese and German firms have shown that strong strategic links between financial and nonfinancial companies help both parties enter new markets successfully.

When Mitsubishi Semiconductor decided to build a plant in the United States, it turned to Mitsubishi Bank North America to provide some of the startup capital. Mitsubishi International Corporation acquired Rockefeller Center with financing provided partly by Mitsubishi Bank; and another member of the Mitsubishi keiretsu turned to the U.S. arm of their loyal home bank for financing when competing against General Electric for control of a U.S. chemical company. In fact, the New York–based Mitsubishi Bank North America would rank among the 20 largest U.S. banks, and it does 10 percent of its business with its Japanese group members who have operations in the United States.

The efforts required to establish overseas operations can be daunting to any company—unknown markets, customs, laws, and people. One of the easiest ways to make the process more manageable would be to have ready access to a network of business relationships, information, and capital in the foreign country. If a U.S. industrial company had close ties to a U.S. bank that operated in the markets it hoped to enter, it might find the process of becoming a global corporation more manageable. Its bank could provide advice on issues such as where to build the plant and the politics of dealing with local government officials and the unions.

Financial institutions across the globe are broadening their skill base and entering new markets to better serve their customers. Deutsche Bank, already a powerhouse in financial services in Germany, is expanding throughout Europe. For example, the large German bank took over the U.K. merchant bank Morgan Grenfell for $1.6 billion. Other banks are entering markets through cross-border investments or joint ventures, rather than through outright acquisitions. These strategic alliances do not entail significant capital, but still position financial firms to take advantage of opportunities created by global banking deregulation. For example, the United Kingdom's Midland Bank is now 15 percent owned by the Hong Kong and Shanghai Bank. And a significant exchange of shares was arranged recently between Spain's Banco Santander and the Royal Bank of Scotland.

In preparation for full global competition, banks in many countries are consolidating. Algemene Bank Nederland and Amsterdam-Rotterdam Bank merged to form an institution with $180 billion in assets that operates about 1,500 branches in the Netherlands and 375 branches overseas. In Denmark, the six largest banks were compressed into two survivors. In 1990, Japan's seventh- and eighth-largest banks combined.

Insurance companies are linking up with commercial banks. Nippon Life, the largest insurance company in the world, now owns a stake in the largest bank in Spain. Nippon Life is also teaming up with European banks to establish new skills. It acquired a 3-percent stake in Banque Swiss whose employees will train Nippon Life employees in portfolio management.

But just as a truly global financial services market is emerging, U.S. banks are pulling out of foreign countries. Chase Manhattan has closed operations in 22 countries in recent years, recently selling its $5-billion Dutch bank to Credit Lyonnaise. Bank of America sold its Italian bank to Germany's Deutsche Bank. Since 1987, First Chicago has closed offices in France, Greece, Ireland, Italy, Singapore, Sweden, and West Germany. And Chemical Bank, which only 10 years ago secured 50 percent of its revenues from abroad, has pulled out of more than 20 of the 30 countries in which it once had offices.

One would expect that having strong relationships with home country customers operating globally would be appealing to the banks as well as to their customers. Confident that they could pay the overhead of a German office, for example, by tapping into U.S. companies that had German operations, more U.S. banks would open foreign offices. These new offices would provide them with an opportunity to broaden their worldwide customer base. But without strong ties to home country customers, it is hard to justify foreign operations needed to establish ties to foreign customers. Today U.S. banks operate only 12 branches with $21 billion in assets in Germany. In Japan, U.S. banks have actually lost market share recently and now have only $32 billion in assets generated by 28 branches owned by a handful of banks. Meanwhile, 39 Japanese banks now operate out of 120 offices in the United States and control $373 billion in assets. In fact, Tokai Bank Ltd. opened an office in Lexington, Kentucky, when one of its principal customers, Toyota Motor Company, built a plant there. Of course, Morgan Bank is prohibited from opening a branch in Kentucky.

* * * *

A lack of closer relationships between financial intermediaries and U.S. corporations has made both parties less competitive and more short-term oriented. Unfortunately, present trends in the United States are making matters worse. The continued disintermediation of banks, securitization of risky business loans, reliance on foreign banks for capital, inefficiencies in the venture capital market, and retreat by U.S. banks from foreign markets all undermine the ability of U.S. companies to adopt a long-term perspective.

Both financial and commercial businesses in the United States have a tradition of independence, at least partly because of the American legal and regulatory systems. We pride ourselves in being able to establish rules that eliminate all potential for collusion or conflict of interest. Our legal and regulatory systems have been designed to provide significant sanctions to companies that cooperate to lessen competition, as they should. But these laws and regulations have gone to such extremes to prevent conflicts of interest that they have not only eliminated the conflicts, they have also removed the interest. They inhibit the cooperation that could lead to more competitive financial institutions as well as stronger global competitors in the commercial sector. The ability to borrow more tax-deductible debt without incurring greater risk, to have more capital flowing to projects with long-term payoffs, and to establish joint efforts by banks and their customers to penetrate foreign markets would all foster a longer-term perspective and help the U.S. economy prosper in the years to come.

The 1992 European Community (EC 92) reforms are upon us. These reforms grant European banks even broader powers,[10] which will make it more difficult for U.S. banks to compete. Unfortunately, efforts to enact meaningful reform legislation in the past have been undermined by a populist sentiment in Congress that we need to further tie the hands of our financial services industry. Many policy makers have concluded that what banks need is a little more regulatory discipline. What they fail to realize is that the primary reason banks have chased so many risky loans is that they lack *market* discipline. Our overregulated banks are prohibited from offering many of the basic products and services that are the mainstay of foreign banks, and the present deposit insurance system subsidizes inefficient banks at the expense of the more competitive institutions.

What the U.S. financial services industry needs is not more stringent regulation, but more *efficient* regulation; not higher deposit insurance rates, but a more sensible deposit insurance system; not fewer powers, but a chance to streamline and consolidate financial services providers to achieve the scale and synergies needed to compete internationally. In a nutshell, banks need the regulatory freedom to better serve their customers and to establish stronger relationships. The proposal presented in Chapter 8 will show that it is possible to offer banks greater freedom and still reduce the exposure of the federal deposit insurance system and the U.S. taxpayer.

6

The Cost-of-Capital Enigma

Any businessperson who has ever tried to justify a capital expenditure to senior management is familiar with the concept of the cost of capital. Typically, the most important criterion in determining which projects will make next year's budget is their net present value or internal rate of return. Both measures are derived from discounted cash flow (DCF) models that are driven by a corporation's cost of capital. Companies regularly reject proposals that they believe would help their competitive strategy but that fail to show a return high enough to meet or exceed the company's cost of capital.

There is a growing belief in American business that we should disregard discounted cash flow techniques in managerial decision making. Critics argue that important strategic decisions ought not be based on these rigid financial formulas. But the problem is not with the analytical framework. If it is too hot outside, we cannot blame the thermometer. Our problem is that America's high cost of capital is giving us answers we do not like, because high capital costs systematically bias against investments with distant payoffs.

Understanding the economic factors that cause short-term behavior requires an analysis of the cost of capital and how it affects investment decisions and corporate strategies. The cost of capital is one of the most talked about but least understood competitiveness issues. Like labor and raw materials, capital comes with a

171

cost. But unlike expenditures for labor and raw materials, the cost of capital is difficult to measure and is never reported in a company's financial statements. Interest payments may be easy to monitor, but a company's cost of equity and overall cost of capital are enigmatic. Academics and businesspeople define the cost of capital differently. Even within each community there is no consensus. In fact, virtually every study on the cost of capital uses a different method to try to quantify a company's capital costs.

What little has been written in the business press about the cost of capital is superficial and in some cases misleading. The solution to lower capital costs in America is commonly believed to be lower interest rates brought about by reducing the budget deficit and increasing personal savings. Others believe that lowering taxes is the solution to America's high capital costs. This chapter will explain that although savings and taxes clearly influence the cost of capital, these macroeconomic factors fail to account fully for the wide disparities in international capital costs that are thought to exist.

A closer analysis reveals that structural factors within our financial system also contribute to America's cost of capital differential. Capital now flows relatively freely across borders. But once that capital enters a country, how it is allocated and monitored influences the returns investors require. In other words, there are ways to lower America's capital costs without changing savings, taxes, or interest rates whatsoever. And each of these structural problems has a common denominator—the U.S. financial system engenders confrontational, rather than cooperative relationships between capital providers and capital users.

This chapter will explore the extent to which capital costs differ between countries, the impact these differentials have on long-term management decisions and corporate competitiveness, and the causes of present international discrepancies in capital costs. We will begin with an important overview of what constitutes the cost of capital.

Defining the Cost of Capital

The cost of capital is not synonymous with interest rates as many people believe. A company has two sources of capital—debt and equity. The returns required by lenders and shareholders both influence capital costs, as does the relative proportion of debt and equity in a company's capital structure. Most small and medium-sized companies secure their debt from banks. Many of the larger companies borrow directly from insurance companies and pension funds, or through publicly issued securities. The interest rate a company pays on its loans is referred to as its *cost of debt*. It is important to note that since interest expenses are deductible for tax purposes, a borrower's cost of debt is lowered by the tax benefit of the interest deduction.

A company can also raise capital by retaining its profits or by selling new shares of stock. When investors purchase stock, they expect to receive a return on their investment through dividends paid out of the company's profits and/or by appreciation in the value of their shares. The combined return investors require from dividends *and* stock appreciation constitutes a company's *cost of equity*.

When I was moderating a joint Treasury and Commerce Department seminar on financing technology investments, one of the most renowned investors in the country stated that companies that retain their profits have a cost of equity equal to zero. Others in the room dropped their jaws. Just because a company does not have to go to the market to secure equity because it is generated from profits does not mean the owners are willing to have their equity invested in projects that produce no return. Unless the company can earn a return on retained profits equal to the total return required by the shareholders, the company should dividend those profits to the owners. In other words, even internally generated capital has an opportunity cost associated with it.

The cost of equity in a given company always exceeds its cost of debt. The main reason equity is more expensive than debt is that the Internal Revenue Service taxes a company's profits twice.

After corporate taxes are paid, the same profits are taxed again when they are paid out in dividends to shareholders or realized through the sale of appreciated stock, i.e., capital gains. Furthermore, the risks of an equity investment are greater than for a debt instrument. When a company's assets are liquidated, the creditors are paid in full before the owners receive anything. The principal and interest a lender is due are contractual obligations of the borrower, but dividends and capital gains are dependent on company performance and market factors.

The overall cost of capital for a given corporation is the weighted average cost of debt and equity in the company's capital structure. For example, if a company were facing a pretax cost of debt of 10 percent and a pretax cost of equity of 15 percent, and were to have half as much debt as equity, its cost of capital would be computed as follows:

Pretax cost of debt	10.0%	
Less tax benefit*	-4.0%	
After-tax cost of debt	6.0%	
Times percentage of debt	33.0%	
equals		2.0%
plus		
Pretax cost of equity	15.0%	
Less tax benefit	-0.0%	
After-tax cost of equity	15.0%	
Times percentage of equity	67.0%	
equals		10.0%
Weighted Average Cost of Capital		12.0%

*Assumes a 40-percent marginal tax rate.

U.S. Capital Costs Are High

The cost of capital has only recently been regarded as a serious competitiveness issue. During the 1970s and 1980s, U.S. business leaders frequently blamed high labor costs for their waning competitiveness. Hundreds of American companies moved production offshore to take advantage of lower wages overseas, building factories from Singapore to Ireland to produce everything from electronic components to tennis shoes. However, during the 1980s American car makers closed seven plants in the United States while Japanese auto producers opened seven, staffing them with U.S. workers. These decisions clearly were not driven by labor cost considerations. Now that average hourly wage rates in the United States are about the same as in Japan and Germany, it is obvious that labor costs do not fully explain the cost advantages of our foreign rivals.

Many of the industries in which the United States is losing ground to foreign competitors are capital-intensive businesses such as consumer electronics, steel, automobiles, and banking. It is not only mature businesses that are ceding market share to foreign competitors; U.S. high-tech industries that require substantial capital for growth are also losing ground. According to the American Electronics Association, the U.S. share of world electronics production plunged more than 10 percent between 1984 and 1987 alone. Table 6.1 shows a few examples of what is happening to the U.S. market share of some specific capital-intensive high-tech industries.

Table 6.1

U.S. Share of World Exports

	1980	1988
Microelectronics	21.2%	17.2%
Computers	55.2%	35.8%
Telecommunications	12.4%	10.7%

Source: Handbook of Economic Statistics (Washington, DC: Central Intelligence Agency, 1989).

Texas Instruments CEO Jerry Junkins stated the problem clearly: "To put the consequences of Japan's cost of capital advantage in numerical terms, in the past five years, Japanese semiconductor companies have invested $10 billion more in R&D, plant, and equipment than U.S. suppliers were able to invest. And they gained more than 10 points of world market share—mostly at the expense of U.S. companies."[1]

The two countries that seem to be achieving the greatest relative growth in global market share of capital-intensive businesses are Japan and Germany. Not surprisingly, studies show that Japanese and German companies pay less than American businesses for the capital needed to construct a manufacturing plant, purchase an assembly robot, or build a salesforce and distribution network.

Table 6.2

Estimated Costs of Capital, U.S. and Japan

	Cost of Capital Year	United States	Japan
Hatsopoulos-Brooks	1980	14.1%	4.0%
	1985	9.7	3.8
McCauley-Zimmer	1980	11.5	8.8
	1985	11.2	7.2
Bernheim-Shoven	1980	18.7	11.0
	1985	11.1	4.1

Note: McCauley-Zimmer estimated Germany's cost of capital to be 8.6 percent in 1980 and 7.0 percent in 1988.

Source: James M. Poterba, "Comparing the Cost of Capital in the United States and Japan: A Survey of Methods," *Federal Reserve Bank of New York Quarterly Review* (Winter 1991), p. 30.

Table 6.2 summarizes the findings of some of the studies that have attempted to measure capital costs in the United States and Japan.

Measuring the cost of capital for a nation is not an exact science. Studies of the cost of capital usually employ different methodologies and data sources. Also, the cost of capital typically varies with the type of investment, so it is not uncommon for different studies to compare apples and oranges. However, putting aside the complexities of real versus nominal rates and the myriad assumptions needed to compute a company's cost of capital, there is consensus that a gap exists between the U.S. cost of capital and the capital costs of companies in Japan and Germany. Generally, studies conclude Japanese and German capital costs are roughly half America's cost of capital. The size of this gap varies, depending on the study's completion date and its assumptions. But what matters most to a company that has to compete in global markets is the relative disparity.

Exhibit 6.1
Real Gross Fixed-Capital Formation
Nonresidential Construction, 1960–1987

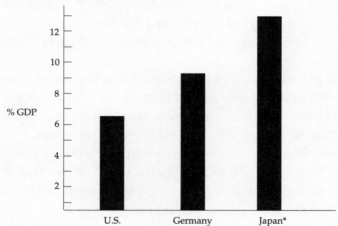

*1970–1987
Source: Council on Competitiveness.

These studies are supported by some convincing circumstantial evidence—the amount of capital investment being undertaken in the United States, Japan, and Germany. As Exhibit 6.1 illustrates, something is obviously very different in these countries when it comes to evaluating the risks and returns of capital expenditures, since far more investments appear to meet the minimum criteria in Japan and Germany than in the United States.

The Cost of Capital and Investment Decisions

To understand just how profound a problem high capital costs can be, it is helpful to look at how investment decisions are made and corporate strategies are developed within an individual company. American businesses typically evaluate investment opportunities based on whether the amount of cash generated by an investment exceeds its cost, which is certainly the most appropriate criterion. Unfortunately, many of the variables that influence a cash flow analysis are difficult to quantify. How will a change in the overall economic outlook influence the project? How about a change in tax laws? What opportunities might the investment provide for the future? How will the risk of the investment affect the overall risk of the company, which will affect its cost of capital for other projects?

Corporate planners attempt to translate these and all other relevant issues into numbers that project the amount of cash an investment will generate over its life. These cash flows are then compared to what it costs to finance a project—which is determined by the company's cost of capital—to assess whether an investment creates value. The formulas used in this analysis are very simple and straightforward; they are taught in every entry-level finance course. The problem is making the right assumptions.

As mentioned earlier, the use of this quantitative approach to make investment decisions has come under increasing criticism in recent years. Many business leaders now argue that some necessary investments can never be justified if they are measured purely on the basis of their ability to cover investment costs, but should be undertaken anyway for strategic reasons to put a company on a faster or longer-lasting growth track. This, they claim, is how the Japanese make investment decisions. For example, Japanese companies poured enormous sums of money into the first generation of semiconductor memory-chip production, which they knew would not be recouped in the short run. The typical explanation for why the Japanese can invest in projects that their American counterparts find financially unacceptable is that Japanese businesses pursue market share rather than short-term profit as a goal.

To someone who does not understand the dramatic impact capital costs have on investment horizons—as illustrated by the robotics investment decision discussed in Chapter 1—it is understandably baffling why two companies in the same business have such different time horizons. But now that the Japanese dominate much of the semiconductor market and are reaping substantial returns, it is easier to understand that their up-front investment may well have been justifiable using a discounted cash flow model all along. What is important is not how many financial analysts the Japanese have running DCF models—presumably very few— but what those models would tell them if they were used. It is very likely that their "strategic" investments with no short-term payoff make perfect economic sense in the long run because of their lower cost of capital.

One of the primary reasons that DCF models are so heavily criticized today is that they are often used improperly. Financial planners have a tendency to ignore the more distant, less quantifiable strategic benefits of an investment such as the merits of market share, the potential benefits of new technologies on future generations of products, and the inherent value of a higher-skilled labor force. Because senior management will press subordinates to justify how they arrived at their numbers, and these sorts of numbers are highly subjective, it is often easier to ignore them than to defend them. It is important to remember that projecting cash flows is an art, not a science. By only considering "hard" numbers,

DCF models are guaranteed to be shortsighted. It is possible to incorporate less tangible benefits of investment by dealing with them separately and using a higher discount rate to compensate for their uncertainty, but this is seldom done. The problem is not the economic integrity of discounted cash flow analysis, but its application. If the use of these models consistently ignores the more long-term strategic merits of investments, gut feel may be a superior approach.

At a 1990 seminar on the cost of capital that involved many of the nation's top economists, business leaders, bankers, and government officials, Paul Volker, former chairman of the Federal Reserve Board, noted that one of the primary differences between Japanese and American companies is that U.S. companies are staffed with hordes of MBAs who focus excessive attention on crunching numbers. Most of the time spent in business schools on the subject of discounted cash flow analysis is focused on how to take a given set of cash flows and properly compute a net present value or internal rate of return. Perhaps an entire course ought to be centered around how to come up with the cash flow numbers in the first place. As they say in the information processing business, "garbage in, garbage out."

But even when the analysis is performed properly, it often produces answers we do not like. As an example, assume that a consumer electronics manufacturer has an opportunity to purchase a new piece of inspection equipment that would improve quality control in the production of videocassette recorders (VCRs). The inspection equipment costs $6 million and is expected to last ten years, at which point it would be worthless. The more consistent quality control in the production of the VCRs would improve the company's cash flow by $1 million each year.

As Exhibit 6.2 illustrates, if the company had a cost of capital of 8 percent, it would be expected to purchase the inspection equipment. However, if the company had a 12-percent cost of capital, the financing cost would more than offset the benefits of producing a product with more consistent quality. For the business with

Exhibit 6.2
Present Value of Future Cash Flows (in $ thousands)

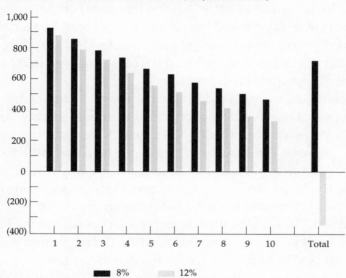

the higher cost of capital, making the investment would reduce the value of the company.

Capital Costs and Corporate Strategies

Although it is commonly acknowledged that the cost of capital influences investment levels, little has been written about how it drives corporate strategies. Continuing with the VCR example, assume the company is also considering a research and development project that would enhance the technology used in manufacturing the VCRs. This project would improve the quality of the VCRs, not just detect defects. Although the R&D project would also require a $6-million up-front expenditure, it would not produce results for five years. However, beginning in year 6, the new technology would enhance the marketability of the product enough to generate an additional $2.5 million in cash flow for the ensuing five years (years 6 to 10).

To keep this illustration simple, assume that two companies—one based in Japan and the other in the United States—make identical VCRs. Also, assume that the Japanese company has an 8-percent cost of capital and the American company has a cost of capital of 10 percent. Since most studies conclude that capital costs are actually about twice as high in the United States as in Japan, a 2-percent differential is conservative.

Both companies are considering either purchasing the inspection equipment that would simply catch mistakes and be worthless in 10 years, or undertaking the research project that would actually improve the quality of their product and add to the company's technology base. The American company would likely purchase the inspection equipment, and the Japanese company would probably choose to invest in the research project.

As Table 6.3 illustrates, the research project produces the highest value for the Japanese company, while the inspection equipment produces the highest value for the American company. The cumulative effect of higher capital costs makes the more distant cash flows from the research project worth less to the American company. By making a decision dictated solely by the numbers, the Japanese executive would be credited with a visionary willingness to invest for the future, and the American executive would be criticized for being shortsighted. Ironically, both executives were making rational decisions to maximize the values of their respective companies.

Table 6.3

Present Value of Alternative Investments

Cost of Capital	Inspection Equipment	Research Project
8%	710	**790**
10%	**145**	(115)

This dilemma transcends individual investment decisions and is embedded in a corporation's overall strategy. In running a business, managers must select among mutually exclusive strategies. One strategy might involve a series of investments producing marginal or no returns early on but eventually providing the business with a competitive advantage that allows it to reap substantial returns in the more distant future. Such an approach might be referred to as a "patient" strategy. The Japanese semiconductor industry is an example. Alternatively, the company might engage in a series of shorter-term projects with quick payoffs but which lack the technology, economies of scale, or market share that provides a sustainable competitive advantage. This second approach might be referred to as a "short-term" strategy.

Assume the "patient" strategy entails building a manufacturing plant, which involves a significant investment in robotics, process technology, and product design. Operating the plant would require substantial work force training. This strategy would produce a finished product only after several years of research, tooling, and training. However, when the product is introduced it would have either the highest quality, the lowest unit cost in the market, or both.

Alternatively, assume that the "short-term" strategy involves bringing a finished product to market more quickly by using a less capital-intensive process. Significant profit would be available in the short run because of higher margins available early in the product life cycle and a lower required investment. However, when a company with a "short-term" strategy later experiences competition from companies with the "patient" strategy that have cost or other advantages, its margins or volumes would decline. Exhibit 6.3 depicts the two alternative strategies.

In the graph, the "patient" strategy is represented by a steep line. The line is steep because the "patient" strategy is characterized by distant cash flows whose values decline precipitously as the cost of capital, or discount rate, increases. The "short-term" strategy line has a more gradual slope—the compounding effect of a high funding cost is not as devastating since cash flows accrue sooner. This strategy is viable for a broader array of competitors because it is not as sensitive to the cost of capital.

Assuming this chart reflects the strategic options available to a company, the firm facing an 8-percent cost of capital would likely choose the "patient" strategy because it creates the most value (point A versus point B). Alternatively, a firm with capital providers that require a return of 10 percent would probably choose the "short-term" strategy because, at that discount rate, the "short-term" strategy creates the most value (point C versus point D). If the "patient" strategy were the only one available, the company with the higher cost of capital should choose to forego the business altogether because it would result in a decline in the value of the company. Hopefully this somewhat tedious academic exercise will bring to light how the cost of capital can dictate corporate strategies.

Exhibit 6.3
Strategic Options

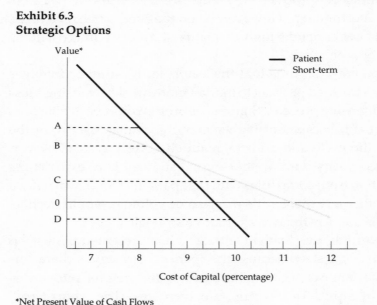

*Net Present Value of Cash Flows

In practice, decisions are not always based solely on the numbers. Executives are paid to apply judgment. However, the problems caused by a high cost of capital present a catch-22 for corporate managers. If American business leaders choose the "short-term" strategy, they are accused of lacking vision, being shortsighted, and managing the company into decline. The company will ultimately find itself with higher-cost or lower-quality products and lose market share to foreign competitors.

Unfortunately, the alternative is not any better. U.S. corporate executives who opt for the "patient" strategy in this example would argue that this strategy is needed to compete with Asian and European companies. Regrettably, they are ignoring long-term economic realities. Since the "patient" strategy in this example produces negative values for the company with the higher cost of capital, those who pursue it will see their company's stock price decline. Consequently, many well-intentioned executives who "invest for the future" become takeover candidates. Eliminating the potential for a takeover does not solve the fundamental economic problem, which is that to enhance the ability of American companies to pursue long-term strategies, we must lower the U.S. cost of capital. In fact, banning takeovers may do just the opposite by raising the cost of equity and driving capital overseas.

One of the reasons the subject of business myopia is receiving greater attention these days is that increasingly U.S. companies are facing foreign competition at home and abroad. When we operated in essentially a domestic economy, all U.S. corporations were subject to the same cost-of-capital constraints. But as markets have become more global, competition from foreign firms facing different constraints has increased. The fact that an overseas competitor can implement a strategy that a U.S. company cannot, frustrates and baffles many Americans.

In a free market, the company with the higher cost of capital will eventually be forced out of a specific business unless it can consistently overcome this handicap. U.S. companies such as Motorola, Conner Peripherals, Nucor Steel, and Coca-Cola have been effective at competing with foreign producers on the basis of superior product innovation, better service, newer technology, more creative marketing, or another advantage. However, when a product can no longer be differentiated and price competition intensifies, the ball-and-chain of high capital costs slows down even the best competitors. That is why the loss of global market share for American companies is most pronounced in capital-intensive industries as they mature and cost becomes a larger issue.

Placebo solutions such as quotas and subsidies may boost the prospects of a company or industry temporarily, but they will not cure the problem of a high cost of capital. In the meantime, protectionist solutions could exact a significant toll on the rest of society, which has to pay for the quotas or subsidies in the form of higher consumer prices. For example, it is estimated that quotas contained in the textile bill passed by Congress and vetoed by President Bush in 1990 would have eventually raised domestic prices by $50 billion each year, which amounts to $200,000 for every job preserved in the textile industry. The Federal Trade Commission estimates that tariffs on textiles already in place inflate by 58 percent the cost of all underwear, towels, and shirts purchased by American consumers.

Similarly, removing antitrust barriers with the primary goal of minimizing competition in the domestic market under the assumption that this enhances a company's ability to compete overseas addresses the symptom rather than the problem. Absent any other changes, merging two companies, each with a high cost of capital, only produces one large company with an uncompetitive cost of capital. As Michael Porter argues in *The Competitive Advantage of Nations,* a lack of competition at home only produces fat, dumb, and happy companies that lack the competitive edge needed to prosper in a global marketplace. The underlying problem of capital costs must be addressed directly if American companies are to be expected to invest for the future.

Causes of International Disparities

Since the cost of capital began receiving so much attention after the publication of George Hatsopoulos's 1983 paper, "High Cost of Capital: Handicap of American Industry,"[2] a number of articles have been written concluding that taxes and the low U.S. savings rate are the primary culprits. However, recent studies, which examine the factors that cause international disparities in capital costs, lead to a different conclusion. Macroeconomic factors such as savings and taxes fail to fully explain the gap.

Savings Is Not the Answer

Equating the cost of capital with prevailing interest rates leads some to conclude that raising national savings—i.e., increasing the domestic supply of capital—is the answer. While nominal interest rates may vary on a country-by-country basis, the fact is that we now operate in a global financial system. Therefore, the traditional theory that the supply and demand of *domestic* savings determines national interest rates no longer applies. Billions of dollars flow across national borders on a daily basis, which tends to level out real interest rates across the globe. As MIT professor James Poterba notes, "The size of the U.S. and Japanese markets and the active cross-border arbitrage in fixed-income markets make large disparities in these markets unlikely."[3]

In earlier days, if the U.S. government drained capital out of our domestic economy by running up deficits, and if individuals failed to save enough to offset the shortfall, the supply of capital for business would dry up and interest rates would skyrocket. With a current annual shortfall in net national savings of more than $100 billion, one would expect U.S. interest rates to be dramatically higher than they have been since the mid-1980s. However, countries now export their excess capital, just like their products, to the nations where the greatest market opportunities exist. Foreigners have been funding a large portion of our budget deficits for years. About one-third of the Treasury securities auctioned during the late 1980s were purchased by Japanese investors. Thanks to this inflow of foreign capital, real U.S. interest rates have been kept in line with most of our competitors'. In fact, as of the end of 1990, real rates were lower in the United States than in Japan and Germany.

This in no way implies that deficit spending or a low personal savings rate does not hurt our economy; they clearly do. Indeed, excess reliance on foreign capital is a risky proposition. Foreign investors, who already hold $650 billion in U.S. debt on a net basis, will not bail us out forever. In fact, the participation of German and Japanese investors in U.S. Treasury securities markets declined considerably in 1990. The ability of both countries to export capital was curtailed as East and West Germany reunited and the Japanese stock market plunged. So although foreign capital pumped into the United States has compensated for the gaping hole in our domestic savings pool in the past, turning off the spigot would cause U.S. interest rates to escalate. Furthermore, the U.S. budget deficit is so large that it raises capital costs across the globe. The drain on the world's savings by our deficit is not inconsequential.

But the point is that although a low U.S. savings rate may be a threat in the future, it does not fully account for the present gap in capital costs. A quick look at how global markets work illustrates further why interest rates have little impact on international competitiveness. Assume, for example, that the prevailing interest rate in Japan is 7 percent in yen and that in the United States the typical corporate borrowing rate is 10 percent in dollars. Thanks to global capital markets that efficiently arbitrage differences in currencies, this means that the market consensus calls for the U.S. dollar to depreciate by 3 percent relative to the Japanese yen over the next year. This expected currency depreciation could be the result of a number of factors; it really does not matter for the purposes of this discussion.

If a Japanese semiconductor company were to sell its products in the United States, it would receive some of its revenues in dollars. Having borrowed in yen to produce its semiconductors, including those sold in the United States, part of its loan payments would have to be made by converting dollar profits into yen. It takes time to produce and ship products, collect on sales, and convert the profits back into one's home currency. Since dollars are expected to depreciate relative to the yen by 3 percent a year, the true borrowing cost to the Japanese company that competes in the United States is not simply its yen-denominated interest rate, but also the depreciation in the value of the dollar revenues it receives for the products sold in the United States. In this case, the cost to the Japanese company to finance its U.S. sales would be its 7 percent annual interest rate plus the 3-percent annual currency depreciation, which would equal 10 percent. This would be the same borrowing cost faced by the U.S. producer who borrows in dollars to manufacture semiconductors in the United States.

On the other hand, if the American company were to sell its semiconductors in Japan, it would receive a currency (yen) that was *appreciating* by 3 percent. This would *lower* its borrowing cost for products sold in Japan from 10 percent to 7 percent, putting the American company on an equal footing with the Japanese competitor.

If you, as a U.S. manager, lacked confidence in the efficiency of the global currency market where over $500 billion is traded around the clock daily, you could simply project how much business your company expected to do in Japan and borrow the amount of capital needed to directly finance that business in yen at a cost of 7 percent. Then your yen profits could pay off a yen loan with no currency risk, and you would have the same interest cost as a Japanese competitor. In other words, based on the way global capital markets function, it is hard to argue that over the long term interest rates produce major capital-cost disparities. Therefore, exclusively blaming low personal savings rates and the federal budget deficit for the current U.S. cost-of-capital problem is misguided.

Taxes Are Not the Answer Either

The other principal scapegoat for global capital-cost differentials is taxes. Taxes get blamed for many of the problems in our economy, but they are just another red herring in the cost-of-capital debate. The tax codes in Japan and Germany tend to tax capital more heavily at the corporate level and more leniently at the investor level than does the U.S. tax code. Unfortunately, comparing all three countries' tax burden on capital is difficult because of myriad differences in aspects of the tax code other than marginal rates. Tax credits, deductions, and allowances also differ a great deal among countries.

One clear differential is frequently blamed for raising U.S. capital costs. The U.S. tax code penalizes equity investments more than most other countries'. In the United States, corporate profits are taxed twice. American investors are virtually the only providers of capital worldwide who effectively receive no tax relief on capital gains income and who are fully taxed on dividend income.

This discrepancy has not gone unnoticed. The capital gains tax was one of the hot political issues in the budget battles of 1990. This debate was waged more over who would benefit directly from capital gains tax relief than on the basis of its economic merits, and the administration's proposal was gutted. Also, the double taxation of corporate profits in the United States will be receiving greater attention following a 1991 Treasury Department analysis of how to integrate the corporate and personal tax systems.

However, proposals to dramatically lower taxes are likely to go nowhere until the deficit is reduced. Even if it were possible from a budgetary perspective, removing the double taxation of corporate profits has surprisingly little support within the business community. Despite the fact that tax integration would lower the cost of capital and make American companies more competitive, executives in low-growth companies generally do not support it because they fear it would put greater pressure on them to pay out excess cash in the form of dividends to their shareholders, which they would prefer to keep and invest.

Providing relief on capital gains taxes and the double taxation of corporate profits would certainly help lower America's cost of capital. But taxes still do not explain the differences in global capital costs. The Germans and Japanese are not happy with their tax codes either. Both corporate and personal tax rates are higher in Germany and Japan than in the United States. In fact, a study by the Federal Reserve Bank of New York on international differences in the cost of capital explicitly rejects the notion that different levels of taxation determine the cost-of-capital gap.[4] This conclusion is also supported by international tax experts with whom I consulted when preparing a policy paper on the cost of capital for the Treasury Department.

Capital Allocation and Monitoring

Some economists argue that if savings and taxes do not cause disparities in global capital costs, these widely discussed differences do not exist. When it comes to debating the cost of capital, semantics is a tremendous handicap. For example, the economic concept of "agency costs," which are the costs incurred when providers of capital invest their money through agents (corporate managers), is regarded by some as a cost-of-capital problem. By others it is not. The same is true with the costs of financial distress, information asymmetries and other concepts presented earlier in this book. Since each of these factors influences the required returns on an investment, I have chosen to include them under the umbrella of the cost of capital. These factors are picked up in the way that the cost of capital is measured in some of the studies because they influence capital structures and the observed, required returns of shareholders.

There are several macroeconomic factors that may partially explain cost-of-capital disparities between nations. For example, a steady national economy with consistent monetary and fiscal policy would reduce economic volatility. Also, the fact that cross-border capital investment generally involves debt, rather than equity securities, may imply that integrated world markets have not arbitraged differences in stock values as well as in the bond markets. However, it is also useful to look beyond macroeconomic factors to how capital is allocated and monitored within each country. Different financial systems in various countries determine how informed capital providers are, how well they are able to target investment opportunities with the greatest promise, and how comfortable they are that their capital is being deployed efficiently. These structural factors, which have been consistently overlooked, can be boiled down into one issue: the relationships between capital providers and capital users in the United States are distant, if not antagonistic, which raises the risks of investing in American companies, thus raising the returns required by providers of capital.

The Role of Leverage

Contrary to popular belief, American companies are actually *underleveraged* by international standards. Although there are various ways to measure leverage, based on either book or market values, U.S. companies appear to use less debt than their German and Japanese competitors.* In the past decade leverage has increased in the United States and decreased in Germany and Japan, so the gap has narrowed, but it still exists.

Debt is always cheaper than equity for reasons discussed earlier. It follows then that companies that operate with more debt and less equity—assuming there is no greater risk in doing so—will have a lower overall cost of capital. A simple illustration will prove this point.

Using the previous example in this chapter, assume that a company can borrow money at a pretax rate of 10 percent (6

---

* The gap on a market value basis was thought to have declined considerably as of the end of 1989; however, a 40-percent drop in Japanese stock prices in 1990 once again left Japanese companies more highly leveraged on a market value basis. They are much more highly leveraged on a book value basis.

percent after-tax), and that its shareholders require a 15-percent return to purchase or hold their stock. Also, assume that a typical American company is capitalized with one-third debt and two-thirds equity, and a German competitor with two-thirds debt and one-third equity. If both companies had the exact same tax rates as well as an identical cost of debt and equity—and because of structural factors each faced identical levels of risk even though one was more leveraged*—the German company would have a substantial advantage in its cost of capital because of its capital structure. The American company would face a cost of capital 33 percent higher than the German company's (12 percent versus 9 percent). This is enough to make a substantial difference in a competitive situation.

Leverage is not patently evil. What is harmful is the risk associated with debt, which restricts a company's ability to pursue a competitive operating strategy. The German and the Japanese systems make debt less risky. In a speech to students at the Harvard Business School, Warren Buffett compared operating a business with large amounts of leverage to driving a car with a dagger in the steering wheel pointed at the driver. Drivers would clearly be much more meticulous in their driving, but if they hit an unexpected bump in the road it could prove to be fatal. Debt in the United States is like a dagger, but in Japan and Germany it is more like a paddle. As discussed in Chapter 5, America's competitors can lower their capital costs through leverage without becoming preoccupied with quarterly cash flows because their debt is more flexible, thanks to closer relationships between borrowers and lenders.

---

* Among the evidence to support this assumption is the fact that both German and Japanese companies experience *fewer* bankruptcies in spite of greater leverage.

The Risks of Ownership

Another reason that capital costs are higher in the United States than in Germany and Japan is that required equity returns are greater. According to most studies, investors in the stocks of U.S. companies command a higher return than investors in the stocks of our foreign rivals.[5] Since U.S. companies operate with a greater percentage of equity than German and Japanese companies, this disparity is particularly alarming.

Some experts regard these studies with great skepticism because there is no universally accepted way to quantify the returns investors in stocks expect in the future. The most popular technique that economists have devised to measure equity costs relies on the fact that price/earnings multiples are dramatically higher in Japan and, to a lesser extent, in Germany than in the United States. This is true even after adjusting for accounting differences. This means that for every incremental dollar a Japanese or German company earns, its stock will go up further than an American competitor's will. Looked at another way, German and Japanese companies do not have to earn as much to make their share prices rise the same amount, which allows them to price their products more aggressively. Other methods besides using price/earnings multiples have shown similar results. Some studies look at return on equity ratios, and one study conducted by Burton Malkiel of Princeton University surveyed the expectations of stockholders.[6] Regardless of which approach is taken, surprisingly similar conclusions about equity costs have been reached.[7]

Perhaps the primary reason that equity is more expensive for U.S. companies is that shareholders in American businesses perceive greater risks. Because of the distant relationships between owners and the executives who run corporations, it is harder for shareholders to monitor a company's performance and to ensure that management is looking out for their interests. This is particularly true for larger public companies in the United States where ownership is highly fragmented, as detailed in Chapters 2 and 3. Additionally, because owners are not actively involved with corporations directly on an ongoing basis, they lack the information to know whether management's plans and strategies make sense, which raises a degree of uncertainty.

The trade-off between management accountability and the return required by investors has always been acknowledged for debt securities. If a company issues two bonds, one with no covenants and the other with restrictions on the company's behavior, to ensure that the bondholders' interests are protected and that bondholders are kept well informed, the bond with no covenants will obviously require a higher yield. The same principle applies to a stock. A stock that has little or no ownership rights involves greater risks, thus requires a higher return, than a share in the same company that enables the owner to influence who sits on the board and to hold management accountable for its performance.

Given the lack of constructive dialogue and accountability between shareholders and corporate officers in the United States, relationships between owners and managers have drifted apart. Business executives detest fickle owners who dump their shares in a heartbeat for a slight profit, and they especially loathe the takeover artists who purchase such shares. Owners, on the other hand, are frustrated by proxy rules that inhibit collective action and feel frozen out of the boardroom by a corporate governance system in which management handpicks directors and then constructs impenetrable barriers to prevent outsiders from replacing board members. It does not matter whether one views this void as contributing to poor corporate performance or raising the risks of stock ownership and escalating the cost of equity. In either case, this problem affects investor time horizons.

One of the fatal mistakes business leaders make is to assume that their cost of equity does not matter unless they plan to issue new shares to finance growth (and few companies have issued stock in recent years). Nothing could be further from the truth. Remember that the value of a company is the sum of all future cash flows that shareholders expect to receive through dividends or stock appreciation, discounted by the return required by the shareholders, which is the cost of equity. A higher discount rate, or cost of equity, translates into a lower stock value even if expectations about a company's future prospects remain constant. That may be why Pennsylvania-based companies saw their share prices plunge when the state enacted a law severely limiting shareholder rights.

Sadly, the strong performance of stocks in the United States in recent years has produced complacency in many quarters. But even the booming U.S. stock market of the 1980s failed to keep pace with securities markets in the rest of the world. Between 1985 and 1990, when the U.S. equity markets more than doubled in value, stocks in Japan, Germany, France, Italy, Switzerland, the United Kingdom, and virtually every other developed country outpaced American equities.

The evidence is overwhelming—America has a cost-of-capital problem. And conventional wisdom about the cost of capital is not going to solve it. Increasing savings and lowering taxes are both important to our nation's economic health. But to achieve competitive capital costs, we must address the structural factors that inflate the U.S. cost of capital. How well informed capital providers are and how much confidence they have in the systems through which the use of their capital is monitored are important components of the cost and availability of capital. As long as our financial system promotes distant relationships between U.S. companies and their capital providers, America will continue to suffer from a high cost of capital which will perpetuate the short-term behavior that is at the heart of our country's competitiveness problem.

7

Management Compensation Plans —Panacea or Placebo?

With shareholders treating stocks more as financial commodities than ownership stakes, corporations and state legislatures dismantling the traditional system of corporate accountability, significant barriers being erected to deter unsolicited takeovers, and the demise of relationship banking, the options for harmonizing the interests of capital providers and capital users are limited. The most popular solution appears to be management compensation plans. By merging their economic fates, the argument goes, corporate managers and their investors will work together to achieve results that enrich them both.

Although this seems intuitively obvious, the evidence indicates that present management compensation systems are not effective in achieving this goal. Furthermore, there is reason to believe that no management incentive system will unilaterally solve the problem of focusing corporate managers' attention on the long-run value of a business. Interestingly, incentive compensation is hardly ever used in Germany and Japan.

In a highly publicized *Harvard Business Review* article titled, "CEO Incentives—It's Not How Much You Pay, But How," Michael Jensen and Kevin Murphy claimed that 1) annual changes in executive compensation fail to reflect changes in corporate performance; 2) compensation for chief executives varies no more than for most hourly and salaried employees; and 3) CEO compensation is becoming less sensitive to performance, rather than the reverse.[1] Jensen and Murphy argue that by making CEOs substantial owners of company stock so that their wealth is tied closely to shareholder returns, corporate values will be maximized. Executive compensation guru Graef Crystal tested this hypothesis. What he found was startling: there is no correlation between pay sensitivity to stock performance and the actual wealth gains that accrue to the shareholders.[2]

How could such a straightforward concept as tying management pay to shareholder value not prove effective in practice? There are three principal reasons:

1. Reward systems that tie compensation to overall corporate success are difficult to implement at levels below senior management.
2. For compensation packages to influence executive behavior, they must be able to affect the lifestyle of top managers who already have substantial incomes and net worths.
3. Existing incentive devices can have undesirable side effects that often prevent them from achieving their intended result.

Performance Pay below the Top

In his book *Rewarding Results*, Kenneth Merchant examines the difficulties in motivating profit center managers through financial rewards.[3] Merchant conducted extensive field studies at 54 profit centers in 12 corporations involved in a variety of industries. He concludes that the ideal "motivational contract" would have the following characteristics:

- Performance measures are consistent with the overall corporate goal of maximizing shareholder value.
- Managers are only measured on factors they can control.

- Measures used to assess performance are accurate.
- Standards are clearly pre-defined and challenging.
- Rewards are meaningful to the employee but not excessively expensive to the corporation.
- The system is simple enough for everyone to understand it.

Merchant concluded that none of the reward systems he studied met all of the above criteria. The inability to measure shareholder value-creation at the profit center level makes most companies rely on accounting measures to assess performance. According to Merchant, accounting measures are inherently shortsighted because they focus on historical results, typically on a quarterly or annual basis. With accounting measurements there is no way to consider strategic position, market share, the value of technologies, employee morale, and other factors that contribute to success and are usually reflected in share prices. Merchant also concludes: 1) that most compensation plans do not differentiate between controllable and uncontrollable events; 2) plans are often complex, which leads to frustration among employees; 3) profit center managers resist standards that are challenging; and 4) often objectives are not preset which breeds uncertainty and distrust. Furthermore, motivational reward systems are frequently used for alternative reasons such as to retain managers or to smooth corporate earnings reports, which biases their initial design and undermines their effectiveness in influencing decisions.

A logical alternative to measuring the performance of mid-level managers based on return on investment or some other accounting standard would be to tie all employees' pay to share prices. However, this approach can also create a number of problems. First, managers below the highest echelon have very little control over the success of the entire corporation. A manufacturing manager in the Buick division of General Motors, for example, would be happy with stock-related bonuses when share prices are rising. But if the stock falls, he or she will complain that it was because of weak results in the Pontiac or Chevrolet division, or that it was the marketing department's fault.

In 1990, Du Pont terminated one of the most ambitious pay-incentive programs in American industry for just such reasons. The company's "achievement sharing" plan was designed to give 20,000 fibers division employees a greater stake in the success of their division. The program provided employees larger-than-average raises when divisional profits exceeded goals and penalized pay when profits fell short of expectations. In the first two years when results were favorable, the employees raved about the program. But in 1990, when results lagged targets, there was an uproar from top managers and plant workers alike as it became obvious that they would lose 2 percent to 4 percent of their income because of weak divisional results. The plan was canceled to prevent a serious erosion in morale.

Obviously, workers who spend what they make experience pain when compensation declines. While this is beneficial in terms of using pay to influence behavior, it also makes these employees far more resistant to any compensation program that has a down-side. Consequently, below the senior management ranks there is tremendous resistance to pay packages tied to results for which an individual is not entirely responsible.

Pay Must Make a Difference

Many of the problems faced in motivating profit center and other mid-level managers to maximize corporate performance should disappear among the ranks of top executives. Those who control corporate decisions have a meaningful impact on the share price, which incorporates factors that cannot be measured solely by accounting norms. Therefore, performance measures can be longer term and simpler just by using share price as a yardstick. Since the overall success of the company is the responsibility of senior managers, uncontrollable events are less of a concern. And since top managers' pay is determined by the board of directors,

theoretically it should be possible to establish challenging performance standards, even if management is resistant.

However, the lack of independence of compensation committees of boards and the fact that compensation consultants are hired
directly by management rather than the board are serious impediments to establishing effective reward packages for top executives. But a more rudimentary problem is perhaps a greater
barrier: it is difficult to pay top U.S. executives enough money to
materially affect their lifestyle. Incentive packages may affect
what senior executives save, but not what they spend.

An incremental 10-percent or 20-percent performance bonus
might change the attitude of someone on the factory floor who
wants to buy a new car, but it is far less likely to alter the perspective of an executive who has received six- or seven-digit incomes
for years and drives whatever car he or she wishes. The typical
chief executive of a large American company now makes more
than 100 times the average wage of a factory worker.[4] That means
it is at least 100 times harder to influence their behavior with an
incremental dollar of pay.

Total Executive Compensation

The drive to link executive compensation with the fate of shareholders has encouraged boards to structure pay packages for
corporate managers that contain greater performance incentives
than in the past. What boards have failed to do is build in any
downside for poor performance. They have simply heaped stock
options, grants, and bonuses on top of salaries, which were already
escalating rapidly in the 1980s. Consequently, there has been an
explosion in executive compensation over the past decade. The
annual growth rate of top management pay outstripped that of
U.S. production workers by a factor of greater than two during the
last 10 years; when compounded over 10 years the actual percentage difference is much greater. According to *Business Week,*
worker pay escalated 53 percent in the 1980s while CEO pay went
up 212 percent. This occurred during a period when the top

marginal tax rate plunged from about 70 percent to approximately 30 percent, causing after-tax income to grow even faster.

Business Week determined that the top two executives in the 500 largest U.S. companies average more than $2 million in salary and bonus a year. After adding in various types of long-term incentives, Graef Crystal found top executives at the 200 largest companies averaged approximately $3 million annually in total compensation, *excluding* fringe benefits and perquisites.

These compensation levels are unmatched anywhere in the world. In terms of purchasing power (net pay adjusted for the cost of goods and services) the compensation consulting firm Towers, Perrin, Forster & Crosby determined that U.S. chief executive pay was over twice that in Germany, France, and the United Kingdom, and over three times that of the average Japanese chief executive in 1989. If TPF&C had used the largest U.S. companies in this analysis, the gap would have been considerably wider.

At the largest Japanese companies, top executives earn about 17 times the average worker's pay; in the United States that multiple is 109.[5] German and French executives receive more pay relative to the work force than the Japanese, and the British even more than their European counterparts. But even British CEOs are paid only 35 times the typical worker, or about a third of the multiple we find in large U.S. companies. Without placing value judgments on whether these levels of pay for the business leaders in America are warranted or proper, the important conclusion is that an incremental amount of income will probably not influence behavior to the extent it might in countries where the disparity is not so great.

Take, for example, a chief executive who earns a base salary of $700,000 a year. Assume that by meeting targets that are readily achievable by merely staying the course, the executive could make another $500,000 in year-end cash bonus and another $800,000 in long-term stock-related compensation, for a total annual income of $2 million. By restructuring the company to get rid of nonproductive business units, and aggressively investing the proceeds in the next generation of technology, the CEO might be able to increase the company's long-term performance significantly and raise the long-term incentive portion of his or her pay by 50 percent, or another $400,000. This strategy, however, might hurt earnings in the next few years, which could cut the cash bonus in half, or by $250,000 (assuming the bonus was highly sensitive to performance, which they typically are not). With only four or five years until retirement, given this scenario the aggressive restructuring would yield the CEO an incremental $150,000 a year when everything is added up, which amounts to a 7.5 percent boost in total compensation.

Is it worth the risk and headaches of upsetting the status quo to receive what translates into an extra 7.5-percent boost in pay, especially if the incremental amount would most likely go into some trust fund rather than affect the spending habits of the executive? The answer for many may well be no, especially if the restructuring involved closing a plant in the company's home town or laying off workers who are members of the CEO's church or country club.

Director Compensation

It may be even harder to influence board decisions through pay schemes. Most directors are high-paid executives of other companies. Board members receive annual retainers that range up to $65,000, plus fees for attending each board or committee meeting. In addition to cash compensation, one-fifth of the companies surveyed by TPF&C provided directors golden parachutes, and about 60 percent offer directors pension plans as well as life, accident, and health insurance, even though these individuals are generally covered elsewhere. Many directors receive special perks. Chrysler provides its boards members with the use of *two* new cars a year, and United Airlines provides directors with unlimited free air travel.

Board fees do not appear to be based on stock performance. The second-highest paid board is that of Time Warner, whose members receive annual retainers of $60,000. These are the directors who refused to let the Time shareholders vote to accept an offer for the company at a substantial premium and then structured an acquisition of Warner—rather than a merger—in order to skirt shareholder approval. The company's stock plummeted as a result.

Institutional Shareholder Services has developed a comprehensive data base on board members of large public companies to assist institutional investors in evaluating corporate board nominees. In its initial research, ISS discovered that 222 of 4,780 directors in its data base owned fewer than 5 *shares* of the company on whose board they serve. The Analysis Group has found that companies whose boards own larger percentages of stock outperform those whose boards own fewer shares. Yet only one of 325 companies surveyed by TPF&C, Primerica, pays its directors' entire retainer in stock. Among the 20 percent of companies that pay directors partially in stock, the median total fee is almost 50 percent higher than the median for all companies, so they too appear to add equity incentives on top of cash payments.[6] In addition to substantial compensation for directors, shareholders of the average company also spend $1.3 million a year on insurance to protect their directors and officers from lawsuits that might be brought by the shareholders themselves.

Pay Packages Can Have Unexpected Side Effects

The other shortcoming in trying to use pay to weave together the interests of corporate decision makers and the company's investors is that no one has yet developed an incentive package that has been proven effective. Since 1980, executive pay has shifted from a mix of 60 percent current pay and 40 percent performance-related to 60 percent performance-driven. Have American executives become more long-term oriented in the past decade as a result? Statistically, the correlation between incentive-based executive compensation plans such as restricted stock and corporate performance is weak.[7]

Each of the typical forms of incentive pay have deficiencies that can lead to perverse behavior. Stock options are a classic example. If an executive stands to make a lot of money by exercising stock options in the future, he or she would obviously be motivated to drive up the price of the stock. On the surface, therefore, it seems like options would promote behavior that maximized returns to the investors. However, option holders do not receive dividend payments, so they would rather see the company retain its profits, reinvesting cash in projects likely to produce even lackluster profits, than pay it out to the shareholders. Shareholders of a mature or declining business that lacks the opportunity to profitably reinvest all the cash it is generating would prefer to have the company pay out its excess cash in the form of dividends; they could then reinvest the cash elsewhere, perhaps in the stock of a growth company. Rather than being motivated to make decisions that maximize the *total* return to shareholders, the executive motivated primarily with options would be inclined to hoard unneeded cash. So what appears to be a logical compensation scheme on the surface has the potential of working against the shareholders' interest and prevents capital from being recycled to industries that need it most for growth and investment.

Executive compensation plans can be the proverbial tail wagging the dog. Ideally, companies should assess their competitive environment, establish the optimal strategy given existing constraints and resources, and then structure a management compensation plan to motivate key employees to behave in a manner consistent with that strategy. In practice, however, it is easy for senior and mid-level managers to take the existing pay system as given, and then craft a strategy that produces results that maximize their pay under the present system. Using pay to drive behavior is a risky proposition since even when compensation plans work, they can promote the wrong behavior if not carefully designed and continuously altered as strategies evolve.

One of the reasons that "performance" packages are often not very sensitive to performance, or are designed to achieve objectives other than value-maximization, is that top executives have substantial influence in how their own pay is determined. The consultants who evaluate and design executive compensation plans are almost always selected and hired by the chief executive, not by an independent committee of the board. Most boards of public companies have a compensation committee, but the consultant seldom reports directly to it. These consultants report to the CEO who pays their bill and determines whether they are rehired. They are not likely to recommend compensation schemes to the board totally out of line with what the chief executive is willing to live with. Otherwise, they could lose a client. Furthermore, the compensation committees of boards that approve pay packages are frequently filled with the CEO's closest allies. Because of the chief executive's significant influence over his or her own pay scheme, many of the so-called performance packages prove to be simply additional income.

Cash Bonuses

Annual cash bonuses are paid at most public companies, and they are usually tied to a mix of year-end performance measures such as net profit, return on equity, or growth in market share. But are these bonuses really subject to performance? In a study by Michael Jensen and Kevin Murphy, the authors concluded that the annual percentage change in cash compensation, i.e., salary plus bonus, for the typical chief executive fluctuated no more than the pay of a group of 10,000 randomly selected workers at all levels.[8] This is because in some cases there appears to be no rhyme or reason to what drives the level of bonus paid to top executives. In 1988, the bonus received by Rand Araskog, the CEO of ITT, surged by 49 percent to $1.1 million from $740,000 the previous year. However, in 1988 the company's return on equity decreased 4 percent and earnings per share before extraordinary items dropped by 17 percent. In 1990, Araskog's total pay skyrocketed to over $7 million on a 4-percent increase in profits. Following the Exxon Valdez incident, Exxon's net profit dropped almost $2 billion. Yet CEO Lawrence Raul's salary and bonus went up. These are not isolated cases.[9]

Many bonus plans kick in at extremely low performance levels, occasionally before a company's return on equity even matches the returns available on riskless Treasury securities. This is not exactly holding management's feet to the fire. Boards that do not make bonus thresholds legitimate achievements tied to peer performance, stock performance, and/or other measures that reflect the creation of value are simply supplementing an executive's base salary and disguising it as an incentive.

Stock Options

The most common form of long-term compensation, and the most rapidly growing form of executive pay, is stock options. Typically, an option grant offers an executive the right to purchase a certain number of shares at any time over the following 10 years at a designated "strike price." The strike price is what the executive has to pay for the shares when the options are exercised, and it is almost always set as the market price at the time the options are granted. Stock options usually are fully vested after three to four years. The average amount of stock optioned to chief executives of the 200 largest American companies from 1986 to 1988 was $5.6 million.

Proponents argue that options are an efficient mechanism for linking executive compensation to changes in shareholder wealth. If the stock price goes up, the executive—along with the owners—reaps the harvest. However, there are shortcomings with option plans, including the incentive to hoard cash, already discussed. Options are a carrot with no stick. Since option holders have no capital at risk, they feel no pain if the stock price declines. So option holders are not really in the same boat as the shareholders.

This problem is compounded by the fact that boards have been known to reissue new options to executives if the price of their company's stock drops after the original grant. Frank Lorenzo, the former chief executive of Continental Airlines, was originally granted options with a strike price of $29 a share. After piloting the company close to a crash landing, he still managed to make money on those options when Scandinavian Airlines System bought out his shares for $10 each. His board had ratcheted down the strike price over the years to an effective level of $4.63 a share. CPA firm Peat Marwick reported in 1991 that 28 companies had made such revisions.

Unfortunately, other shareholders cannot exchange their shares for ones with a lower basis. In fact, one study of option plans at more than 150 large companies concluded that profits on options are more closely correlated to the size of the grant than to the movement of the stock price.[10] In other words, the way to make money on options is through a generous board rather than by improving the market value of the company.

One way to address this problem would be to tie the strike price of management stock options to a scale reflecting minimum performance, so that the option only pays off if the stock rises above a certain threshold. For example, the strike price might ascend each year by the interest rate on long-term government securities. The option holder, therefore, only benefits to the extent that his or her company's stock outperforms a riskless investment.

Perhaps one reason the use of options has escalated in recent years is that stock options have a stealth effect on the company's financial statements. It is possible for generous grants to go undetected in reported results. Unlike salaries and bonuses, stock options are not reflected as a compensation expense in the company's income statements. Instead, the stockholders bear the cost of options in the form of dilution to their existing ownership. Because of this accounting treatment, stock options are clearly not a "pay as you go" incentive plan. The shareholders pay only a small portion of the expense of options each year because they are, in effect, charged off in perpetuity by a slightly lower earnings per share because of the incremental number of shares. These shares never go away, even after the executive retires.

This disclosure is much less likely to catch people's attention than if the value of option awards was reflected as a reduction in company earnings at the time they were issued. In fact, if the executive does not exercise his or her options until after he or she retires, the amount made on them is not disclosed in the proxy statement, where details as to executive compensation are provided. Consequently, the shareholders may never know how well they have compensated top management.

Stock Grants

Rather than issue options, many companies simply prefer to issue shares of restricted stock to key employees. Stock grants are the quickest way to increase the equity ownership of corporate managers. The need to increase executive shareholdings has become a particular concern in recent years because equity ownership by top executives had actually declined during the decade leading up to 1985. The median dollar value of shares held by CEOs fell from $2,022,000 to $1,777,000 from 1974 to 1985 in constant 1985 dollars.

During this same period NYSE stocks more than doubled, which means there was a much greater decline in the proportion of an executive's net worth tied up in shares of his or her own company. In fact, in 1987, the median stock holdings by CEOs in the companies they ran represented less than two years' income according to a *Forbes* Executive Compensation Survey.

With restricted stock grants, the recipient has full voting privileges and the right to receive dividends. However, the grantee cannot sell these shares for a designated time period, and if the employee leaves the company prior to the vesting of the shares, the stock is forfeited. In essence, restricted stock is a deferred equity bonus that is contingent upon the executive's continued service. The goal of restricted stock plans is to encourage executives to focus on longer-term stock appreciation.

Critics claim, however, that stock grants are another example of supplemental rewards without risk. To the extent that executives do not contribute any of their own money or forego any salary to secure the grants, they have no real downside. And unlike options, which can become worthless if the stock drops below the strike price, restricted stock will still have some value as long as the company is solvent.

During the three years leading up to his attempted leveraged buyout of RJR Nabisco, Ross Johnson's board granted him over 200,000 shares of restricted stock that was worth about $20 million when the company was ultimately sold to Kohlberg Kravis Roberts. Because of a loophole in SEC reporting requirements, RJR's shareholders never learned about most of these grants until after the takeover. Martin Davis, CEO of Paramount Communications, received a stock grant worth approximately $24 million in a single year. Although the company's stock dropped by 50 percent over its previous year's high in the ensuing 12 months, these shares were still worth a princely sum.

One suggestion to overcome the fact that executives have none of their own money at risk when granted stock options or restricted stock is to make them pay for all or part of the grants. The problem with this remedy is that the executive may end up with all his or her eggs in one basket. If their income and investments are tied up in a single company, their net worth is undiversified. The only way to minimize financial risk, therefore, would be to diversify the company, which has proven to be an ineffective way to create value for the shareholders. In other words, there is no easy remedy to many of the shortcomings with management compensation schemes; otherwise, they would have already been tried.

Golden Parachutes

Golden parachutes have now been granted to one-half of the CEOs of large public companies. A golden parachute guarantees an executive a significant sum of cash in the event that there is a change in control of the company. Among the more celebrated golden parachutes are those granted to six executives of Beatrice

Corporation before it was purchased in a 1985 LBO. One officer, who had been at the company only 13 months, received $2.7 million. Another received $7 million, although he had already retired from the company and had just returned seven months earlier. That same year, the chairman of Revlon received a $35-million package to turn over the keys of a company many thought was not being well run.

While not technically a golden parachute, perhaps the most egregious executive pay plan that was triggered by a change in control involved Stephen Ross of Warner Communications, who did not even lose his job. When Time Inc. merged with Warner, Ross retained his position, pocketed $75 million in cash, and had another $93 million allocated to a trust fund.[11] While golden parachutes are common for senior executives, only one in 60 factory workers receives similar protection.

Golden parachutes theoretically allow an executive to be willing to sacrifice his or her job for the sake of the shareholders by agreeing to a takeover. But since most takeover targets are underperformers, rewarding executives in vulnerable companies essentially eliminates one of the primary risks of poor performance. Some people argue that golden parachutes even provide an incentive for top executives to sell the company when they approach retirement age rather than continue to maximize its value as an independent entity.

* * * *

Executive compensation plans are not a panacea for America's shortsightedness. In many ways they are simply a placebo. After assessing how these plans work in reality, not just in theory, it is easy to conclude that management pay is not an effective motivator. When it does work, it often motivates the wrong kind of behavior. Perhaps if we had more compensation consultants who told boards what they needed to hear rather than what senior management wanted them to say, it would help. Then perhaps we might find better ways to tie executive rewards to the long-term performance of their enterprise. But pay alone will never prove to be a substitute for effective accountability.

8

A Cure for Myopia

The preceding chapters have shown that shortsightedness in the business and investment communities is not a myth, but a very dangerous reality—one that needs to be addressed for America to remain the most competitive nation on earth. We all like simple solutions to difficult problems. Unfortunately, what is needed to cure the chronic myopia undermining America's competitiveness is a complex solution to a simple problem. Short-termism will not go away by simply thinking longer term. We also need to address the business practices, investment strategies, and government regulations that make up the Rubik's cube of business myopia.

In recent years the goals of our economic system have become murkier. Should companies pursue profits or market share? Should boards attempt to maximize shareholder value or give priority to the immediate needs of employees, customers, and communities? Should institutional investors use their power to promote social objectives or economic goals? Should the government become more involved with directing business decisions or leave businesses alone? Should the economy be structured to conform to our legal system, or should we reconfigure our legal system to promote our economy? Confusion breeds indecision; indecision breeds atrophy; and in a rapidly changing world, atrophy breeds failure.

Many people believe we need to rethink the capitalistic ideals that have served as the underpinning of the U.S. economy for centuries. Today these ideals no longer seem to be working. American corporations are losing ground both at home and abroad. U.S. workers have seen real wages decline. And most people believe their children will not have the same level of opportunity they had.

But the problem is not that capitalism no longer works. The problem is that the United States no longer practices capitalism. Despite all the economic and military successes of our country during the "American Century," we have become complacent and lost discipline. We have stretched ideals, laws, and regulations to the point that their purpose is no longer being served. Without recognizing how our financial system has evolved, we run the danger of dismissing as flawed principles we are not even practicing.

America's economy was founded on the belief that markets work. Yet the United States now operates the most heavily regulated financial system on earth. Banks cannot underwrite securities or own stocks. A simple loan agreement that is two pages in Japan requires hundreds of pages in the United States. Investors cannot talk to each other about companies they own without disclosing their discussions to federal regulators. Stockholders cannot vote the shares they own if they accumulate a significant percentage of certain companies' stock. Institutions that should be long-term investors are prohibited from owning a meaningful stake in any individual company or trying to influence its behavior. This is not capitalism. Yet most of the solutions surfaced so far to deal with these sort of problems entail *more* regulations or new taxes to change existing behavior.

The system designed to provide constructive tension between suppliers of capital and users of capital has been dismembered. The goal of capitalism never has been—and never should be—to perpetuate the existence of specific corporations. Rather, the objective of capitalism is to deploy the limited resources of our country in the most efficient manner possible, to create the greatest wealth possible, and to produce the highest standard of living possible for our citizens.

How can we say that the unbridled pursuit of value-maximization has undermined our country's ability to compete when many of our competitiveness problems began during an era in which corporations were turned into mutual funds, destroying shareholder value in the process. The conglomerates of the 1960s and 1970s were formed in spite of the fact that share prices declined in a majority of the cases after these transactions were consummated.[1] The market said then that most of these deals did not make sense. Yet when deals were announced in the 1980s to disassemble these conglomerates and share prices rose, corporations and policy makers implemented measures to prevent those transactions from occurring, once again ignoring the market.

U.S. banks are in serious trouble, and as the primary suppliers of capital to business, that does not bode well for our economy. The reason banks have embarked on risky lending junkets is that they have been severely handcuffed and are unable to establish close relationships with their traditional corporate customers. The emergence of global financial markets and new technologies in recent years has illuminated the problems of excessive regulations and made U.S. commercial banks anachronisms. Yet many in Congress want to solve the problem by burdening banks with heavier shackles. Meanwhile, small uncompetitive banks that exist only because the federal government insures their deposits argue for the status quo, as do many insurance companies that convinced Congress to enact legislation exempting them from federal antitrust laws in 1945.[2]

Every year the vast majority of professional money managers and mutual funds produce results below what a monkey could achieve by selecting stocks randomly out of a barrel. Yet the United States spends up to $25 billion annually to shuffle stock certificates. The solution most often proposed to curb excessive stock trading is to tax stock transactions; there has been very little interest in removing the barriers that prevent professional investors from behaving as long-term owners in the first place.

Business managers and investors are *not* irrational people. They do not operate with a short-term focus for mysterious reasons. They are reacting rationally to the system in which they operate. Short-term behavior will not disappear unless that system is changed.

Relationships and Common Goals

The economic fate of our nation is in the hands of those who provide capital and those who use capital. As long as their relationship remains distant or antagonistic, they will be unable to establish shared objectives that will be mutually beneficial in the long run. Today's self-serving practices inhibit communications and erode trust, making it harder to channel capital in the direction of the greatest opportunities and escalating the cost of capital by imposing unnecessary risks on investors. As Chapter 6 has shown, our nation's high cost of capital makes investments with long-term payoffs economically unattractive and imposes short-term strategies on corporations.

Throughout the preceding chapters, several of the business practices, laws, and regulations of other countries, particularly Japan and Germany, have been cited. These comparisons have been made simply to illustrate the superiority of cooperation over confrontation in the building of competitive enterprises. They are not intended as a template for reform in the United States. To simplemindedly attempt to mimic the financial system of a foreign country would be a mistake. Americans do not want a banking system like Germany's, where banks totally dominate the economy; where the power of Deutsche Bank's top executive rivals that of the chancellor. Nor would we ever be able to replicate the keiretsu system in which many Japanese companies operate, even if we wanted to. These cross-shareholdings and strong business ties are the product of generations of historical relationships and a much different culture. Besides, just because this system has worked in recent years does not mean it will continue to flourish as markets become more open. As stated at the outset, we need solutions that are uniquely American.

However, there are lessons to be learned from Germany and Japan that can be applied in any financial system. Obviously, a long-term perspective beats a short-term mentality, but there are more specific principles. The dominant investors in Japan and Germany are sophisticated owners with long-term horizons; banks work closely with their customers through good times and bad; corporations are held accountable for their performance; and poor performers are restructured in an *evolutionary* manner with the participation and consent of owners and creditors, rather than through *revolutionary* changes brought on by a takeover. Government regulators work cooperatively with business, often facilitating investor/manager relationships rather than enacting measures to insulate them from one another and letting the courts intervene to resolve disputes. Executive pay schemes are not the primary mechanism to encourage business leaders to make long-term decisions because the whole financial system discourages myopic behavior.

For many Americans there is a mystique to the long-term approach of investors and businesses in Japan and Germany. But if we take an objective look at how dramatically the practices and regulations that dictate economic behavior in our country have changed over the years, it becomes clear that America's shortsightedness is not simply the product of a cultural bias. We used to do what they do, only better.

The growing rift between capital providers and capital users in the United States has been a slow, gradual process. Perhaps for that reason it has gone largely unnoticed. Twenty-five years ago if you had told business leaders that by 1990 a corporation's most important constituent would no longer be its owners, that banks were going to abandon their customer relationships in pursuit of transactions, that investors would churn stocks through computer programs and ignore their voting responsibilities, and that companies would try to create value by buying and selling other companies rather than by building competitive, focused enterprises, they would likely have observed that this is a prescription for competitive disaster. But that is exactly what has happened.

Although we need to look back to those aspects of the past that made our economic system successful, we must also recognize that the world has changed dramatically. We live in a global economy with markets and technologies that were unthinkable a generation ago. We cannot ignore the evolutions of the past few decades, or the likely changes in the years to come, as we establish policies to guide our future.

The mission is achievable. America still has the people, the resources, and the desire to remain the world's greatest economy. What we are lacking are the right public policies, business relationships, and investment practices to keep us competitive. Harmonizing the interests of investors and corporate managers will take time and require leadership. But we must begin the process immediately. Instead of simply blaming other countries for our economic problems, we need to reform the laws and practices that we do have control over.

As we approach the next millennium, business leaders, institutional investors, bankers, and government policy makers each have a vital role to play in redirecting our financial system to provide an environment more conducive to cooperation. After spending a couple of years meeting with leaders in each of these groups, it is clear that no one thinks the problems are of their making. But someone must take the initiative. As we have seen with the restructuring of the savings and loan industry and the 1991 budget fiasco, bold measures by the government are often too little, too late. So the first steps must come from the private sector.

Within the private sector, the most likely group to initiate change is our nation's new powerful class of owners—institutional investors. They have the least to lose. Their current investment practices are an abysmal failure no matter how you measure them.

Furthermore, they are the obvious candidate: banks are even more hamstrung by regulations; and too many corporate leaders vehemently oppose working more closely with shareholders and lenders because it means that managers will be held more accountable for their performance by groups they do not trust.

When I was at the Treasury Department and the press picked up on the fact that I was reviewing corporate governance policy, I was invited to lunch by representatives of one of the most powerful business organizations in America. The message they conveyed—in no uncertain terms—was that corporate America liked things exactly the way they were with regard to corporate governance, and they would prefer that I not get the administration involved in reassessing the present system. The takeover market had been squelched, and there was no reason, in their view, to wake up the sleeping dogs—institutional investors. Later, when the SEC began a review of the proxy system, with the goal of improving shareholder/manager communications, the Business Roundtable sent a letter to the director of the SEC's Division of Corporation Finance, saying that the proxy system works just fine; reform is unnecessary. There is a lot of political power against progress. The business community has some very real fears that pension fund managers untrained in corporate strategies will take control of their companies. If institutional investors are going to be allowed greater involvement, they need to allay these fears.

A New Way to Invest

The United States desperately needs a class of long-term, sophisticated investors capable of working with corporations and providing constructive accountability. The principal owners of American corporations—pension funds and other institutional shareholders—face major hurdles in serving in this capacity. The most obvious one is that institutional investors currently lack the expertise to fill this role. Today's pension fund managers are trained in investment strategies and fiduciary law, not corporate strategies and corporate governance.

Some large investors are trying to improve these skills. New advisory services such as Institutional Shareholder Services and the Investor Responsibility Research Center have been formed to provide them with information and guidance on corporate governance matters. Perhaps the most powerful investor in the nation, the California Public Employees Retirement System, has spent a significant amount of time and money to take a more active role in corporate governance. With $60 billion in assets—$17 billion of which is invested in U.S. equities—CalPERS can afford to commit resources to this effort. But few others are following its lead for political and other reasons.

Although it has taken no steps as dramatic as initiating a proxy contest to replace a board, CalPERS has been the target of substantial criticism in the corporate community. How can these people who have never run a business (and none of whom earns more than $100,000 a year) tell large company boards what is right for their business, many ask. Institutional investors have a credibility problem. What they need is a surrogate that possesses the skills they lack and can circumvent many of the onerous laws and regulations that prevent institutions from taking a more active role directly.

Without waiting for the government to change any laws, institutional investors could bring about radical change in the way they interact with the corporations they own by investing in a new manner. Rather than allocating equity investments to money managers who constantly trade stocks, or to index fund managers who ignore the ownership component of investing, they could support the establishment of a new breed of investment firms whose approach is to make significant long-term investments in a limited number of companies. Such an investment firm would raise money from several pension funds and/or insurance companies, which it would then use to purchase a meaningful percentage, e.g., 10 percent to 20 percent, of the shares of one to two dozen corporations in unrelated businesses. By investing in this manner, these firms would limit their portfolio to a number of companies that could be actively monitored, have influence with each company, avoid antitrust problems, and achieve portfolio diversification. The firm would hold these stakes indefinitely, and its partners would become actively involved in learning each company's business. Their energies would be focused on improving the companies they own rather than changing which companies they own. A representative of the investment firm could sit on each company's board and have access to the confidential data that would allow them to provide informed, meaningful guidance. They would not simply scan a board book on the plane to a bimonthly board meeting. Since they would not be selling their stock regularly, having access to detailed inside data would not run afoul of securities laws.

These investors would have no interest in taking over the company, so they would not be a threat to corporate management. In fact, given their focus on long-term results, corporations should welcome them as the patient owners that are so desperately lacking today. And by combining a meaningful ownership stake with active involvement, these firms would provide the accountability that is so visibly absent from our present financial system.

Obviously, the backgrounds of the people who would manage this type of investment firm (the general partners) would need to be such that they could add value as board members and be respected by company management—not people trained in technical stock market analysis, but people trained in corporate strategy and corporate governance. By investing in this manner in a dozen or two companies in dissimilar businesses, the firm's assets would be well diversified. A portfolio of 15 stocks properly selected provides almost the same level of diversification as a portfolio of 500 stocks. By placing money with several such investment firms, institutional investors could, in effect, achieve the same level of diversification they now have by purchasing stocks in thousands of companies over which they have no influence. And by owning meaningful stakes through a surrogate, they would avoid the regulatory barriers (such as antitrust laws) that a pension fund would face if it tried to take on this role directly. In other words, by divvying up their equity investments to several such investment firms, institutional investors could have the best of both worlds—meaningful ownership stakes and broad diversification.

At the present time there is only one organization that invests in a manner similar to this, but it is not typically thought of as an investment firm. Berkshire Hathaway, the company controlled by Warren Buffett, essentially applies this investment philosophy. Most people credit Buffett's success to an uncanny ability to pick the right stocks, but if you read the annual reports of Berkshire Hathaway, you will find a very strong investment philosophy—one that relies on more than being able to outguess the market. How Buffett invests—large stakes with board representation in unrelated businesses—may be as important as which companies he selects. There is no reason that Buffett's investment vehicle could not just as easily be a private partnership rather than a public corporation. Most of the outside investors in Berkshire Hathaway are institutional investors, the same ones that the investment firms I am describing would go to for capital.

The investment banking firm Lazard Frères established an investment firm known as Corporate Partners, which operates somewhat along the lines I suggest. Corporate Partners raised $1.6 billion in 1988 to make large investments for extended periods. Representatives of the firm usually are represented on the boards of the companies in which it invests. However, Corporate Partners does not purchase common stock like the other shareholders. Because it invests in newly issued securities with terms superior to the other shareholders, and because it helped to rescue Polaroid when it was under siege, Corporate Partners has acquired a reputation as being used by companies as a takeover defense rather than as committed to the interests of all shareholders.

The version of this concept I propose is starting to receive some attention. Citing a speech I gave, a fall 1990, *Harvard Business*

Review article entitled, "Can Big Owners Make a Big Difference?" concluded:

> Such partnerships are as close as anyone has come to devising new mechanisms that begin to suggest the shareholder relationship that served GM so well in the 1920s. They deserve more attention and experimentation.[3]

Many of the institutional investors and business leaders with whom I have spoken about this concept think it is an idea whose time has come. However, it may take some time to catch on because the investment industry is extremely resistant to change. Institutional investors generally only invest through firms with a proven track record. Since no firm such as I describe exists, no one has a track record. Those who do have track records, i.e., traditional money managers, do not have the backgrounds and skills to make the concept viable.

Another impediment is the fact that many in the investment industry have a lot to lose if this concept becomes popular. As mentioned, the advisers used by institutional investors to approve new investment techniques are often paid in soft dollars, which would dry up if this method became popular. This investment approach would also erode the traditional business of money managers, brokers, and research analysts. Stocks would be traded less, generating fewer commission dollars, and these new investment firms would have little use for third-party research if they had access to better quality, firsthand information.

Finding the right people to put such a firm together will not be easy. A few former corporate raiders and LBO firms have made an attempt to raise investment money somewhat along these lines, but they have been unsuccessful. Those who participated in the takeover binge of the 1980s have a reputation of being too adversarial to be welcomed by corporate America. The managers of such a firm would have to be respected by corporate managers and institutional investors alike.

Some might argue that for an institutional investor to commit large sums of money to long-term investments would unduly expose them to equity risks since it would be difficult to shift funds to cash or bonds if they saw a declining stock market on the horizon. But in today's market, large portfolio managers have no reason to shy away from investing long-term in equities; if they want to reduce their exposure to equities, they can do so synthetically through the futures market rather than by selling stocks. Ironically, the stock futures that so many in corporate America abhor might prove to be part of the solution to patient capital. Further, there is no need for all investment to take this form. As in Japan and Germany, if enough stock was held by "permanent" owners, speculators could trade all they want—providing market liquidity—without having a meaningful impact on corporate decision making.

The Labor Department could help expedite adoption of this concept by reminding the private pension funds that having three-fourths of their money managers perform below average is not consistent with their fiduciary duty of investing for the sole benefit of plan beneficiaries. The Internal Revenue Service and the Federal Trade Commission could also help by constraining their zeal to regulate, and refrain from accusing institutional investors that invest in this manner of trying to engage in a business. The Unrelated Business Income Tax and Hart-Scott-Rodino should have no application for pension funds and others engaging in pure investment through such an investment firm.

Investors should not be asked to invest in this manner out of the kindness of their hearts or forced into it by legal mandate. By reducing transactions costs and injecting greater accountability into our economic system, the returns to investors should improve. In fact, when CDA Investment Technologies ranked 261 money managers based on their performance for the five-year period ending in 1990, the one that came out on top had invested the firm's $800 million in capital in only 10 stocks, holding each one for a lengthy period. Similarly, Berkshire Hathaway, has outperformed market averages by many multiples in five-, ten-, and fifteen-year comparisons. This investment approach appears to offer both investors and corporations enormous benefits.

Corporate Governance Reform

Simply changing the way investors behave will not fully bridge the gap between owners and managers. Many companies are now so heavily insulated from their owners that no rational investor would want to invest sufficient capital to acquire 10 percent to 20 percent of their stock. Unfortunately, it is often the very companies that need the most outside direction that have erected the greatest barriers to shareholder influence, inhibiting the market discipline that produces a competitive economy.

If business leaders are serious about addressing the shortsightedness problem in America, it is imperative that they take steps to lower their cost of capital. Otherwise, long-term investments will not be economically viable. The cost of equity is among the greatest sources of disparity in global capital costs. Reducing the risks of stock ownership would lower the required returns of shareholders. Without serious efforts to reform the corporate governance process to make managers more accountable to the board, and directors more accountable to the owners, shareholders will continue to lack confidence that their money is being deployed effectively. Even if they have confidence in the stewardship of present management, a lack of faith in the system to effect change should things go awry still produces uncertainty.

One of the most sophisticated private pension funds in the country recently reviewed its portfolio of privately held corporate securities to determine the principal causes of success and failure. The firm attributed three out of four cases where it had recognized losses to management failures, not to market factors, foreign competition, or a host of other potential causes. Without the ability to intervene in the event of poorly performing management, this fund obviously requires a higher return on an investment.

Corporate governance reform does not mean that companies will be subject to micromanagement by uninformed shareholders. Reform efforts should focus on a "board-centered" model. Virtually the only right that should matter to shareholders is the ability to elect and replace directors. With effective representation, all other issues will fall into place. But until the owners believe that the board is truly responsive to their needs, they will continue to be hesitant to turn over their capital for extended periods to corporate managers, and they will continue to fight for the right to make more decisions directly.

Many in corporate America are resisting corporate governance reform because the measures that are needed to restore the rights of ownership to shareholders would reduce the control enjoyed by entrenched boards and managers. Control is power, and power—as history demonstrates—is seductive. It is time to remove the suits of armor donned by corporate management during the past decade. The business community must begin to embrace shareholders as partners rather than treat them as adversaries. Those who do will be rewarded by a lower cost of equity. Meanwhile, the companies that seek protections provided by poison pills and onerous state anti-takeover laws will see their investor base continue to dry up. Institutional investors, and even groups of individual investors such as the United Shareholders of America, have begun to perform corporate governance "audits" to guide their selection of stocks.

The private sector has the opportunity to take the lead on this issue, but if it fails to do so there will be increasing pressure on the government to intervene. Richard Breeden, chairman of the SEC, was so incensed by the disenfranchisement of corporate owners during the late 1980s that he suggested a "shareholder bill of rights" might be necessary. The Business Roundtable made an important first step to improve the situation in March 1990 by publishing a brochure entitled, "Corporate Governance and American Competitiveness." In this document, the BRT encourages members to establish boards comprised of a majority of independent directors and to establish nominating and compensation committees comprised exclusively of nonmanagement directors. But the Roundtable failed to address the fundamental problem—corporate executives still select "independent" directors. Just because a board member is not an employee of the firm does not mean he or she is independent, nor does it mean that the individual is accountable to the owners. The BRT handbook stopped short of endorsing most of the reforms that shareholders have been lobbying for to give owners a greater say in who is nominated to represent them and to improve the integrity of how directors are elected.

When the California Public Employees Retirement System, the United Shareholders of America, and the American Bar Association sent letters to the SEC expressing various views on how the proxy system should be reformed to enhance dialogue between owners and managers, the Business Roundtable balked. To justify its position that proxy reform was unnecessary, the BRT hired a proxy solicitation firm to study the outcome of 190 proxy contests that occurred between October 1984 and September 1990.[4] The study concluded that in 74 percent of the proxy battles shareholders obtained "significant gains." In the study, a significant gain was defined as virtually any concession, almost all of which fell short of replacing a majority of the board (except in cases where a proxy contest was used as an aid to a hostile tender offer). In addition to subtle biases in data presentation, the study failed to address the primary issue: proxy contests are so expensive and involve such extensive regulatory hurdles that shareholders seldom engage in them. Why were there only 190 proxy contests in a study that covered a six-year period in which there were thousands of changes in control? The answer is that it is virtually unheard of for a group of ordinary shareholders to be able to replace a majority of the board. Our corporate governance system should not require selling a company to a hostile bidder to change the direction of a company. If shareholders could replace the boards of poorly performing companies, they would not be forced to rely on the takeover market.

The longer individuals who control America's corporations continue to resist extending a hand of partnership to their owners, the more likelihood there is that the government will unilaterally initiate change by reforming the cumbersome and counterproductive regulations that now handcuff shareholders. The first step would be to restore the board of directors as the functional centerpiece of corporate governance through reform of the proxy system. Specifically, the SEC should eliminate the need of owners who communicate among themselves to file the content of their discussions with the federal government. This Orwellian rule has no place in a capitalist system. The Business Roundtable claims that eliminating this rule would lead to "back room" discussions among shareholders. That is exactly what occurs in Germany and Japan by design. Why should shareholder disputes with management be aired in *The Wall Street Journal*?

Rather than grant "gadfly" shareholders space in a proxy statement to discuss their views on social issues, the proxy ought to be limited to a discussion of the important economic matters such as who will represent the shareholders on the board. Any group constituting at least 5 percent of the outstanding shares of a company should be allowed to nominate someone to serve as a director and provide a brief statement in the proxy as to why they have proposed this person for the board. The proxy statement should not be the exclusive domain of management as long as it is paid for out of the shareholders' equity account.

The present "race to the bottom" in state anti-takeover laws can be addressed without federal intervention by simply injecting some market discipline into the process. As long as management selects the state of incorporation, state laws will obviously cater to management. Shareholders seldom receive a fair hearing. When Massachusetts passed its law mandating staggered boards in 1990, only one representative of the investment community, Nell Minow of Institutional Shareholder Services, was allowed to testify in opposition to the bill. Because state laws have been radically altered in recent years, most shareholders are governed by rules in which they had no say. Shareholders should be allowed to decide by a majority vote to reincorporate in another state. Management and the unions would still have the upper hand politically because they control powerful political action committees and jobs. But perhaps then the states would consider the impact their laws have on the owners and on the cost of capital before they rearrange corporate law to protect a single company. This change alone would dramatically improve corporate governance because it would create a market for balanced laws rather than protectionist laws. And it would not involve the federal government meddling in corporate affairs.

If there is a role for the federal government, it would be to pass a law that unequivocally supports the capitalist system by abolishing multiple constituencies statutes that permit boards to put the interests of various parties ahead of those of the owners. Like socialism, taking care of the short-term needs of a host of constituents may sound noble, but it is in no one's long-term interest because it can undermine a market economy. Managers should unabashedly seek to maximize the value of their companies. If they feel the market is not properly valuing the company, they should attempt to either better inform their present owners or find owners who are willing to listen. Peter Drucker claims that the goal of a corporation should be to "maximize the wealth-producing capacity of the enterprise."[5] If corporations achieve this goal, and investors are well informed, would this not be one and the same with maximizing the value of the firm? Shareholders will pay more for stock if they expect the company to generate more wealth. Also, a federal law stipulating that a victory is determined by the percentage of votes *cast* would be useful. It defies logic that abstentions and unreturned ballots are allowed to be counted in favor of management, as they are in many states.

The emergence of significant owners in the form of the investment firms previously mentioned, coupled with a corporate governance system that encouraged active, ongoing dialogue between owners and managers through the board, would eliminate *the need* for most takeovers. As a result, lowering barriers to changes in control would not expose companies to the whims of overzealous financiers. First, significant long-term investors who had strong bonds with the companies they owned would not sell their shares to a financial buyer who offered them only a small premium for their stock. Second, because companies would be more responsive to their shareholders, they would be more fully valued. This would reduce the likelihood of being able to offer large premiums. Lowering takeover defenses would then allow strategic transactions to occur, where true economic synergies do exist. In our rapidly changing global economy it is imperative to consolidate declining industries and redeploy labor and capital efficiently. Many of today's takeover defenses prevent this from happening.

Not only would most hostile tender offers disappear, proxy battles would also be replaced by candid, tough, and productive debates in the boardroom. These debates would not air the dirty laundry of a company as proxy contests often do. Instead, they could be argued on the merits since all parties would have access to detailed firsthand information on the performance of the company. Differences of opinion between owners and managers would be handled in a more civilized, and far more efficient manner than they are today.

In spite of the thorny relationship between owners and managers in recent years, there is reason to be optimistic. In a January 1991 address, the chairman of Armstrong World Industries (the company that initiated the 1990 Pennsylvania anti-takeover law that stripped many traditional rights of owners) stated:

> Institutional investors and corporations have many common goals. They should—and they ultimately will—focus on that which they can accomplish together with a united front, not on the few issues on which thoughtful people may not agree....Corporations and

investors should be allies in the fight to enhance American competitiveness.[6]

With the 1980s behind us, hopefully this will be the attitude of the 1990s.

Banking Reform

Lowering the cost of equity is vital, but it alone will not solve the cost-of-capital problem. The inability of U.S. corporations to operate with the same level of leverage as their foreign competitors without incurring undue risk also needs to be addressed. As described throughout the book, the present banking system in the United States makes debt a much riskier source of capital than it is elsewhere in the world. Since debt is the cheapest source of capital, this presents a problem. Regulations governing the financial services industry in the United States are out of step with those of the rest of the world, particularly the European Community. In order to promote a longer-term perspective in banks, and lower the risks of borrowing, it is essential that banks be granted broader powers to address a wider range of their customers' needs. Perhaps more important, banks need greater ability to own stock in their customers. All this can be done while lowering the risks to the American taxpayer imposed by the federal deposit insurance system.

On the heels of the savings and loan debacle, few members of Congress have the appetite to grant banks the freedom to engage in anything that even implies "riskier" investments and activities. But nothing would make U.S. financial institutions less risky than a solid dose of profitability and market accountability. Profitable institutions do not have to be bailed out. And the best way to ensure that banks survive as competitive enterprises in the future is to grant them the freedom to establish stronger relationships with their customers so they can differentiate themselves by some method other than price.

The primary principles that should drive any efforts to reform the financial services industry are to:

- minimize the risks to American taxpayers of providing deposit insurance;
- allow financial institutions to capitalize on synergies within the financial services arena to better serve customers, lower costs, and improve profits;
- strengthen the bonds between financial and nonfinancial entities by allowing limited cross shareholdings without eliminating the constructive tension that holds them both accountable; and
- regulate the industry in the most efficient manner.

Streamline Regulation

The U.S. financial services industry is the most heavily regulated in the world. Today commercial banks are regulated by the Federal Reserve Board, the Office of the Comptroller of the Currency, the Federal Deposit Insurance Corporation, and 50 separate state regulators. Savings and loans are under the jurisdiction of the Office of Thrift Supervision as well as the 50 states; and insurance companies that operate throughout the nation must comply with more than 50 separate sets of rules with *no* central coordination. Securities firms that underwrite stocks and bonds need not only comply with the Securities and Exchange Commission rules, but also follow separate state securities standards, which vary widely. Based on the present performance of the U.S. financial services industry detailed in Chapter 5, this regulatory scheme is neither efficient nor effective.

Despite the presence of more bank examiners per institution than in any other country, our fragmented regulatory system has been unable to address clear warning signals with early and decisive action. The Task Force on the International Competitiveness of U.S. Financial Institutions established by the U.S. House of Representatives concluded in its comprehensive report issued in late 1990:

A more cooperative relationship between regulators and the regulated is typical in competitor countries while the U.S. system is of a far more adversarial nature. The cooperative relationships evident in other countries permit earlier intervention to identify problems and seek solutions with significant cooperation between the public and private sector, offering better protection to deposit insurance funds.[7]

The present conflicts between state and federal regulations and the ability to skirt oversight by playing regulators off against each other need to be eliminated. All financial institutions should be categorized as either state or national and regulated as such. An institution that conducts business in more than one state would be regarded as national. Institutions that operate exclusively within the boundaries of a single state would be regulated by state regulators. Each state would be free to establish whatever banking, insurance, and securities regulations it wished in order to preserve the concept of regulatory innovation, but states should not be allowed to let the costs of lax regulations spill over into other jurisdictions. Accounts insured in a state-regulated institution should be insured by the state, not the federal government. It is important to remember that most of the losses to federal taxpayers caused by the savings and loan scandal were incurred by state-regulated thrifts. If the states had been liable for the tab, they would not have permitted such egregious behavior.

Federal institutions should be regulated in a more consistent and coherent fashion. Presently, the FDIC insures banks against losses, yet it is also the principal regulator of all state-chartered banks that are not members of the Federal Reserve System. The FDIC should stick to insuring accounts. There should be one regulator that oversees all commercial banking activities (including the thrifts); one securities regulator that regulates securities operations, regardless of what type of institution they are conducted in; and a body responsible for setting national standards for insurance regulation that could be implemented at the state level. (The lack of federal involvement with insurance regulation in the past would make a wholesale conversion to federal oversight imprudent at the present time.) Similarly, state securities regulators should continue their efforts to detect and punish securities fraud and review offerings conducted exclusively within state borders. But they should not be allowed to review and approve documents already cleared by the SEC. Current state securities review practices simply add bureaucratic delays, increase the cost of raising capital, and drive securities transactions offshore. The one exception to the above regulatory scheme would be that the Federal Reserve should be allowed to serve as the primary regulator of the 50 largest banks in order to maintain control of the money supply.

The distinctions between banks and thrifts ought to be eliminated. Healthy thrifts should be converted into banks; the unhealthy ones should be acquired by banks or closed down. Given present mortgage-lending activities within commercial banks, and the expanding role of government-sponsored enterprises (GSEs) such as the Federal National Mortgage Association and the Federal Home Loan Mortgage Corporation, which add tremendous liquidity to the home mortgage market, there is no need to preserve an entire industry that has been effectively restricted to offering only one product, real estate mortgages. In today's marketplace, thrifts are dinosaurs.

Federally regulated financial institutions would operate under a holding company structure if they wished to participate in more than one business area. The holding company would be used to consolidate and orchestrate the activities of each subsidiary, but regulators of each subsidiary would be responsible for ensuring that assets are not upstreamed in a way that might compromise the health of the subsidiary. Holding companies would not need to be regulated since each subsidiary would be functionally regulated. In the case of disputes between regulators, the Federal Reserve would resolve issues. An institution that desired to operate in only one of the permitted areas could do so without a holding company and would be subject to regulation only by its functional regulator.

Establish Insured "Deposit Banks"

The enormous barrier to market discipline of deposit insurance should be scaled back. A narrow subsidiary called a "deposit bank" could be established to take deposits of individuals, corporations, pension funds, and so forth, and invest those deposits in a highly safe manner. These accounts would be fully insured by the federal government with *no limitation* on the size of the account. Since 1985, 99 percent of the uninsured deposits at failed banks have been fully protected by the FDIC in an effort to avoid runs at other banks. This coverage should be made explicit. But deposit banks should be made so safe that there is no chance of failure short of a national catastrophe. The only acceptable investments these institutions could make would be in U.S. government securities, high-grade corporate bonds (AAA or AA), commercial paper (A1-P1 only), and government agency securities (AA or better equivalent).

Today deposit insurance fees paid by U.S. banks are substantially higher than elsewhere in the world. One reason that deposit insurance in so expensive in the United States is that our regulatory system de facto insures institutions rather than accounts, thereby making the taxpayers liable for all the mistakes of the entire financial institution. Deposit insurance was originally designed to protect depositors only, not mismanaged banks and thrifts. By insulating only the insured accounts for protection, the health of the deposit insurance system would be greatly improved, and the exposure of the American taxpayer virtually eliminated. This modification would also inject much greater market discipline into our present system, which perversely privatizes the successes and nationalizes the failures of financial providers. If a bank wanted to engage in any activity beyond accepting deposits that are invested in safe securities, it would have to raise the capital to do so from the market. This would entail convincing investors that the bank could make money in these other areas. Today banks can raise money without proving their competence by paying higher interest rates to depositors whose accounts are fully insured regardless of the quality of the bank.

Expand Uninsured Activities

Because the risks involved with owning high-grade investments would be negligible, deposit banks would be required to hold only a minimal amount of capital. The majority of bank capital could be invested in other subsidiaries that engage in "riskier" activities, where it is needed. The major functions performed in these other subsidiaries would include

- investing the institution's own capital in customers in the form of debt or equity (acting as principal);
- raising capital from third parties for customers (acting as agent); and
- providing advisory services, money management, and other nonbanking products and services such as insurance brokerage and mutual funds.

The functions of principal and agent should logically be split because different skills are required. Principal activities would entail investing capital in corporations at any level, including senior debt, subordinated debt, and equity, much as a firm such as GE Capital does now. With this structure, lenders would take the perspective of owners, giving them an incentive to capitalize businesses in a manner that most efficiently lowers their cost of capital. Lenders would also be more prone to encourage corporate customers to take calculated risks to maximize performance since they would share in the upside benefits. At the same time, equity ownership would provide banks with an incentive not to over-leverage their customers, since the bank would stand to lose as a shareholder if the customer went bankrupt.

Equity investments by banks in a single company should be limited to 15 percent of the company's voting shares so that commerce and banking would not become so inextricably interwoven that a consolidation of economic power would occur, a problem many believe exists today in Germany. Laws discouraging access to insider information by long-term owners should be relaxed. Similarly, lender liability reform *must* be a part of bank reform because banks will not take advantage of the opportunity to own equities as long as doing so exposes them to significant liability.

A separate agency function would be established to raise capital from third parties for customers, providing many traditional investment banking functions such as underwriting debt and equity, selling stocks and bonds, providing advisory services, and privately placing securities with institutional investors. The reasons for separating the agent and principal functions are many. First, when a single institution provides both services, as under the German universal banking system, it tends to undermine the breadth and quality of the capital markets. This occurs because banks that have the choice to either lend a company money or issue public bonds on its behalf will often prefer to do the former. The same is true with equities. If separate functions competed within an institution to offer the customer the financing option best suited to its needs, markets would be more efficient.

Second, the skills required are quite different. Agents are generally more promotional by nature, while principals are more analytical. Mixing tasks can undermine the effectiveness of both functions, and in some cases even prove to be dangerous. This is one reason why commercial bankers have had limited success in providing merger and acquisition advisory services. They tend to be more risk averse and less effective as "deal makers." Investment bankers, on the other hand, have invested poorly in junk bonds and bridge financings because they failed to understand the credit risks and overlooked concerns that more conservative lenders would have raised. Separating the principal and agent function would not, however, preclude a U.S. financial institution from competing against merchant banks based in Europe. The same institution could provide advice, capital raising services, and direct capital investments by coordinating subsidiary activities.

Additional subsidiaries could be established to provide other financial products and services to corporate and retail customers. Examples would include brokering personal and corporate insurance, managing mutual funds, trust services, and financial consulting.

One of the ways in which the uninsured subsidiary could raise capital would be to offer money market mutual funds that function much as these accounts do today. They would offer a higher yield than insured deposit accounts, but clearly entail the risk of principal loss. Depositors could decide within a single institution which mix of safety and yield they prefer rather than only finding insured accounts at banks and higher-yielding money market funds at brokerage firms or through the mail.

The capital requirements of the uninsured subsidiary should be determined on a case-by-case basis rather than mandated across the board. The principal criteria for assessing the necessary level of capital would be the quality of the investments made by the institution. Today, with capital standards applied uniformly across all institutions, there is an incentive for banks to invest in the riskiest assets because the potential returns are higher and no additional capital is required to serve as a buffer against potential losses. Under the proposed scheme, the failure of uninsured subsidiaries would expose the owners, rather than the deposit insurance system and the American taxpayer, to losses.

Benefits of the New Structure

The primary objective in restructuring the financial services industry would be to provide more stable and less risky sources of capital to commercial enterprises. But this new structure would also benefit individuals. From the retail customer's perspective, such a structure would greatly enhance the convenience and efficiency of purchasing financial services. Customers could go to a single bank branch in their neighborhood, or across the country, to take care of their financial needs because banks would be allowed to branch nationwide. Individuals would be able to open an insured depository account, an uninsured depository account, and a securities account. They could take out a car loan, a mortgage loan, or secure a credit card. And they could also purchase their life, auto, and property insurance. Each month one statement would summarize all their accounts.

Similarly, the business customer could have unprecedented service from its financial providers. Each customer could be assigned a relationship manager whose only job would be to see that all the customer's financial needs were addressed by the various bank subsidiaries and divisions. The relationship manager—along with the appropriate specialists—could help the customer decide whether a direct equity investment was appropriate given present market conditions or whether a public stock offering would be preferable. They could help the customer weigh the trade-offs between cost and operating flexibility provided by a bond offering and a direct loan. Banks could invest the deposits of corporate customers in insured or uninsured accounts or even in the equity markets, depending upon the customers' investment parameters.

Under such an arrangement financial institutions would have the flexibility to work closely with customers in helping them address the challenges faced in raising and deploying the capital needed to compete. At the same time, because they would have much more at stake with a given customer than any single institution does today, banks would be more rigorous in providing accountability to ensure that corporations are managed efficiently.

The one risk that needs to be guarded against is that close relationships not become incestuous. The constructive tension between capital providers and capital users could disappear if businesses became dominated by financiers or if banks became the puppets of businesses, subsidizing their credit costs to the detriment of the other shareholders. The savings and loan debacle, caused partly by commercial real estate investors using financial institutions as their private piggy banks, should be instructive. For this reason, commercial enterprises should not be allowed to own more than 15 percent of a bank. If both commercial and financial enterprises owned 15 percent of each others' stock, relationships could be solidified without removing market discipline from either party.

Some will argue that commercial enterprises should be free to own 100 percent of a bank holding company because this would provide a new source of deep pockets for the financial services industry. However, if banks are capable of generating acceptable returns, they should be able to raise money in the capital markets. If they are unable to produce sufficient returns, commercial enterprises have no business buying them. Interestingly, of the major investment banking firms, those that required substantial capital infusions in 1990 were owned by a corporate parent; those that were run independently fared better. The ability to establish strong relationships without compromising independence provides corporations the best of both worlds—a stable source of capital and careful monitoring and discipline.

The U.S. institution that most closely resembles those that would flourish under the proposed regulatory scheme is General Electric Capital Corporation. Because GE Capital does not raise funds through government insured deposits, it is able to own meaningful equity stakes in the companies it lends to. And because regulators do not dictate how the firm categorizes its assets, GE Capital is willing to work with distressed companies to resolve problems.

GECC not only invest in corporations, it also operates the country's largest leasing company, owns a major investment banking firm, insures residential mortgages, and supplies retail credit through a nationwide credit card operation.

With $70 billion in assets, GECC has become one of the six largest financial services organizations in the United States. The firm has also achieved a triple-A credit rating, a feat accomplished by only one traditional U.S. bank. During 1990, when the overregulated banking system was crumbling, GECC turned in over $1 billion in profits, a 21-percent increase over the prior year. Although bad commercial real estate loans forced major write-offs and bank failures across the nation, less than 2 percent of GECC's commercial real estate protfolio was delinquent. Although it is not necessarily a prototype for the bank of the future, the GECC model certainly looks better than the status quo in today's banking industry.

Providing True Long-Term Compensation

Improving the way corporate managers and boards are compensated may not be a cure-all for business myopia, but it certainly would not hurt. It is possible to do a much better job than we do today of tying the economic well-being of senior executives and directors to the long-term performance of companies.

Two primary principles need to be added to most compensation plans now in existence. First, pay has to be significantly affected by marginal changes in performance, not marginally affected by significant changes in performance. Second, incentives need to be meaningfully tied to *long-term* performance.

Specifically, boards should first establish what the appropriate level of total compensation should be for a senior executive if the company achieves its objectives. A plan should be devised that emphasizes long-term incentives over current income. As an example, the amount of total pay could be broken down as follows: one-fourth in base salary; one-fourth in annual bonus; and one-half in long-term incentives tied to the stock price. In other words, if the appropriate pay for a chief executive is deemed to be a million dollars, he or she would receive a base salary of $250,000, which is far less than most present salaries. Law partners, investment bankers, and entrepreneurs all take relatively small draws to pay the monthly bills and count on distributions based on their performance to make them wealthy; why shouldn't corporate executives?

In this example the annual bonus might range anywhere from zero to $500,000, depending upon year-end results, with the expected level of performance pegged to a bonus of $250,000. The expected level of performance must be meaningful, e.g., not a return on equity of 6 percent when Treasury bills are yielding 10 percent. In good years the executive will make more than his or her expected level of cash compensation, in poor years less.

Another half a million dollars would be accrued (not necessarily paid) each year in the form of a long-term incentive pegged to results over a longer time horizon such as five or ten years. This incentive should be equity-based to keep executives focused on the company's stock price, which is the best reflection of value-creation over time. Whether it be straight stock, stock options, or another equity-related incentive matters less than the fact that it is customized to the circumstances of the company. Perhaps a growth company that paid no dividends would use stock options while a mature business with a high dividend-payout rate might prefer restricted stock.

One company that has attempted to tie its long-term performance pay to the fate of the shareholders is Georgia Pacific. Georgia Pacific's restricted stock plan works as follows:

- Each executive covered by the plan is "allotted" a specific number of shares based on his or her position in the company and compensation level.
- None of the allotted shares actually belong to the individual until the company achieves certain milestones.
- The company defines milestones in terms of the appreciation of the stock price over the ensuing five-year period.
- After Georgia Pacific's shares increase in value by 20 percent, the executive receives one-fifth, or 20 percent of the shares in the form of restricted stock. In other words, at that point the executive can vote the shares and receive dividends, but he or she cannot sell the shares until the end of the five-year period.

- Each successive increase in share price by the same amount (20 percent above the original price) triggers another grant, until the stock price has increased 100 percent and all allotted shares are granted.
- If the stock price does not double within the five-year period, the executive forfeits the balance of his or her allotment.
- At the end of the five-year period, the executive receives a cash bonus to defray a portion of the taxes due upon receiving shares so that managers will not be forced to sell their shares in order to pay income taxes.

This specific plan may or may not work for other companies, but it has the benefit of ensuring the owners that senior management is going to do what they can to at least double the stock price during the five-year period.

Director fees should be paid exclusively in stock—no options, no pensions, no health or retirement benefits that cause directors to lose sight of their job of representing the owners. The government does not need to mandate this, but the shareholders should; there is evidence that board stock ownership is correlated to company performance.[8] Directors who have a tax problem because of noncash compensation should be allowed to opt for a partial cash payment to cover taxes. But given the other income sources of most corporate directors, few will fall into this category. Any director who is not interested in owning the company's stock should resign.

Incentive compensation plans should be more clearly disclosed in the annual proxy statement so that the owners would have a clear idea of what management's expectations are for themselves. Rather than only requiring disclosure of how much money top managers make, the SEC should mandate that companies explain in narrative form how executive incentive plans are devised. Investors would then be able to discriminate between companies whose top officers get paid to achieve token levels of performance and those who have meaningful objectives. This would provide an incentive to provide better incentives.

SEC Composition

One final recommendation would be to encourage the Securities and Exchange Commission to establish a tradition of allocating certain commissioner posts to nonlawyers. At the time this is being written, all five SEC commissioners are lawyers. Several of them are friends of mine, so this is not meant personally. But the interests of our financial system would be better served if one seat was designated for an economist, one for a businessperson, and one to represent the investment community. Then it would be easier to debate securities laws and regulations in the context of how they affect our economy.

* * * *

As many others have done, in the spring of 1991, the Center for Strategic and International Studies (CSIS) held a symposium on capital formation and time horizons. Hosted by two prominent senators and attended by top policy and business leaders, virtually the entire day was spent rehashing the same issues that have been talked about for years—increasing savings, lowering taxes, and income redistribution. These are obviously important issues. But they are not the only issues. It is time to start focusing on the structural issues that affect the allocation and monitoring of the capital that already exists.

I do not doubt the merits of higher savings and lower taxes. But until Congress can agree on our nation's economic priorities, the intense partisanship on Capitol Hill will prevent significant progress on these macroeconomic issues. In the meantime, we continue to ignore the critical barriers to longer time horizons imposed by our corporate governance system, investment practices, and financial institutions' regulatory scheme. Fixing these problems will not impact the federal budget by a dime, so the deficit cannot be used as an excuse for inaction.

People invest money on the basis of risk and reward trade-offs. Yet when it comes to encouraging investment, all we talk about is increasing rewards. We never address the issue of how to lower the risks of investing. To be sure, tax breaks can be used to lengthen investment horizons. Looking at all the empty office buildings in our country we can see that through the tax code you can induce investors to do almost anything. But the goal is not to establish long time horizons; it is to provide for the *right* time horizons. Rather than artificially motivating people to invest in one direction or another, we should concentrate on eliminating the impediments that prevent capital from naturally flowing to where it will generate the greatest amount of wealth.

Business myopia is undermining the economic future of the United States. We must begin to confront this problem. Self-flagellation will not help; neither will arrogance or apathy. Business leaders, bankers, institutional investors, and government policy makers need to work together to craft a financial system in America that promotes a more cooperative environment between capital providers and capital users. Only then will they be able to work together to accomplish goals that are in our nation's collective, long-run well-being and stop focusing on their parochial short-term interests. And only then will America regain the competitive edge necessary to compete in the tough global markets of the twenty-first century.

Notes

Chapter 1

1. Mark Vamos, "What Americans Think of Japan Inc.," *Business Week* (August 7, 1989), p. 51.
2. National Science Board, *Science & Engineering Indicators—1989* (Washington, DC: U.S. Government Printing Office, 1989), p. 397.
3. "U.S. Report Card: Trends," *Emerging Technologies: A Survey of Technical and Economic Opportunity* (U.S. Department of Commerce, Technology Administration, Spring 1990), p. xiii.
4. Robert Reich, "Who Is Us?," *Harvard Business Review* (January–February 1990), pp. 53–64.
5. Tom Steinert-Threlkeld, "Unfocused Outlook—Chips Are Down; Other Areas of U.S. Electronics Industry May Follow," The *Dallas Morning News* (December 17, 1990), p. 15A.
6. John Curran, "Japan Tries to Cool Money Mania," *Fortune* (January 28, 1991), p. 66.
7. "Capitalism—In Triumph, in Flux," *The Economist* (May 5, 1990), p. 8.
8. Louis Lowenstein, "The Changing Role of the Stock Market in the U.S." Speech presented to 16th Congress, European Federation of Financial Analysts' Societies, Stockholm, June 8, 1990.
9. Frank Lichtenberg, "Industrial De-Diversification and Its Consequences for Productivity." National Bureau of Economic Research, Working Paper No. 3231, January 1990.
10. Mark Mitchell and Ken Lehn, "Do Bad Bidders Become Good Targets?," *Journal of Political Economy*, vol. 98, no. 2. (1990), pp. 372–398. This article concludes that "the motive behind many takeovers is to undo inefficient acquisitions previously made."
11. Milo Geyelin, "Feuding Firms Cram Courts, Study Says," *The Wall Street Journal* (December 31, 1990), p. 9.

Chapter 2

1. Several articles have been written about the conflicting objectives and potential biases of stock research analysts, including the following: Jeffrey Laderman et al., "How Much Should You Trust Your Analyst?," *Business Week* (July 23, 1990), pp. 54–56; Mary Lowengard, "Pursuing the Buy Side," *Institutional Investor* (November 1990), pp. 175–176; and "Confes-

sions of an Ex-Analyst," *Investment Dealers' Digest* (April 27, 1990), pp. 29–31.

2. Ken Froot, Andre Perold, and Jeremy Stein, "Shareholder Trading Practices and Corporate Investment Horizons." Paper prepared for the Time Horizons of American Management project sponsored by the Council on Competitiveness and the Harvard Business School (September 17, 1990 draft).

3. Robert Rose, "Motorola Profit Report Depresses Stock," *The Wall Street Journal* (October 10, 1990), p. A8.

4. Gary Hector, "Yes, You *Can* Manage Long Term," *Fortune* (November 21, 1988), pp. 66–75.

5. The statistics relating to the asset size and equity portfolios of institutional investors are taken from various papers written by Dr. Carolyn Kay Brancato, President of Riverside Economic Research in Washington, DC. Her paper, "The Pivotal Role of Institutional Investors in Capital Markets," presented at the Conference on the Fiduciary Responsibilities of Institutional Investors in New York on June 13, 1990, contains most of these data.

6. Philip Maher, "Why Wall Street Can't Bank on Soft Dollars," *Investment Dealers' Digest* (October 23, 1989), pp. 18–21. For a detailed discussion of the soft-dollar business, including its origination, current practices, and abuses, see Betty Linn Krikorian, *Fiduciary Standards in Pension and Trust Fund Management* (Boston: Butterworth Legal Publishers, 1989), pp. 119–150.

7. Jeffrey Laderman and Tim Smart, "Wall Street Falls in Love with Soft Dollars," *Business Week* (April 24, 1989), pp. 127–128.

8. John M. Sipple, Jr., prepared remarks before the New York State Bar Association, Antitrust Law Section, New York, January 16, 1990.

9. See "Competitive Plus—Economically Targeted Investments by Pension Funds." A study of the feasibility of implementing recommendations made by the Cuomo Commission Task Force on Pension Fund Investment, published in February 1990 by the New York State Industrial Cooperation Council. Also see the original study, "Our Money's Worth," which was published in June 1989.

Chapter 3

1. George Anders, "Morgan Stanley Found a Gold Mine of Fees by Buying Burlington," *The Wall Street Journal* (December 14, 1990), p. A1.

2. Ibid.

3. Frederick Rose and Roger Lowenstein, "How Will Occidental Fare after Hammer? Traders Bet Both Ways," *The Wall Street Journal* (December 12, 1990), p. A1.

4. The discussion of the Japanese and German corporate governance systems was taken mainly from *International Corporate Governance,* published by Euromoney Books (London, 1990), edited by Joseph Lufkin and David Gallagher; from *Shareholder Rights Abroad* by Stephen Davis, Investor Responsibility Research Center, Washington, DC; and from unpublished papers written by Jonathan Charkham, adviser to the Bank of England, who interviewed numerous government officials and companies in both countries.
5. Peter Drucker, "Reckoning with the Pension Fund Revolution," *Harvard Business Review* (March–April 1991), pp. 316–324.
6. Jay Lorsch, *Pawns or Potentates* (Boston: Harvard Business School Press, 1989), p. 22.
7. John Byrne, "Kiss and Tell Proxies for the Persevering," *Business Week* (May 21, 1990), p. 48.
8. SEC Rule 14a-8 covers the restrictions placed on shareholder proposals. This rule details 12 specific reasons that corporate management can cite to disregard a shareholder proposal.
9. The results of these two studies of the economic impact on shareholders of the 1990 Pennsylvania anti-takeover law are discussed in the September–October 1990 *Corporate Governance Bulletin,* published by the Investor Responsibility Research Center, Washington, DC.
10. *Amanda Acquisition Corporation* v. *Universal Foods et al.,* U.S. Court of Appeals for the Seventh Circuit, 1989.
11. "A Dangerous Game in Pennsylvania," *Business Week* (January 29, 1990), p. 106.
12. Jason Zweig, "Socialism, Pennsylvania Style," *Forbes* (May 14, 1990), pp. 42–43.

Chapter 4

1. For further discussion of the conglomerate era see Roy C. Smith, *The Money Wars* (New York: Dutton, 1990), pp. 84–99.
2. John McConnell and Chris Muscarella, "Corporate Capital Expenditure Decisions and the Market Value of the Firm," *Journal of Financial Economics,* vol. 14 (1985), pp. 399–422.
3. For an analysis of stock price reactions to "strategic investment," see Randall Woolridge, "Competitive Decline and Corporate Restructuring: Is a Myopic Stock Market to Blame?," *Journal of Applied Corporate Finance* (Spring 1988), pp. 26–36. The two-day market returns to 45 announcements of R&D expenditures averaged a positive 1.2 percent.
4. In 1988, several members of the Office of Economic Analysis at the SEC tested the hypothesis that companies subject to a takeover would reduce

R&D expenditures to boost current earnings. They examined whether: 1) firms facing a high probability of takeover had relatively low R&D expenditures, and 2) firms passing takeover protections increased R&D expenditures afterward. Either of these might indicate that firms cut back research spending because of the takeover market. The evidence did not find that either of the above factors occurred.

5. See John Pound, "On Motives for Choosing a Corporate Governance Structure," published by the Analysis Group and Harvard University in December 1990. Pound studied which Pennsylvania-chartered corporations opted out of the protections provided by that state's 1990 anti-takeover law. He found that the market placed a 25-percent higher multiple on the cash flows of firms that chose to opt out of Act 36, i.e., to not seek the protections provided by the new law.

6. Eric Patel (Manager in the U.K. office of Marakon Associates), "What Europeans Can Learn from Colonial Raiders," *The Wall Street Journal* (January 8, 1990), p. A13.

7. Michael Jensen, "Eclipse of the Public Corporation," *Harvard Business Review* (September–October 1989), pp. 61–74.

8. In 1988, Polaroid successfully used an employee stock ownership plan (ESOP) as a defense against a hostile bidder. The company guaranteed a loan to an ESOP established to acquire 14 percent of Polaroid's outstanding shares. Under Delaware law (where Polaroid is incorporated) a bidder must acquire 85 percent of the company's shares or it can be prevented from merging with a Delaware corporation for three years. With 14 percent of the shares held in a trust whose votes could be assured to support management, Shamrock Holdings (an investment company formed by Roy E. Disney) had no chance to gain control of 85 percent of Polaroid's shares. After the Delaware Supreme Court upheld Polaroid's use of an ESOP, a number of other companies including J.C. Penney and Procter & Gamble quickly established or expanded ESOPs.

9. "Icahn on Icahn," *Fortune* (February 29, 1988), p. 54.

10. In their paper, "Original Issue High Yield Bonds: Aging Analysis of Defaults, Exchanges and Calls" (1988), Paul Asquith, David Mullins, and Eric Wolff argued that the surge in new issues of junk bonds in the late 1980s covered up the real default rate on these securities. Over time the default rate grew from 0 percent to 8 percent after three years, to 18 percent to 26 percent after seven years, and to more than 34 percent after eleven years. Since newly issued bonds seldom defaulted, and the market was growing rapidly, junk bond underwriters were able to convince people that the risk was low because as a percentage of total high-yield debt outstanding, the percentage of defaults was minimal (largely because most bonds were recent issues). This analysis failed to recognize the risks

inherent in these bonds, which relate to the likely default rate over time as correctly pointed out by Asquith et al.

11. Carol Loomis, "The Biggest Looniest Deal Ever," *Fortune* (June 18, 1990), pp. 48–72.

12. Frank Lichtenberg and Donald Siegel, "The Effects of Leveraged Buyouts on Productivity and Related Aspects of Firm Behavior." National Bureau of Economic Research, Working Paper No. 3022, June 1989.

13. "BLS Report on Mass Layoffs in 1988," U.S. Department of Labor, Bureau of Labor Statistics (August 1, 1989).

14. For example, see Steven Kaplan, "The Effects of Management Buyouts on Operations and Value," draft for *Journal of Financial Economics*, August 1989.

15. Michael Jensen, Steven Kaplan, and Laura Stiglin, "Effects of LBOs on Tax Revenues of the U.S. Treasury," *Tax Notes* (February 6, 1989), pp. 727–733.

16. Ben Bernanke and John Campbell, "Is There a Corporate Debt Crisis?," *Brookings Papers on Economic Activity,* 1:1988, pp. 97, 98, 103.

17. Kathleen Madigan, "O.K., So the Debt Spree Wasn't All That Risky," *Business Week* (November 26, 1990), p. 22.

Chapter 5

1. See J. Bradford DeLong, "Did J.P. Morgan's Men Add Value? An Historical Perspective of Financial Capitalism." National Bureau of Economic Research, Working Paper No. 3426, August 1990, for a discussion of the role played by Morgan bankers in corporate accountability. The author shows a statistically significant stock price increase (estimated to be 30 percent) associated with the presence of a Morgan banker on a corporate board.

2. See the February 1991 Treasury Department proposal for banking reform, "Modernizing the Financial System," for a discussion of bank failures and the origins of the present federal deposit insurance system. The report notes that over 5,000 banks failed from 1930 to1932, costing depositors the equivalent of $6 billion in 1990 dollars.

3. Robert McCauley and Steven Zimmer, "The Cost of Capital for Internationally Active Banks" (December 1990 draft).

4. W. Carl Kester, *Japanese Takeovers* (Boston: Harvard Business School Press, 1990).

5. See Robert McCauley and Steven Zimmer, "Explaining International Differences in the Cost of Capital," *Federal Reserve Bank of New York Quarterly Review* (Summer 1989), pp. 22–23, which states that the frequency of bankruptcies is 1.6 percent for U.S. firms, 1.3 percent for U.K. firms, 1.1 percent in Japan, and 0.7 percent in Germany.

6. William Murray, "Polly Peck's Fall Signals Banking Shift," *The Wall Street Journal* (November 2, 1990), p. B4F.
7. Takeo Hoshi, Anil Kashyap, and David Scharfstein, "Corporate Structure, Liquidity and Investment: Evidence from Japanese Industrial Groups," Federal Reserve Board Discussion Series, No. 82 (May 1989).
8. For a discussion of the Revco case and and its impact on fraudulant conveyance see Aaron Pressman, "Bondholders Get Tough," *Investment Dealers' Digest* (November 5, 1990), pp. 18–23; and George Anders, "Revco Can Sue Its Ex-Advisors Over Buy-Out," *The Wall Street Journal* (January 3, 1991), pp. A3, A7.
9. For a discussion of concerns regarding this program see the record of hearings before the Committee on Small Business, United States Senate, pertaining to the SBA's Small Business Investment Companies (SBIC) Program (Washington, DC: U.S. Government Printing Office, 1990).
10. For a discussion of the changing global regulatory structure governing financial institutions, including the likely outcome of harmonized banking laws in Europe, see the report of the Task Force on the International Competitiveness of U.S. Financial Institutions prepared by the Committee on Banking, Finance and Urban Affairs, U.S. House of Representatives (Washington, DC; U.S. Government Printing Office, 1990).

Chapter 6

1. From remarks by Jerry R. Junkins to the Japan Society, New York, November 8, 1989.
2. George Hatsopoulos, "High Cost of Capital: Handicap of American Industry," Waltham, MA: Thermo Electron Corporation, April 26, 1983.
3. James M. Poterba, "International Comparisons of the Cost of Capital: A Survey of Methods, with Reference to the U.S. and Japan," *New York Federal Reserve Bulletin* (October 1990 draft).
4. See Robert McCauley and Steven Zimmer, "Explaining International Differences in the Cost of Capital," *Federal Reserve Bank of New York Quarterly Review* (Summer 1989), p. 16, which states that "different overall income tax wedges do not explain differences in the cost of capital." Poterba also concludes, "Tax considerations do not appear to be central explanators of cost of capital disparities between the United States and Japan " (1990 draft).
5. For example, see McCauley and Zimmer, "Explaining International Differences in the Cost of Capital," and Poterba, "International Comparisons of the Cost of Capital."
6. See Burton G. Malkiel, "The Influence of Conditions in Financial Markets on the Time Horizons of Business Managers: An International Comparison." Paper prepared for the Time Horizons of American Management

project sponsored by the Council on Competitiveness and the Harvard Business School (1990 draft).

7. Poterba, in "International Comparisons of the Cost of Capital," concludes, "This survey of previous work suggests that several different methodologies point to a similar conclusion: the cost of equity has been lower in Japan than in the United States for most of the last two decades."

Chapter 7

1. Michael Jensen and Kevin Murphy, "CEO Incentives—It's Not How Much You Pay, But How," *Harvard Business Review* (May–June 1990), pp. 138–153.

2. In his May–June 1990 executive compensation newsletter, *The Crystal Report,* Graef Crystal tested the Jensen–Murphy hypothesis on various samples of companies including the sample listed in the *HBR* article. Crystal "ran some regression analyses . . . and concluded, rather astoundingly, that knowing the sensitivity of CEO pay and CEO shareholdings as measured by Jensen and Murphy's Total CEO Wealth measure helped hardly at all in explaining differences in shareholder return among the 50 companies." According to Crystal, the dollar value of shares owned by the CEO is a better predictor of shareholder wealth than the percentage of a company's shares owned by the top executive. Still, only 11 percent of the compensation level of 200 top CEOs could be explained by shareholder return.

3. Kenneth A. Merchant, *Rewarding Results* (Boston: Harvard Business School Press, 1989).

4. Statistics relating to the relative pay of top executives and factory workers were provided by Graef Crystal.

5. Ibid.

6. Leslie Eaton, "Corporate Couch Potatoes," *Barron's* (December 24, 1990), p. 24.

7. See Graef Crystal, "Incentive Pay That Doesn't Work," *Fortune* (August 28, 1989), pp. 101–104, for the results of a survey on the performance of companies that granted top executives restricted stock. In every category measured, these companies underperformed other companies in the survey during the five-year period studied.

8. Michael Jensen and Kevin Murphy, "Performance Pay & Top-Management Incentives," *Journal of Political Economy,* vol. 98, no. 2 (1990), p. 47.

9. Among numerous other examples are Phillips Petroleum where return on ending equity (ROEE) dropped from 31 percent to 10 percent in 1989 yet CEO pay rose from $760,833 to $1,239,880; Tenneco where ROEE declined 31 percent in 1989 yet pay rose 52 percent; and Manufacturers Hanover

Trust where ROEE was 42 percent, 29 percent, and 15 percent from 1987 through 1989, yet total current compensation increased each year. See *The Crystal Report* (May–June 1990), p. 10.

10. Thomas Stewart, "The Trouble with Stock Options," *Fortune* (January 1, 1990), pp. 93–95.

11. John Byrne, Ronald Grover, and Robert Hof, "Pay Stubs of the Rich and Corporate," *Business Week* (May 7, 1990), p. 61.

Chapter 8

1. See Malcolm Salter and Wolf A. Weinhold, *Diversification Through Acquisition* (New York: Free Press, 1979) for a discussion of the influence of unrelated diversification on corporate performance and stock price performance. From 1967 to 1976, the Standard & Poor's 500 index increased, yet the S&P index of conglomerates dropped by more than 40 percent. Also, see Victor You et al., "Mergers and Bidders' Wealth: Managerial and Strategic Factors," in *The Economics of Strategic Planning*, Lacy Glenn Thomas, III, ed. (Lexington, MA: Lexington Books, 1986), which concludes that a majority of bidders making acquisitions also experienced negative stock price returns in the period 1975 to 1984.

2. The McCarran-Ferguson Act of 1945 specified that virtually all regulation of the insurance industry would take place at the state level and that insurance companies, for all intents and purposes, would be exempt from federal antitrust statutes including the Sherman Act, the Clayton Act, and the Federal Trade Commission Act.

3. See William Taylor, "Can Big Owners Make a Big Difference?," *Harvard Business Review* (September–October 1990), pp. 70-80.

4. The study, entitled, "Proxy Contest Study—October 1984 to September 1990," was conducted by Georgeson & Company, Inc., a proxy solicitation firm based in New York, and dated December 14, 1990.

5. Peter Drucker, "Reckoning with the Pension Fund Revolution," *Harvard Business Review* (March–April 1991), p. 322.

6. Remarks of W.W. Adams, chairman of Armstrong World Industries, to the CEO Roundtable Conference, Naples, Florida, January 19, 1991.

7. Report of the Task Force on the International Competitiveness of U.S. Financial Institutions, Committee on Banking, Finance and Urban Affairs, U.S. House of Representatives, November 1990, p. 12.

8. See Leslie Eaton, "Corporate Couch Potatoes," *Barron's* (December 24, 1990), p. 24, which notes that the Analysis Group in Belmont, MA, in studying the relative performance of companies in 16 industries has found that a higher percentage of the shares are owned by directors at the best-performing companies.

Index